UNIX™
Shell Programming

UNIX™
Shell Programming

SECOND EDITION

Lowell Jay Arthur

John Wiley & Sons, Inc.
NEW YORK / CHICHESTER / BRISBANE / TORONTO / SINGAPORE

TAB BOOKS offers software for
sale. For information and a catalog,
please contact TAB Software Department,
Blue Ridge Summit, PA 17294-0850.

Copyright © 1990 by Lowell Jay Arthur.
Published by John Wiley & Sons, Inc.

Library of Congress Cataloging in Publication Data:

Arthur, Lowell Jay, 1951–
    UNIX Shell programming   /   Lowell Jay Arthur.—2nd ed.
        p.   cm.
    Includes bibliographical references.
    ISBN 0–471–51820–4. — ISBN 0–471–51821–2 (pbk.)
    1. UNIX (Computer operating system)   2. UNIX Shell (Computer
programs)   I. Title.
QA76.76.063A765   1990
005.4′465—dc20   90–12088
                                                        CIP

Printed in the United States of America

10 9 8 7 6 5 4 3 2 1

Upon a mountain height, far from the sea,
I found a shell,
And to my listening ear the lonely thing
Ever a song of ocean seemed to sing,
Ever a tale of ocean seemed to tell.

                    Eugene Field

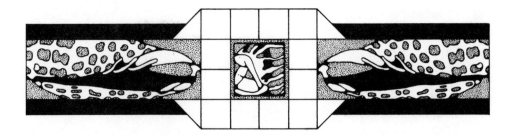

Contents

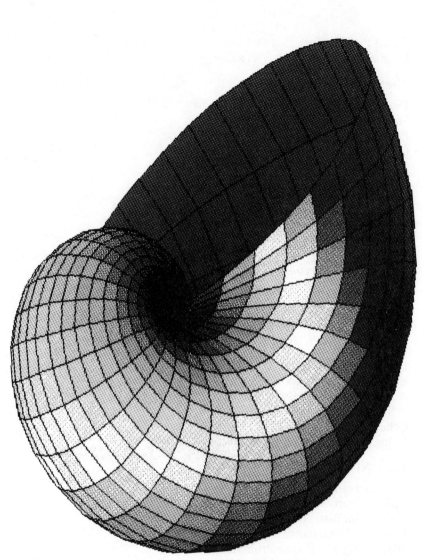

Courtesy of Prescience Computer Corporation, 814 Castro Street #102, San Francisco, CA 94114.

Preface

This book is like the shell of a chambered nautilus—sheltering you during your evolution from a novice to a power user of Shell programming. Along the way, you will learn the basics and travel the avenues to knowledge and wisdom. In Shell as in life, there are three stages to growth: childhood, adolescence, adulthood; apprentice, journeyman, master; and so it is with this book—novice, user, and power user. Fourteen chambers of knowledge and experience will guide you with examples.

Shell unlocks the power of UNIX. It presumes that users can and will do remarkable things. Shell teaches productivity; one line of Shell can do the work of 100 lines of C language. Shell teaches programming through *composition* of existing programs, not through coding of complex, custom software. Shell teaches *reuse* in ways that support such advanced concepts as object-oriented programming.

To enable everyone to derive the maximum benefit from using the Shell, I have designed this book to carry you from beginning Shell usage all of the way through power user status. There are three major sections:

1. Shell for the Novice

2. Shell Programming for the User

3. Shell Programming for the Power User

Shell for the Novice leads you through files and processes and the power of Shell. It teaches you how to use Shell, from simple commands to more complicated programming.

Shell Programming for the User teaches you how to use these basic skills to create whole applications. People do things every day that could benefit from automation, but do not require a sophisticated data base system. This section of the book will teach you how to master using Shell to automate your everyday needs. It also establishes the foundation for building more exotic applications as you evolve toward Shell mastery.

Shell Programming for the Power User steps into the world of software developers and systems administrators. This part of the book discusses rapid prototyping and other crucial software engineering activities in detail. Throughout, the attention will be on UNIX and the varieties of Shell.

There are two major flavors of UNIX: AT&T and Berkeley. From AT&T Bell Labs, we received the Bourne and Korn Shells. Berkeley gave us the C Shell. Bourne is the most common. C Shell is widely available in all Berkeley UNIX systems. Korn retains the power of the Bourne Shell while adding the power features of the C Shell. This book will address all three shells. So regardless of your environment, it will support your growth and development. Unless otherwise noted, the Bourne and Korn Shell examples will appear on the left-hand side of the page, and the C Shell examples will be on the right-hand side of the page. In other instances, the C Shell examples will be prefaced by 'csh:'. Rather than retrain their customers, most vendors are providing all three shells with their UNIX systems. Now you can choose the shell that suits your needs the best.

For personal computer users, the Korn Shell and most of its tools are also available on MS-DOS. PC users can now have access to most of the power of the Shell.

When I wrote the first edition of this book in 1984, UNIX was still a four-letter word and Shell was not far behind. You couldn't find a reference to either of them in any of the industry journals or magazines. Now references shine from almost everywhere. Through the growth in popularity of UNIX, the use of Shell, the UNIX command language, has grown as well. I want to show you why.

Step-by-step, this edition will lead you through the depths of the Shell and its usage. I hope you find the book as readable and enjoyable as I found the experience of writing it. I know that you will benefit greatly from the use of Shell to make your job more effective and efficient.

LOWELL JAY ARTHUR

Denver, Colorado
July 1990

UNIX™
Shell Programming

PART ONE

Shell for the Novice

The mind of the beginner is empty, free of the habits of the expert, ready to accept, to doubt, and open to all the possibilities.

Shunryu Suzuki

Chapter One

The Power of Shell

The Shell is the key to improving productivity and quality in a UNIX environment. The Shell can automate repetitive tasks, find where you left things, do things while you are at lunch or asleep, and a host of other time-saving activities. The use of the Shell can double, triple, or quadruple your productivity, making you more effective and more efficient. The Shell accomplishes these results by letting you create tools to automate many tasks. It enables you to construct prototypes of applications, programs, procedures, and tools. The speed with which you can build a working prototype, enhance it to provide exactly what you need, or just throw it away and begin again, will allow you the flexibility to create exactly the right tool or application without a lot of coding, compiling, and testing. It will rarely be necessary to do things manually, because the Shell can grapple with almost any problem.

WHY SHELL?

Before we get into the core of Shell, let's look at a few key reasons for using the UNIX Shell.

1. More and more data exists in a mechanized format all over the world. For people to benefit from this data, however, it must be transformed into information, knowledge, and wisdom (Figure 1.1). Data can become these higher forms of understanding in only a few ways:

   - *Selection* of data separates the wheat from the chaff. Selection, like light, illuminates key pieces of information. Shell filters accomplish this function.

3

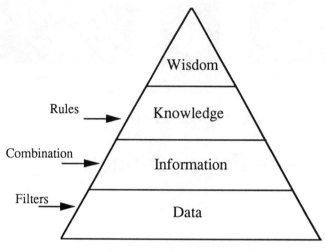

Figure 1.1   The evolution of data

- *Combination* of data creates a collision course for two or more groups of data, and, in this collision, information is created and knowledge is gained. Other Shell commands help scrub information and data, to gain further insight.
- *Decisions and rules* help us further analyze the resulting information to gain knowledge. Shell control structures help evaluate information to create knowledge.
- *Serendipity* causes a person to mentally combine ideas, data, and information in totally unexpected ways. Shell commands offer so many ways to examine and evaluate existing information that serendipity is almost guaranteed.

2. UNIX was the first fully integrated CASE (computer-aided software engineering) toolkit. Integration of tools is the cornerstone of UNIX Shell. UNIX will continue to be the platform of choice for IPSE (integrated project support environment).

3. There simply isn't enough power and room in a personal computer platform running a single program to automate the complex tasks of software engineering and development, or any other human task, for that matter.

4. Shell is a full programming language. It has:
   - variables,
   - conditional and iterative constructs, and
   - tailorable user environment.

UNIX Shell is the original rapid prototyping tool, teaching such key concepts as modularity, reuse, and development through *composition* instead of coding. The Shell library of tools is the most widely reused library in the world, other than perhaps a few FORTRAN math libraries. The UNIX philosophy is: Build on the work of others. Stand on the shoulders of those who have gone before you.

5. UNIX Shell is one of the original fourth-generation programming languages (4GL). Whole applications can be built quickly and effectively in Shell. Compare the power of Shell; what takes one line in Shell may take 10 or more lines in C++ or 100 lines in C (or COBOL). Some people complain that Shell has an awkward syntax; it does, but no more so than most 4GLs.

6. Machines are cheaper than people. With Shell you can optimize your investment in people by creating look-alike environments for new users and developing an environment that can grow as the users grow.

WHAT'S IN IT FOR ME?

"So what?" you might ask. "I've heard these claims before." Or you might be a user rather than a developer of systems. "What's in it for me?" How about the following:

1. Would you like to be more successful, more confident, and more productive; receive more praise; and take more pride in your work? Shell is the key to personal satisfaction and success. Shell allows you to compose in hours or days applications that would take months or years in conventional environments. Completion of projects provides a major source of psychic income—self-esteem, recognition, and reward.

2. Would you like to be more effective and take advantage of opportunities? Shell gives you the ability to solve problems quickly and effectively. Programmers tend to think that they must program in C or COBOL or some language. This is unnecessary. Composing systems from Shell programs will accomplish almost any task. Instead of waiting months or years for the "perfect solution," prototype Shell applications can be developed, refined, and implemented. They can then be used as the requirements specifications for the development of a "real" system, if needed. The ability to apply the full power of the UNIX Shell toolkit to immediate problems outweighs the efficiency penalties of using Shell.

3. Do you need more time? Every job has its exciting parts and its dull parts. Shell frees you from the drudgery of dull, typically repetitive tasks.

4. Do you need more timely information? Shell can extract and massage huge quantities of information to meet your needs. Why look through a whole report when Shell can scan and retrieve important information for you effortlessly?

5. Do you need to integrate information from various existing systems? Using the communication facilities of UNIX and the power of Shell, integration can be done at a fraction of the normal cost.

6. Are you having a hard time creating the applications that you or your clients really need? With UNIX Shell, you can rapidly prototype applications to make sure you have the requirements right, before you build the production system. Even at that early stage, the Shell version may be completely satisfactory.

7. Would you like to be more creative? Are you having enough fun at work? Tinkering with Shell programming can be great fun for both the novice and the expert.

Beaten paths are for beaten men.

Shell's vast arsenal of tools can be easily combined to automate much of your repetitive activity. When I was at Bell Labs, I had the excellent good fortune to work with John Burgess, a bearded, spectacled wizard, who was our resident UNIX toolsmith. All one needed to do was complain about something and by the next morning John would automate it with Shell. The project I was on was successful in many ways because of his tool building support.

8. Would you like to avoid retraining to use UNIX? Would you rather use familiar command names instead of UNIX commands? Shell lets you emulate any environment that you have used in the past. Shell can easily imitate DOS (which I call "baby" UNIX) or an IBM MVS TSO environment. Using the smorgasbord of Shell tools, you can create commands that emulate the functionality of most systems. No need for retraining!

How can the UNIX Shell do all of these things? It must be complex! On the contrary, it is simplicity that allows this to happen, not complexity. Processing, interfaces, and data management are all dirt simple, which is why Shell is such a pleasure to use.

SHELL SIMPLICITY

Shell commands talk to one another through a simple and consistent interface called a *pipe*. Shell uses the UNIX file system (a hierarchy much like an organizational chart), which lets you organize files into cabinets and folders (directories). This hierarchy of directories and files yields a simple, clean view of all information in the system.

The UNIX system is another key to the Shell's ability. UNIX is portable; it runs on almost any computer hardware made today. Your investment in training, education, and development of Shell programs will be portable to system after system as you move around. Because UNIX supports multiple users and multiple tasks, your investment in Shell programming will support dozens of other users and allow for hundreds and even thousands of repetitive tasks to be done in the "background" while you work on something else.

The Shell is almost exactly what it sounds like—a friendly environment that protects each user from every other one. It allows users to do whatever they want without affecting anyone else. When a user logs into a UNIX system, the operating system automatically starts a unique copy of the Shell, under which the user can perform any function available. This protected yet powerful environment gives each user the ability to be more productive.

THE UNIX SHELLS

There are two major flavors of UNIX: Berkeley (BSD 4.3) and AT&T System V. With POSIX looming on the horizon as a standard, the best of both will come together to make a stronger environment. Within these two UNIX environments, there are three Shells: Bourne, Korn, and C (Table 1.1). All of these support processes—both foreground and background, pipes, filters, directories, and other similar standard features of UNIX. The original Shell was rewritten by S. R. Bourne about 1975. The Bourne Shell runs on most UNIX systems. Bill Joy and students on the University of California at Berkeley campus created another version of the Shell known as the C Shell, which is useful for C language programmers. It runs under Berkeley UNIX, BSD 4.3. David Korn, at AT&T, created the Korn Shell, which preserves the functionality of the Bourne Shell and incorporates many of the powerful features of the C Shell. Which of these Shells will dominate the market is yet to be seen; I predict it will be the Korn Shell. I expect to see all three Shells provided in future releases of UNIX because it's easier and less expensive to support users' existing knowledge than it is to retrain them. This book will describe all three Shells.

TABLE 1.1   The UNIX Shells

Shell	Originator	System Name	Prompt
Bourne	S. R. Bourne	sh	$
Korn	David Korn	ksh	$
C	Bill Joy	csh	%

Bourne Shell

The Bourne Shell is the most common of the three shells (Table 1.2). Almost all UNIX implementations offer the Bourne Shell as part of their standard configuration. It is smaller than the other two shells and therefore more efficient for most shell processing. It lacks, however, the interactive bells and whistles of either the C or the Korn Shell.

The Bourne Shell allows exception handling using the **trap** command, which is unique to the Shell. Input/output redirection is more versatile. For example, it allows redirection of standard input and output into and out of whole control structures, unlike the C Shell. The Bourne Shell can also take advantage of System V's *named pipes*.

The Bourne Shell supports both local and global variables. Global variables must be **export**ed. The Bourne Shell offers the **if-then-else**, **case**, **for**, **while**, and **until** control structures. It relies, however, on the UNIX utilities **test** and **expr** to evaluate conditional expressions, unlike either the C or the Korn Shell which evaluate expressions directly.

C Shell

Developed at the University of California at Berkeley, the C Shell offers some advantages over the Bourne Shell: **history**, and direct evaluation of conditions and built-in commands. Interactively, the C Shell **history** feature keeps track of

TABLE 1.2   Shell Functions

Function	Bourne	Korn	C
Availability	most	least	Berkeley UNIX; some System V
Variables	local	local	local (`set`)
	global (`export`)	global (`export`)	global (`setenv`)
Control	`if-then-else-fi`	`if-then-else-fi`	`if-then-else-endif`
Commands	`case-esac`	`case-esac`	`switch-case-endsw`
		`select`	
	`for-do-done`	`for-do-done`	`foreach-end`
	`xargs`	`xargs`	`repeat`
	`while-do-done`	`while-do-done`	`while-end`
	`until-do-done`	`until-do-done`	
Conditional evaluation	`test, expr`	direct	direct
Interactive		`history`	`history`
Aliasing	functions	functions	`alias`
Signals	`trap`	`trap`	
Efficiency	fast	medium	medium

the commands as you enter them and allows you to go back and execute them again without reentering the command. Or, if you want to, you can recall them, make modifications, and then execute the new command.

The C Shell offers *aliasing,* which allows the user to create aliases for command names. The C Shell also offers control over background and foreground tasks. In the Bourne Shell, if you start a command in background or foreground, it stays there until it ends. In the C Shell, you can move commands from foreground execution to background execution as required.

The C Shell offers two kinds of variables, regular (local) or environment (global), which are established by using **set** and **setenv**.

The syntax of the C Shell is more like C language programming and offers all of the C conditional operators (= =, >, and so on), which C programmers might find useful. The C Shell offers the **if-then-else**, **switch**, **foreach**, **repeat , and while** control constructs and evaluates conditional expressions within these control structures directly.

Korn Shell

The Korn Shell retains the complete functionality of the Bourne Shell and combines many of the key features of the C Shell. The Korn Shell is faster than the C Shell but slower than the Bourne, for most processing.

The Korn Shell offers improved **history** management which provides direct access to past commands. It also offers, like the Bourne Shell, *aliasing* using shell *functions.* The Korn Shell evaluates conditional expressions directly for efficiency and adds a **select** control construct (like **case**) for menu-driven shells.

Choosing a Shell

For a novice, I would choose the Korn Shell. I find the Korn/Bourne Shell syntax simpler and therefore preferable to the C Shell. More experienced users, familiar with either the Bourne or C Shell, will benefit from staying with what they already know. Bourne Shell users, however, can benefit from the interactive power of the Korn Shell. Throughout this book, Bourne and Korn examples will be displayed on the left side of the page and C Shell examples on the right. Otherwise, C Shell examples will have a leading "csh:" to help users find them.

WHEN TO USE THE SHELL

Any time you enter a UNIX command, you are using the Shell. To increase productivity, use the Shell whenever you are faced with:

1. doing something to many files,
2. doing the same task repeatedly,
3. doing a task automatically, on schedule

It's as simple as that. People, by necessity, perform repetitive tasks:

- Dates or names in a group of documents must be changed.
- Reports must be produced every month.
- Status must be entered daily and reported monthly.

Each of these tasks, and a host of others, can be automated with a Shell program.

You can also use the Shell interactively at your terminal to automate one-time tasks. Many situations could benefit from use of the powerful features of Shell, but they do not require the creation of a separate Shell program. These problems can be solved with interactive use of Shell. We'll look at interactive Shell usage in more depth in Chapter Four, Shell Control Structures.

> Choose your weapons to match the war.
>
> *Brad Cox*

You should not use the Shell when the task:

- is too complex,
- requires high efficiency,
- requires a different hardware environment, or
- requires different software tools.

Use the Shell to automate anything that requires text manipulation: selecting data, adding numbers, printing statistics, or whatever. Finding the right information in a mound of reports is simple for the Shell but cumbersome for people. Manipulating data and putting it into printable form is also tedious and unreliable. The Shell, as you will soon see, can do all of these things quickly and reliably.

PRODUCTIVITY AND SHELL

Studies (Thadhani 1984) have shown that an average programmer may spend 20 to 25 hours a week at a terminal. "Human-intensive" activities like editing and data manipulation consume 95 percent of that time. As homes, offices, and businesses become increasingly automated, 20–25 hours may climb to 30–35. To make people more productive:

1. Response times must be kept to a minimum (under one second), and
2. People must be allowed to automate their human-intensive activities.

The Shell and its tools have been designed and optimized to automate many of these activities. It requires some insight into the Shell and its usage to derive these benefits, but it only takes a little ingenuity to become more effective and efficient.

Since the Shell can automate most of the recurring tasks, which encompass 50 to 80 percent of the human-intensive activities, it is little wonder that the Shell can double or triple productivity. The simplicity of UNIX files and the file system design makes this possible.

Chapter Two

Shell Basics

A good beginning makes a good ending.

English proverb

In today's rapidly evolving technological environment, UNIX must be one of the arrows in your quiver. There is no way to separate a discussion of the Shell from UNIX (although some single-tasking versions run under MS-DOS). Without the simplicity of the UNIX architecture, the Shell could not exist. The Shell derives much of its power from UNIX.

WHAT IS UNIX?

Is UNIX an operating system? A philosophy? Or a red-hot environment for personal productivity that runs on every hardware platform from a personal computer to the Cray Supercomputer? Answer: All of the above.

UNIX is a time-sharing operating system. UNIX departed from most traditional approaches to operating systems in that it simplified the reading and writing of files—input/output (I/O). All files and devices look the same to any command that uses them. Files contain data as streams of characters—no records, no varying record sizes, and therefore none of the associated problems. This unique design allows every program to accept input from any other program. Each program can perform a single, unique function and be connected to other programs, devices, or files via the operating system. This simple design gives UNIX and the Shell much of their power.

Following the development of UNIX, many software developers contributed additional user-oriented tools. Originally packaged as an extension to UNIX called the Programmer's Workbench (PWB), these tools have since been included in the standard package, UNIX.

UNIX FILES

UNIX files are unique because they are basically free form. Each file is just a sequence of characters (see Figure 2.1). Lines or records are delimited by the newline (\n or nl) character. The end of a file is delimited by an end-of-file (\0 or EOF) or end-of-tape (EOT) character. Since every file can be read character by character and output the same way, every Shell tool has been designed to handle this simple file architecture. This design choice made it possible for the originators of UNIX to create simple, modular programs to perform single functions. Each function, although trivial when viewed as a single entity, becomes vastly more important when combined with other singular functions to do virtually any kind of activity.

UNIX files reside in a hierarchical file system or inverted tree (similar to an organization chart), like the one shown in Figure 2.2. To implement this structure, UNIX uses a special file known as a directory. You can think of a directory as a file cabinet, file drawer, or file folder. Each directory is a fork in the hierarchy, from which other branches may grow. This facility is useful for organizing files and information. In Figure 2.2, my user identification, lja, resides under the file system, /enduser. Under my ID there are directories for shell commands (bin), documents (doc), and source code (src). These names are short because most people are terrible typists. Longer names like source code or documentation can rarely be typed without error, and typing them is time-consuming. Even my ID, lja, is nothing but initials. Under src are directories for C language (c.d) and COBOL (cobol.d). The convention of using the ".d" suffix makes them readily identifiable as directories. Some people put directory names in all caps (e.g., C or COBOL). Under each of these directories are a variety of files (shown as rectangles). Just by use of directories and their names, I can usually find what I need in short order. Finding where you left something in a UNIX file system is often a challenge, especially if you have 30 to 100 files in a directory.

Directories and data files are not the only types of files UNIX offers. There are other special "files" that are not really files at all, but devices like terminal handlers, disk drives, tape drives, and so on. These will be discussed in detail in the advanced material. Any of these files can be processed using a Shell command to filter or enhance the data.

The UNIX Shell is the key to improving your productivity\n
and quality in a typical UNIX environment.\n
The Shell can automate repetitive tasks,\n
find where you left things,\n
do things while you are at lunch,\n
and a host of other time-saving activities.\n \0

Figure 2.1   A UNIX file

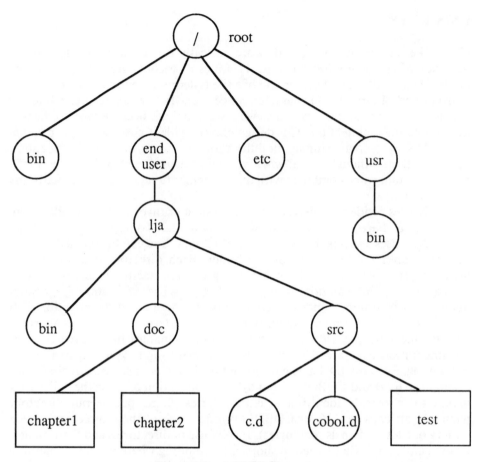

Figure 2.2   A UNIX file system

FILTERS

As we discussed briefly in Chapter One, a key way to turn raw data into useful information is to filter out the extraneous data. You should think of most Shell commands as filters, like the one shown in Figure 2.3. They have a single input, called standard input (abbreviated as *stdin;* see Table 2.1), that gives them a single character at a time. Each command also has two outputs: standard output (*stdout*) and standard error (*stderr*). Each command filters data from the standard input or refines it in some fashion, and passes it to the standard output. Any errors that it encounters are passed to *stderr*. Errors rarely occur, however, because most UNIX commands are designed to take intelligent default actions in most situations. If, for example, you don't assign a file as *stdin,* then the Shell assumes that your terminal is *stdin.* If you don't assign a file as standard output, then the Shell again assumes that the terminal is *stdout.* One of the dumbest

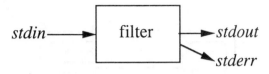

Figure 2.3   A Shell filter

things you will ever do is type a command like **cat** (concatenate and print) followed by a return and then wonder what happened:

```
cat
```

What is happening? See Figure 2.4. The Shell is waiting for you to type input from the screen, and it will display it back to you when you are done. To get out of this command, you have to hit the "break" or "delete" key, or hold down the control key and hit "d" for end-of-file (EOF).

The **cat** command is the simplest of the Shell's filters. It does not change the data; it takes the standard input and reproduces it on the standard output. At first glance, this seems worthless, but if you want to view a file on your terminal all you have to do is type the command:

```
cat file
```

The Shell will open the file and reproduce it on *stdout* (your terminal). Messages about any errors detected, like a missing file, will be passed to *stderr* (again, your terminal).

Some filters extract only the data you want to see; others add or change the data per your instructions. The **grep** command (Globally look for a Regular Expression and Print) will find every occurrence of a word or phrase in a UNIX file. For example, the following command will find all occurrences of my name in a document:

```
grep "Arthur" chapter1
Author: Lowell Jay Arthur
King Arthur and the Knights of the Round Table
```

TABLE 2.1   File Descriptors

Name	I/O	File Descriptor
stdin	input	0
stdout	output	1
stderr	error output	2
user-defined	input/output	3-19

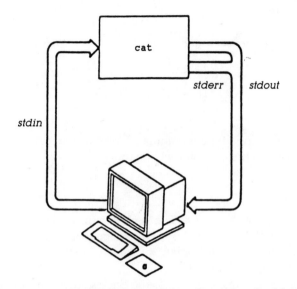

Figure 2.4   A terminal as *stdin*, *stdout*, and *stderr* (Reproduced with permission from John Wiley & Sons, New York, 1984. From *Application Prototyping* by Bernard Boar.)

Two occurrences were found; **grep** filtered out all of the other lines in the file chapter1. Please notice that all Shell commands are *case-sensitive*: upper case and lower case letters are different. To illustrate how the Shell can use commands to modify and enhance data, imagine that I need to change all occurrences of 'shell' to 'Shell.' The **sed** (stream editor) command is useful:

```
sed -e "s/shell/Shell/g" chapter1
```

Sed will open chapter1 as *stdin* and pass the file to *stdout* (the terminal) while changing all occurrences of 'shell' to 'Shell.' Well, you might say, that is certainly useful, but I need the output in a new file. To create a new file with Shell, you need to use a facility called input/output redirection.

INPUT/OUTPUT REDIRECTION

Input and output redirection allows you to:

1. create files
2. append to files
3. use existing files as input to the Shell
4. merge two output streams
5. use part of the Shell command as input.

You can use I/O redirection to change the direction of *stdin, stdout,* and *stderr,* or any other user-defined file descriptor (Table 2.1). Twenty files may be open at one time; their file descriptors are 0 through 19. The first three file descriptors are reserved for *stdin* (0), *stdout* (1), and *stderr* (2).

The syntax of the two most frequent redirection activities is as follows:

```
file-descriptor-1  operator  file-name          (e.g.,  2> errorfile)
file-descriptor-1  operator  file-descriptor-2  (e.g.,  2>&1)
```

The first format opens a file as either input or output and assigns it to a specified file descriptor. The second format duplicates or assigns one file descriptor to another. The Shell recognizes the operators shown in Table 2.2.

In the previous example, I could have used I/O redirection (see Table 2.3) to save the output in a new file as follows:

```
sed -e "s/shell/Shell/g" chapter1 > newchapter1
```

The **sed** command knew to open the file, chapter1, as *stdin,* but I could have also written the command as:

```
sed -e "s/shell/Shell/g" < chapter1 > newchapter1
```

But what about *stderr?* Isn't it still directed to the terminal? Well, yes. Redirecting *stderr* into a file is occasionally useful to debug a Shell command. To do so, however, the Bourne and Korn Shells recognize the file descriptor for *stderr* (2) and the output symbol (>) to mean that *stderr* should be placed in a file:

```
sed -e "s/shell/Shell/" chapter1 > newchapter1 2> newerrors
```

Any errors will be put in the file, newerrors. (Note: This syntax will not work with the C Shell.)

TABLE 2.2 Redirection Operators

Operator	Action
<	open the following file as *stdin*
>	open the following file as *stdout*
>>	append to the following file
<<del	take *stdin* from here, up to the delimiter
m<&n	use file descriptor *n* as input wherever file descriptor *m* is used
m>&n	merge file descriptor *m* with file descriptor *n*
m>>&n	append file descriptor *m* to file descriptor *n*
|	pipe *stdout* into *stdin*

TABLE 2.3   Input/Output Redirection

Bourne/Korn	C Shell	Action
< file	<file	take *stdin* from a file
> file	> file	put *stdout* in a new file
>> file	>> file	append to an existing file (or create it)
<<delimiter	<<delimiter	take *stdin* from the Shell up to delimiter
4< file		open file as file descriptor 4
<&4		read from file descriptor 4
2> file		put *stderr* in a new file
>&3		write to file descriptor 3
0<&4		use file descriptor 4 as *stdin*
2>&1	>&	merge *stdout* with *stderr*
2>>&1	>>&	append *stderr* to *stdout*
	>! file	override *noclobber* and create new file
	>>! file	override *noclobber* and append to a file
<&-	<&-	close file descriptor 0 (*stdin*)
2>&-		close file descriptor 2 (*stderr*)
2|		pipe *stderr* into the next command
2>&1|	|&	merge *stderr* and *stdin* and pipe the results

Sometimes, it is useful to combine *stdout* and *stderr* into one output stream and put it into a single file. To do so is simple:

```
        sed -e "s/shell/Shell/g" chapter1 2>&1 > newchapter1
csh:    sed -e "s/shell/Shell/g" chapter1 >& newchapter1
```

The expression '2>&1' tells the Shell to assign *stderr* (2) to the same file descriptor as *stdin* (&1). Then, the Shell redirects both outputs into the file, newchapter1.

The Shell has two other special features—appending to a file and using part of the Shell command as input—to handle special situations. The output redirection symbol, '>', creates a new file if the file name does not exist. If the file already exists, the Shell writes over it. Sometimes, it is useful to write some text into a file and then add text to it as required. To do this, you use the symbol to append, '>>'.

- If the file does not exist, then the Shell will create it.
- If it exists, the Shell will append text to the file.

A common example involves writing Shell procedures. Often, when using a Shell procedure, you want to create a file of errors and mail them to the person executing the command:

```
echo "First Error" > mailfile   # create a new error file
echo "Second Error" >> mailfile # append errors to the error file
echo "Third Error" >> mailfile  # append more errors
mail lja < mailfile             # mail the error file
```

The first error is detected and stored in a new mail file. The use of ' > ' creates a new file and avoids appending new errors to old errors in a similar file. All subsequent errors are appended to the mail file. Finally, the mail is sent to the person executing the command—one message is usually better than three separate ones.

The remaining redirection device, '<<', uses lines of data *within* the Shell command as input. Using data within the Shell command is most often useful with the editor. Rather than having a separate file as input to the command, you can include it directly with the Shell command:

```
ed mailfile <<EOF!
g/Error/s//Terminal Error/
/First/d
w
q
EOF!
```

This command will edit the mail file using the subsequent lines, up to the first occurrence of delimiter line 'EOF!', as input. The editor will replace all of the occurrences of "Error" with "Terminal Error", delete the next occurrence of "First", write the mailfile, and quit. This ability is useful when you need to edit more than one file and make the same changes to each.

By the way, you do not have to use 'EOF!'; any word or character will do. For example, you could use 'de' (ed spelled backward).

```
ed mailfile <<de
s/Error/Terminal Error/
/First/d
w
q
de
```

Anything else will work equally as well.

To close an open file descriptor, use '&-':

```
exec 4>&-    # Close file descriptor 4
exec 1<&-    # Close stdin
```

REDIRECTION USING C SHELL

The C Shell handles input/output redirection almost identically except for a couple of minor exceptions: combining standard output with standard error and overwriting existing files. To combine *stderr* with *stdout,* add an ampersand at the end of the redirection sign:

```
command arguments >& outfile
command arguments >>& outfile
```

The output file will contain all of the standard output and standard error data created by the shell command.

The C Shell has a variable, *noclobber,* which can be set to prevent accidental destruction of existing files:

```
setenv noclobber
```

When *noclobber* is set, it is an error to try to overwrite an existing file. To override this protection, use the exclamation point:

```
command arguments >! outfile
command arguments >&! outfile
command arguments >>! outfile
command arguments >>&! outfile
```

Outfile will be rewritten or appended whether the output file exists or not. If the variable *noclobber* is not set, the exclamation points are ignored without concern for the format of the files or their existence. The Shell handles all of this for you. As you will see in the next chapter, input/output redirection gives you great flexibility to manipulate text.

Sometimes, however, it is unnecessary and somewhat inefficient to create a file for everything. Occasionally, you will want to pass the output of one Shell command directly to the input of another. Rather than create a file and have the second command read it, you can pass the data from one command to another using the Shell facility called *pipe.*

PIPES

The *pipe* is exactly what it sounds like—a conduit to carry data from one command to another. (See Figure 2.5.) It connects the *stdout* of one command to the *stdin* of another—no messy temporary files to deal with, fewer errors, and greater productivity. Besides eliminating temporary files, the *pipe* allows the two commands to operate at the same time (asynchronously). As soon as the first command creates some output, the second command can begin execution. Figure 2.6

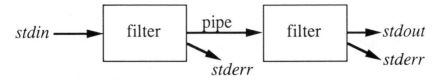

Figure 2.5   A Shell pipe

shows the difference in execution time between processes that execute syn-
chronously and asynchronously. The *pipe* is not only useful but efficient as well.
In an earlier example in this chapter, I changed all occurrences of 'shell' to 'Shell'
in Chapter One. Suppose it were useful to change all occurrences in all of the
chapters and put them into a single file. The *pipe* would let me combine the **cat**
and **sed** commands to do this simply:

```
cat chapter1 chapter2 chapter3 | sed -e "s/shell/Shell/" > book
```

Cat concatenates the chapter files and puts them on *stdout*. The *pipe* passes the
data from the **cat** command to the stream editor command (**sed**), which then edits
the data and writes it into the file, book.

It is also possible to redirect standard error into standard output and then *pipe*
them both into another command as follows:

```
      command arguments 2>&1 | nextcommand
csh: command arguments |& nextcommand
```

Aside from this minor difference, the Bourne and C Shells both handle *pipe*s in
the same way.

Because it may be necessary to save the data passing through a *pipe*—to test
that the command is passing correct data or just to retain the data for future
use—there is a facility to save the information in a file. What better name for a
pipe fitting than **tee**. **Tee** writes the standard input into a file and onto the
standard output. **Tee** is as simple to use as a *pipe*:

```
cat chapter? | tee book | nroff -cm
```

In this example, **cat** pulls together all of the chapters, **tee** creates the compiled
book, and **nroff** formats the chapters.

Pipes connect shell commands, creating complex functions that improve efficiency and effectiveness. There is no need to code some new command to handle
a needed function; shell commands can be reused, coupled together, and shaped
to handle even the most difficult information applications. Information passing
through *pipes* can be saved in files with **tee**. *Pipes* are a key component of the
Shell's flexibility and usability.

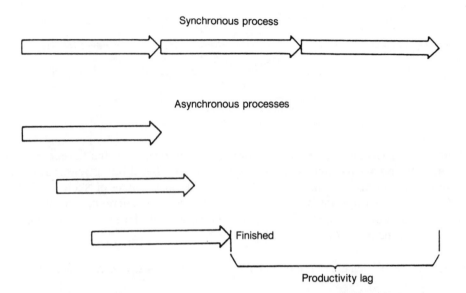

Figure 2.6 Asynchronous versus synchronous processes (Reproduced with permission from John Wiley & Sons, New York, 1984. From *Application Prototyping* by Bernard Boar.)

Named Pipes

Using Bourne or Korn Shell, you can create special devices called *named pipes.* Instead of accepting input from one program, they can accept input from any commands that write to them. Typically only one *background* command will read the input, however. To see how this works, let's create a *named pipe* called **LOG** using the **mknod** (make node) command and run a background process **runlog** that will write log records to the logfile:

```
/etc/mknod LOG p

#  log < LOG
while TRUE
do
   read line
   echo `date  +'%H%M%S'` $line >> /usr/local/logfile
done  < LOG

nohup nice log&
```

Now, all of the other commands we have running can write to the *named pipe,* **LOG**, and the **log** command will then read and create records with the output from these commands:

command1 > LOG
command2 > LOG

The handy thing about *named pipe*s and their background commands is that they can be running all day while other commands come and go. This is a great way to reuse applications like writing logs or error files.

SUMMARY

The simplicity of UNIX files, the file system structure, and the input/output subsystem gives the Shell much of its flexibility and power. Its vast arsenal of reusable commands, or filters as they are often called, further enhances the power of the Shell. The Shell *pipe,* by use of asynchronous processes, makes Shell commands more flexible, efficient, and responsive.

The Shell and all of its facilities allow users to become more productive, automate routine tasks, and pursue more creative, fulfilling work.

EXERCISES

1. When should the Shell be used:

   a. Interactively?

   b. For programming?

2. Describe UNIX file and file system structures.

3. Diagram and describe a typical Shell filter.

4. What are standard input (*stdin*), standard output (*stdout*), and standard error (*stderr*)?

5. What is input/output redirection?

6. Write a simple interactive Shell using I/O redirection to accept input from file1, put *stdout* in file2, and collect *stderr* in file3.

7. Write a simple Shell to redirect *stderr* into *stdout* and put the combined output in *outerr.*

8. Write a simple Shell to append to an existing file.

9. Write a simple Shell, using the *pipe,* to sort a file both before and after using **grep** to extract information from it. Which form is more efficient?

10. Use a *pipe* and **tee** with exercise 9 to put the output of **grep** into a file before sorting the information selected.

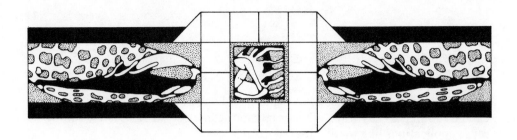

Chapter Three

Shell Commands

Almost any UNIX command is available for use with the Shell. This chapter will explain how the Shell finds commands and files. It will also introduce some of the most useful, but simplest commands. They fall into several key categories:

File and directory
Selection
Combination and ordering
Printing
Security
Builtin

Before we get into these various kinds of commands, I need to explain that I'm not going to attempt to reiterate the UNIX manual pages for each command discussed. If you would like to know more, and believe me, there is much more to most commands than we have space to discuss in this book, then you will need to look up the commands in either your documentation or interactively on the UNIX system. To view the documentation for a command, use **man**:

    man *command_name*

If you need to view it page by page, *pipe* the output into **more** or **pg**:

    man *command_name* | **more**

Or, if you absolutely need a paper copy, you can *pipe* the output into either **lp** or **lpr**—the standard line printer commands—or whatever printing command is appropriate for your system:

```
man command_name | lpr
```

Now that we've handled the administrative details, we need to examine the typical syntax for a Shell command.

COMMAND SYNTAX

The syntax of English is *subject-verb-object.* Using Shell, the syntax is *verb-modifier-object*:

```
command -options object
```

The command can be any one of the hundreds of commands available to the Shell. The commands covered in this chapter are shown in Table 3.1. Their many uses will be explored further in subsequent chapters.

Options, like adverbs in English, modify the operation of the command. Most options are single letters or numbers prefaced by a minus sign:

```
command -a -l object
```

Not all commands use options in the same way. Some command options work differently in System V and Berkeley UNIX and in MS-DOS. If you get surprise results, check the system documentation for a description of how the command works in your environment.

Shell commands operate on files, directories, and various devices—tapes, disks, printers, and so on. You will need to choose your tool to match the task at hand.

You will discover one of the pleasures of Shell commands: they all tend to take an intelligent default action. By that I mean, if you use a command incorrectly it might:

- give you a help message

```
rm
syntax: rm -(rf) file(s)
```

- exit gracefully with a return code
- do whatever will cause the least damage (e.g., leave a file unchanged).

Intelligent default actions prevent defects and can save you a lot of effort and rework. Now let's look at the key file and directory commands.

TABLE 3.1   Shell Commands

Type	Command	Purpose
Directory	`cd`	change directory
	`ls`	list a directory's contents
	`pwd`	print working directory
	`mkdir`	make a new directory
	`rmdir`	remove an existing directory (if empty)
File	`cat`	concatenate file(s)
	`cp`	copy file(s)
	`csplit`	split a file based on arguments
	`ln`	link two names to one file
	`mv`	move file(s)
	`rm`	remove file(s)
	`split`	split a file into n line chunks
Selection	`awk`	pattern scanning and processing language
	`cut`	select columns
	`diff`	compare and select differences in two files
	`grep`	select lines or rows
	`head`	select header lines
	`line`	read the first line
	`sed`	edit streams of data
	`tail`	select trailing lines
	`uniq`	select unique lines or rows
	`wc`	count characters, words, or lines in a file
Joining	`cat`	concatenate files
	`join`	join two files, matching row by row
	`paste`	paste multiple files, column by column
Ordering	`sort`	sort and merge multiple files together
Transform	`sed`	edit streams of data
	`tr`	transform character by character
Printing	`awk`	pattern scanning and processing language
	`cat`	concatenate and print
	`pr`	format and print
	`lp`	print on system printer
Security	`chmod`	change security mode on a file or directory
	`umask`	set default security mode

FILE AND DIRECTORY COMMANDS

Directories are like file cabinets and file folders; they allow you to organize your information effectively in various files. The standard length of all file and directory names is 14 characters. File and directory names can include any of the following characters: '. a-zA-Z0-9'.

File	`cat`	concatenate file(s)
	`csplit`	split a file based on arguments
	`cp`	copy file(s)
	`ln`	link two names to one file
	`mv`	move file(s)
	`rm`	remove file(s)
	`split`	split a file into *n* line segments
Directory	`cd`	change directory
	`ls`	list a directory's contents
	`pwd`	print working directory
	`mkdir`	make a new directory
	`rmdir`	remove an existing directory (if empty)

Figure 3.1   File and directory commands

The Shell file and directory commands are shown in Figure 3.1. The most elementary directory commands are **pwd**, **ls**, **cd**, **mkdir**, and **rmdir**. Elementary file commands include **cat**, **cp**, **mv**, and **rm**.

Directory Commands

Since it's easy to get lost in the file system, you will occasionally need to ask the question: Where am I? The **pwd** command does this for you:

```
pwd
/unix1/lja
```

Another common question is: What's in this directory? The **ls** (list) command, without any options or arguments, gives a listing of all of the files and directories in the current directory:

```
ls      ls
bin     bin     doc     src
doc
src
```

The **ls** command can be combined with numerous options, most commonly -l and -ld, to give a more detailed listing of the current directory and its contents:

```
ls -l
drwxrwx---      3       lja     adm      992 Dec 1 05:39 bin
drwx------     28       lja     adm      496 Dec 4 12:28 doc
drwxrwxrwx     32       lja     adm     1008 Dec 3 18:22 src


ls -ld
drwxrwxrwx     32       lja     adm      437 Dec 3 18:22
```

It is possible, however, that there may be some hidden files in a directory. Hidden files have a period (.) as the first character of their name. To see all of the files in a directory, including those deliberately hidden, you should use the -a option:

```
ls -a        ls -a
.            .              .cshrc     .profile doc
..           ..             .login     bin      src
.cshrc
.login
.profile
bin
doc
src
```

Once you know where you are and the directories beneath the current one, you may want to move into another directory. The **cd** (change directory) command moves you from one directory to another:

```
cd  directory_name
```

You should put related files in different directories (cabinets, drawers, or folders) to make them easier to find. Proper naming of directories and files will help you locate them.

Using the **cd** command without any arguments will transfer you to your home directory:

```
pwd
/unix1/lja/src/application
cd
pwd
/unix1/lja
```

To make a big leap and change to any other directory in the system, you would use the full path name to the other directory. For example:

```
cd /usr/bin
pwd
/usr/bin
```

You will also need to create and delete directories. This is simple using **mkdir** and **rmdir**:

```
mkdir new_directory
rmdir old_directory
```

Rmdir, however, will not let you remove a directory if it still holds any files. To delete the directory, you first have to delete all of the files within it. More about deleting files in the next section.

Using the Shell interactively or with actual procedures often requires changing directories. Determining the current directory is also important. Both the **cd** and the **pwd** command can be used anywhere at any time. You can then use **mkdir** and **rmdir** to create and delete directories as you require.

Pwd, **ls**, **cd**, **mkdir**, and **rmdir** handle most of the basic file and directory handling needs. **Ls** and **pwd** are especially important; they produce their output on *stdout,* so they can be coupled with other commands via pipes to create more complex commands. Once you have directories set up, you will need to begin working with files of data and information.

File Commands

The most common file commands are: **cat**, **cp**, **mv**, and **rm**. The **cat** command takes its arguments, opens the indicated files, and copies them to standard output. **Cat** allows you to display them on your terminal or redirect them into other files:

```
cat .profile
PATH = ${PATH}:${HOME}/bin
export PATH

cat january february march > status_1Q_90
```

The move (**mv**) and copy (**cp**) commands work similarly. You can move or copy one file to another:

```
mv file1 file2
cp file1 file2
```

Or you can move or copy many files into another directory:

```
mv file1 file2 file3 directory
cp file1 file2 file3 directory
```

At other times, you may want to remove (**rm**) one or more files:

```
rm file_name
rm file1 file2 file3
```

Metacharacters

The Shell assumes that anything on a command line that is not a command or an option is a file, directory, or special file. To simplify handling files and directories there is another facility, called metacharacters, which:

- reduces the amount of typing necessary,
- encourages good naming conventions, and
- simplifies Shell programming.

The Shell provides the user with special characters (* ? \ [...]) to allow automatic substitution of characters in file names. These special characters, sometimes called metacharacters, are shown in Table 3.2. In a previous example, I used the **cat** command to copy the first three chapters of this book into a single file:

```
cat chapter1 chapter2 chapter3 > book
```

This could have been handled more easily in any of the following ways:

```
cat ch* > book
cat chapter? > book
cat chapter[123] > book
```

Metacharacters can significantly reduce the keystrokes required to access a series of file names. There are a few drawbacks, however. In the previous example, I would have gotten different results if the following files existed in the directory:

```
chapter1 chapter2 chapter3 chapter4 charles
```

The first command would have concatenated all five files. The second command would have concatenated the first four. The last command would have been the only one that worked exactly as required. Metacharacters can reduce typing effort, but can give unexpected results, depending on the files in a directory.

Other special Shell characters are shown in Table 3.3. We'll demonstrate how to use them as we progress through the book.

TABLE 3.2   Metacharacters

Metacharacter	Description
*	matches any string of characters (including none)
?	matches any single alphanumeric character
[...]	matches any single character within the brackets
\m	matches any single metacharacter
[a-z]*	matches anything that consists of lower case alphabetic characters
chap?	matches any five-letter name that begins with 'chap'
*	matches the character '*'

TABLE 3.3   Special Characters

Character	Purpose	Example
;	sequential command separator	*cmd1*; *cmd2*; *cmd3*
&	background command	*cmd&*
()	groups the *stdout* of commands	(*cmd1* | *cmd2*; *cmd3*)
| ^	create a pipe	*cmd1* | *cmd2* ^ *cmd3*
<	input redirection	*cmd1* < *file*
>	output redirection	*cmd2* > *file*
${*var*}	variable	${*variable*}
`cmd`	substitute *stdout*	*var*=`cmd2`
\	quote a character	*
'*string*'	quote all characters in string	'$1,000'
"*string*"	quote but allow substitution	"${var} $1"
*	match any string of characters	`cat ch*`
?	match any single character	`cat chapter?`
[*characters*]	match enclosed characters	`cat chapter[0-9]`
#	comment	`# execute command`

File Splitting Commands

Having put the files together, you may need to split them apart. There are two key System V programs to support splitting files: **split** and **csplit**. Split chops files into smaller ones that contain a user-specified number of lines. To split **book** into 100-line files, I could use the following command:

```
split -100 book
ls
book
xaa
xab
xac
```

This might not give me exactly what I want, however. To split the book back into chapters, I could use **csplit**—a context split. Csplit splits files wherever it finds a match between its arguments and the content of the file. For example, to split the file by chapter, I could use the following:

```
csplit -f Chapter book "/Chapter 1/" "/Chapter 2/" "/Chapter 3/"
ls Chapter*
Chapter00
Chapter01
Chapter02
Chapter03
```

In this example, **csplit** created four files; using the prefix (-f Chapter), it divided the chapters wherever it found the chapter headers. **Csplit** always begins numbering the created files from 00. The first file, in this example, would be a null file.

Now that you know how to find and manipulate files and directories, it is important to learn how to extract information from either.

SELECTION COMMANDS

Every Shell user will need to select, extract, and organize information from existing files, thereby transforming data into information. Several Shell commands make it easy to select information (by row and column) and prepare it for printing or processing. The commands to handle this important task are shown in Figure 3.2.

To begin to understand why these commands are important and how they work, we must again look at how to structure data files. All files are simple, "flat" files, but through the addition of delimiters like the tab character, these flat files become transformed. What was once a flat file can become a relational data base (Figure 3.3) or a spreadsheet (Figure 3.4). Why not use a true relational data base or a spreadsheet, you might ask? If you have access to one, do so. Most relational data base management systems (RDBMS) and spreadsheets, however, do not keep their data in a form that is directly accessible by Shell. You may have to export data from the software packages to get them into a simple format that is usable by Shell. We'll discuss how to do this in later chapters, but for now you can keep the same data in simple files that are easily accessible.

To get data from a spreadsheet or an RDBMS, you need to be able to select information by row (horizontal) and column (vertical). **Grep**, **head**, **line**, **sed**, **tail**, and **uniq** operate on rows. **Cut** operates on columns.

awk	pattern scanning and processing language
cut	select columns
diff	compare and select differences in two files
grep	select lines or rows using a single matching criterion
egrep	select lines or rows using multiple matching criteria
fgrep	select lines or rows that exactly match the criteria
head	select leading lines or rows
line	select the first line or row of a file
sed	edit streams of data
tail	select the trailing lines or rows in a file
uniq	select unique lines or rows
wc	count characters, words, and lines in a file

Figure 3.2   Selection commands

Social						
Security	\<tab\>	Last	\<tab\>	First	\<tab\>	Middle
Number	\<tab\>	Name	\<tab\>	Name	\<tab\>	Initial
527964942	\<tab\>	Arthur	\<tab\>	Lowell	\<tab\>	Jay
234567890	\<tab\>	Doe	\<tab\>	John	\<tab\>	D.

Figure 3.3   Relational table

Month	\<tab\>	Income	\<tab\>	Expense
Jan	\<tab\>	10000	\<tab\>	9000
Feb	\<tab\>	12000	\<tab\>	10500
Mar	\<tab\>	11500	\<tab\>	9800

Figure 3.4   Spreadsheet

Line or Row Commands

There are some simple ways of getting information from files. The first is System V's **line**, which can easily get the first line from a file. The first line is an excellent place to put any heading information:

```
line < employee_file
SSN Name Street City State
```

Or you may want to look at only the first few lines of a file. Two commands support previewing files: **head** and **sed**. **Head** is not available on most System V UNIX systems, because it can be implemented by **sed**. If you wanted to view the first 10 lines of a file, the following two commands would be equivalent:

```
head file
sed -e '11,$d' file
```

Similarly, you could use **tail** to view the last 10 lines of a file:

```
tail file
tail < file
```

Although these commands are simple methods of extracting information from a file, there are other, more exotic ways of selecting information. The **grep** command finds and selects information that is often hidden deep within files. It looks for character strings in files and writes the requested information on *stdout*. You might, for example, want to determine each of the chapters that has the word PATH in it. To do so, you would enter the command on page 34:

```
grep PATH chapter?
chapter2: PATH = ${PATH}:${HOME}/bin
chapter2: export PATH

  .

  .

chapter9: the PATH variable.
```

Unfortunately, **grep** also provided all of the lines in each of these files that contain PATH. To get just the name, you would use the -l option:

```
grep -l PATH *
chapter2
chapter9
```

Or, you may want to know which lines in the files contain PATH. You could use the -n option and enter the following command:

```
grep -n PATH chapter2
28:PATH = $PATH:$HOME/bin
29:export PATH
```

When using **grep**, if you are looking for strings of more than one word, you must enclose the string in double quotes; otherwise **grep** thinks that the spaces or tabs between words separate the search string from the file names:

```
grep -l export PATH *
cannot open PATH
```

```
grep -l "export PATH" *
chapter2
```

There are two other forms of **grep**: **egrep** or extended **grep**, and **fgrep** or fast **grep**. **Egrep** looks for more than one string at a time; **fgrep** looks for many strings that *exactly* match a line of the file. These two variations of the command provide efficiency when looking for multiple strings in the same files. For simplicity, however, I find it most useful to stick with **grep**.

Another useful command, word count (**wc**), can count the number of characters, words, and lines in a file. The counts of characters and words are useful for determining speed, productivity, and document content. The number of lines in a file, however, is often useful in Shell programs to determine the scope of a file. Sorts work more efficiently when they know the exact number of lines or records in the file. Also, if a command should create only 10 records instead of 10,000, you could use **wc** to check the outcome of the processing. To find out how many files contain the word PATH, for example, you could couple **grep** with **wc**:

```
grep -l PATH chapter? | wc -l
2
```

Grep is the key tool for extracting information from fields of data. Another useful command is **uniq**. In its simplest form, **uniq** removes identical lines or rows from a file. Invariably, data is duplicated throughout files and data bases. **Uniq** gets rid of the redundancy. For **uniq** to work, however, the file must be sorted. We'll see how to do this a little later in this chapter.

Column Commands

Cut does exactly what its name suggests—it cuts files into columns that can be pasted back together in some other usable fashion. **Cut** can operate on a character-by-character or field-by-field basis, or some combination of both. These columns can be put back together later, using a command called **paste**. **Paste**, unlike **cut**, works line by line to put new files together.

One of the simplest examples of using **cut** involves finding a person's name in the /etc/passwd file using just his or her *logname*. If you entered the following commands you would get the lines shown:

```
who
root console Jan 2 6:00
lja ttyp0 Jan 2 8:30
```

```
grep lja /etc/passwd
lja:password:user#:group#:Jay Arthur x9999:/unix1/lja:/bin/sh
```

This is more information than needed. **Cut**, however, can extract the required fields. Fields in /etc/passwd are delimited by a colon (. Field one is the login name; field two, the password; and so on. All you really need are fields one and five. **Grep** and **cut** can retrieve this information:

```
grep lja /etc/passwd | cut -f1,5 -d:
lja:Jay Arthur x9999
```

When creating files using Shell, use delimiters to take advantage of **cut** and a command we'll discuss in a moment, **paste**. Most files currently created or maintained in the UNIX system have delimiters to facilitate their use.

Even without delimiters in a file, **cut** can be useful. For example, some of the outputs from Shell commands are not delimited. The output of the **ls -l** command has no delimiters. **Cut** can be used, on a character-by-character basis, to extract only the data required:

```
ls -l | cut -c1-15,55-
drwxrwx---           3          bin
drwx------          28          doc
drwxrwxrwx          32          src
```

Like **grep**, **cut** is an incredibly powerful command for operating on tables of data; it removes the fat from the meat of the information you require. Having looked at ways of selecting information, let's look at ways of combining and ordering the selected data to create even more useful information.

COMBINING AND ORDERING COMMANDS

When you have selected the data you need, the next logical step is to refine it further, using the commands shown in Figure 3.5. Using selection commands, you can extract information from a file in any form required. Once the files are cut into several slices, however, you will want to recombine them in a different order to present the information in a more usable form.

Paste

Paste can put files together in useful ways. **Paste** works on single files, multiple files, or the standard input. The syntax of the paste command takes several forms:

```
paste file(s)              #paste two or more files together
paste -d"list" file(s)     #paste files using specified delimiters
paste -s -d"list" files    #paste subsequent lines of files
paste - -                  #paste two subsequent lines from stdin
```

Using the **ls** command, for example, you can easily create a multiple column listing of a directory's contents:

```
ls -a | paste - - - -
.            ..          .cshrc .login
.profile  bin         doc    src
```

The dashes tell **paste** to use one line from standard input in each of those positions. The same result could have been obtained with the following commands:

```
ls -a > dirlist
paste -s -d"\t\t\t\n" dirlist
.            ..          .cshrc .login
.profile  bin         doc    src
```

join	joins two files, matching row by row
paste	pastes multiple files, column by column
sort	sorts and merges multiple files together

Figure 3.5   Combining and ordering commands

The -s parameter tells **paste** to merge subsequent lines from the same file. The -d parameter tells **paste** to use the characters between the double quotes as delimiters between subsequent lines. In this case, the first three delimiters are tabs(\t); the last delimiter is the newline character (\n). The following command would produce an output with two items per line:

```
paste -s -d"\t\n" dirlist
.cshrc    .login
.profile  bin
doc       src
```

Paste can also put two files together once they have been separated. Using the passwd file, let's extract two of the fields and put them back together in a different order:

```
cut -f1 -d: /etc/passwd > temp1
cut -f5 -d: /etc/passwd > temp2
paste temp2 temp1 > loginlist
pr -e20 loginlist

Jay Arthur x9999 lja
Paula Martin x9999 pgm
```

This could also be accomplished using **awk**:

```
awk -F: '{print $5 $1}' /etc/passwd
Jay Arthur x9999 lja
Paula Martin x9999 pgm
```

The secret to making people more productive is to select the right data and present it in a usable format. **Grep**, **cut**, and **paste** provide a tremendous facility to extract only the data needed, recombine the fields, create a new file, or print the information with another command. **Grep** and **cut** select the data required. **Paste** combines selected data into a usable format.

These commands provide the basic tools of a relational database: select and join. It takes a while to gain an understanding of the use and relationships among these commands, but once acquired, you will wonder how you ever got along without them.

Sort

In many cases, sorting the data makes the resulting output easier to use. In other cases, it may be necessary to merge two files that have already been sorted on a common key. The **sort** command performs both of these functions. Sorted output often contains duplicate lines of data; **uniq** will remove them or display only the repeated lines. **Uniq** facilitates the removal or selection of duplicate data—a common requirement in Shell programming.

The **sort** command, as you might have guessed, works character-by-character, field-by-field, or in some combination of the two. Once again, **sort** is designed to work easily with **grep**, **cut**, and **paste**. For efficiency, **sort** should be used after the data has been selected with **grep** and **cut**. Why sort a whole file when you can sort a small subset of the total data? For example, I could sort the passwd file by user ID and then extract all of the users under the file system /unix1:

```
sort -t: +0 -1 /etc/passwd | grep unix1 | cut -f1 -d:
lja
pgm
```

This example forces the Shell to sort the entire passwd file and then extract the pertinent information. It would have been more efficient to extract the data and then sort it:

```
grep unix1 /etc/passwd | cut -f1 -d: | sort
lja
pgm
```

Looking at the previous two examples, you might wonder why the first one had the options: +0 -1. These options told **sort** to use field 0 as the sort key. Since there was only one field in the second example, no options were necessary. Why does **sort** count from field 0 and character 0? I don't know. It has confused more people than it has helped. I presume that because C language counts from 0, **sort** was designed to take advantage of humans instead of the opposite. Figure 3.6 shows a variety of **sort** commands and the sort keys that will be used.

To specify that the fields are delimited by other than white space—blanks or tabs, you must specify the character using the -t option. In the passwd file example, the delimiter was a colon(:). In some files, it may be a blank: -t" ". If there are no consistent field delimiters in the file, use 0.(character position) to

`sort -nr file`	sort in reverse numerical order
`sort -t: +0 -2 file`	sort on fields 1 and 2 delimited by a ":"
`sort +0.20 -0.25 file`	sort on characters 20–25
`sort -rt" " +3 -4 file`	sort on field 4 delimited by blanks
`sort -m file1 file2`	merge file1 and file2

Figure 3.6 Various sort commands

identify the start and end positions. To sort a long listing of a directory by the number of characters in each file, in descending (reverse) sequence, use the following command:

```
ls -al | sort +4nr
-rwxr-xr-x          1      lja      adm      12839    Jun 23 05:12 .profile
-rwxr-xr-x          1      lja      adm       4839    Jun 23 05:12 .cshrc
-rwxr-xr-x          1      lja      adm       4139    Jun 23 05:12 .login
drwxrwxrwx         32      lja      adm       1008    Dec 3 18:22 src
drwxrwx             3      lja      adm        992    Dec 1 05:39 bin
drwx               28      lja      adm        496    Dec 4 12:28 doc
```

Merge

Sort can organize any UNIX file by fields or characters. Occasionally, the need arises to combine two or more files that are already sorted. In these cases, it is more efficient to merge the files. The output of the **ls** command, for example, is already sorted. To get a sorted listing of the commands available to a user under the /bin and /usr/bin directories, the following commands would provide equivalent outputs:

```
ls /bin > binlist
ls /usr/bin > usrbinlist
sort binlist usrbinlist > cmdlist

ls /bin > binlist
ls /usr/bin | sort -m binlist - > cmdlist
```

Since merging is more efficient than sorting, the second set of commands is preferable. The last command uses the dash (-) to tell **sort** to look for one of its inputs on *stdin* (the output of "ls /usr/bin"). This eliminates one temporary file, another efficiency consideration. The cmdlist file can now be printed or included in a memo or user guide.

As previously mentioned, problems can occur when there are duplicate command names in /bin, /usr/bin, and user bins. To identify these potential problems, you could manually compare the three listings of /bin, /usr/bin, and $HOME/ bin. This is nothing but drudgery and prone to error. It can be automated using **join**, which reads two files as input and puts out a single file containing a "join" of only those lines from both files that match on a specified field (normally the first and in this case the command names):

```
ls /bin > binlist
ls $HOME/bin > homebinlist
join binlist homebinlist
cat
sort
```

Sort and **uniq** can automate this analysis when more than two files are involved:

```
ls /bin > binlist
ls /usr/bin > usrbinlist
ls $HOME/bin > homebinlist
sort -m binlist usrbinlist homebinlist | uniq -d
cat
sort
```

There are two commands, **cat** and **sort**, that are duplicated in two of the three directories. These could be easily located:

```
egrep cat\|sort *binlist
binlist:cat
binlist:sort
homebinlist:cat
homebinlist:sort
```

Similarly, **uniq** could have been used to create a merged listing of the three directories, excluding all duplicate command names:

```
sort -m binlist usrbinlist homebinlist | uniq > cmdlist
```

In other instances, use **uniq** to show only those lines that are not repeated. When comparing two directories that should have identical contents, the only concern is the files unique to each directory. To list them, use the following command:

```
ls dir1 > dir1list
ls dir2 | sort -m dir1list - | uniq -u > differences
```

Sort, **join**, and **uniq** are powerful tools for manipulating information and preparing it for human consumption. Combined with selection commands, they provide a marvelous facility to automate the common functions of data selection, combination, and ordering. The remaining needs of a Shell programmer are to transform or translate the information into another form, and to print the results.

TRANSFORMERS AND TRANSLATORS

Two of the main facilities for transforming or translating data (see Figure 3.7) are **sed** (the stream editor) and **tr** (translator). **Sed** transforms incoming data by executing editor commands on the standard input. **Tr** translates incoming data, character by character, based on conversion tables specified by the user. In Chapter Thirteen we'll look at ways to build custom filters that go beyond these two; for now, let's look at ways to use these standard transformers.

```
sed    edit streams of data
tr     transform character by character
```

Figure 3.7   Data transformers and translators

Sed is used in pipes in place of the standard line editor (**ed**). For simple substitutions, you can put the editor commands on the command line:

```
sed -e "s/shell/Shell/" Chapter1 > newchapter1
```

For more complex transformations involving many substitutions, you can put the editor commands in a file and specify them as input to **sed**:

```
sed -f sedfile Chapter1 > newchapter1
```

where sedfile contains the following:

```
s/shell/Shell/
s/c language/C Language/
```

Sed is an efficient method of transforming a file into some other usable format. For example, the output of the word count command (**wc**) looks like this:

```
wc -l file
   35 file
```

The file has 35 lines in it. Using **sed**, the numbers can be extracted by removing blanks, tabs, and the characters "a-z" as follows:

```
wc -l file | sed -e "s/[\ta-z][\ta-z]*//g"
35
```

```
wc -l < file
    35
```

The translate command **tr** works similarly to the **sed** command, but it changes the standard input character-by-character rather than string-by-string. **Sed** operates on strings but is hard to use on a character-by-character basis. Use the following command to translate a file from upper case into lower case:

```
tr "[A-Z]" "[a-z]" < uppercase > lowercase
```

The expression "[A-Z]" signifies the upper-case letters from A to Z. The second expression "[a-z]" tells **tr** to replace the lower-case letters, on a one-for-one basis, with the upper-case letters. Doing this with **sed** would take a file with 26 editor commands; **tr** is much simpler.

Tr can also be used in other situations that require transformations. If I wanted to change a file called chapter1 into a file of just words and obtain a sorted listing of the words and the number of times they were used, I could issue the following command:

```
tr "[ ]" "[\012]" < chapter1 | sort | uniq -c
```

In this example, **tr** translates blanks into newline (\012) characters (one word per line). These are then sorted in alphabetical order and counted by **uniq**. This output would show all of the words in the document and the number of times they occur. The sequence can be used to identify overused words that should be varied to improve the quality of the prose.

Similarly, to convert a file delimited by colons(:) to a file delimited by tab characters, you could use either of the following commands:

```
sed -e "s/:/\t/g" < colonfile > tabfile
tr "[:]" "[\t]" < colonfile > tabfile
```

Many more transformations are possible and will be introduced in subsequent chapters.

Both **sed** and **tr** are useful for translating and transforming a file or input stream. **Sed** is stronger for use with strings, words, or lines. **Tr** is stronger when operating on characters. Each plays an integral part in the use of the Shell.

EDITORS

UNIX editors (and there are a slew of them; see Figure 3.8) are also commands available to the Shell. The specifics of using each editor have been left out of this section because editor usage varies from installation to installation.

Sometimes it is not possible to **grep**, **cut**, **paste**, **sed**, or **tr** a file into a required format. A few additional lines or human analysis will be needed. In these cases, you can use the editor of your choice from within a Shell command. Editors are an important tool to manipulate text. When used repetitively within a Shell procedure, they become more beneficial.

ed	line editor
emacs	a screen editor
se	another screen editor
vi	the most common screen editor

Figure 3.8   UNIX editors

Ed

As previously described, the standard UNIX line editor **ed** can use commands typed in-line as follows:

```
ed file <<eof!
/First/
a
These are the times that try men's souls
And mine too for that matter.
.
w
q
eof!
```

This would find the line with the first occurrence of "First" and append the next two lines after that line. This facility is occasionally useful in Shell commands.

Vi, Se, Emacs, and Other Editors

From the terminal, **vi** or any of the other editors can be invoked interactively. They can also be used in Shell commands to present a file to a user for editing:

```
vi chapter?
```

The UNIX line and screen editors offer an easy way to create or modify a file. They have many uses in Shell programming.

PRINTING

The previous sections have discussed various ways of selecting information from files, translating the information into other forms, and sorting the information into a meaningful order. These are the essential steps in preparing information for use. The final step displays the information on the user's screen or printer.

All of the Shell commands have *stdout* and *stderr* files that can be displayed on the screen or a printer. These outputs can be redirected into files or devices, but these outputs are rarely formatted for easy human consumption. The facilities for formatting output are **cat**, **more**, **pg**, **pr**, **nroff**, and **awk**. Some are screen-oriented; others are more paper-oriented.

Screen-Oriented Displays

Cat, as we have seen, reads a file and "prints" it exactly as found. **Cat** is effective for simple viewing of a file. For more relaxed viewing, **pg** or **more** will display the file one page at a time.

The commands to display a C language file on a screen and pause between pages are:

```
pg file.c or more file.c
```

Paper-Oriented Displays

Regardless of how much people talk about "paperless" offices, there seems to be no end to the amount of reports that need to be printed and distributed. Shell provides you with many ways of formatting reports.

Pr prints files with simple headings and page breaks. Where **cat** lists a file exactly as it exists, **pr** provides the file name and date of last modification in the page header and provides facilities to break the output every so many lines for clarity. The command line to print a C language file is:

```
pr file.c
```

The command to display the file on a 25-line terminal screen and pause between pages is:

```
pr –124 –p –t –w79 file.c
pg file.c or more file.c
```

To print a file, delimited by colons(:), with a special heading and 20-character-width fields, the command is:

```
pr –e:20 –h "Special Report" file
```

To obtain a more attractive listing, use the print command (**pr**):

```
ls –a > dirlist
paste –s –d"\t\n" dirlist | pr –e20
.            ..
.cshrc       .login
.profile     bin
doc          src
```

Or more simply:

```
ls –a | pr –2 –e20
.            ..
.cshrc       .login
.profile     bin
doc          src
```

Nroff is a text-formatting program that prints documents using **nroff** and various formatting macros, but it can be used with files whose fields are delimited by unique characters, like the password file. **Tbl**, the table preprocessor, creates the input to **nroff**.

Tbl requires a text file like the following:

```
.TS
tab(:) ;          ⎫
1 1 n n 1 1 1.    ⎬   tablestart
                  ⎭

text file

.TE               } tableend
```

The password file can be formatted with **tbl** and **nroff** as follows:

```
tbl tablestart /etc/passwd tableend | nroff
```

Awk For those users who have even more rigorous reporting requirements, **awk** (a pattern scanning and processing language named after its developers, Aho, Kernighan, and Weinberger) provides many of the capabilities of C language. It allows variable definition and control flow, but is interpretive and therefore more responsive to users' needs than compiling and testing C language programs.

One of the previous examples formatted the /etc/passwd file using **awk** to print the first and fifth items in the file:

```
awk -F: '{print $5 $3}' /etc/passwd
```

This example could be expanded by creating a file called passwdprnt to print the other fields of the /etc/passwd file as follows:

```
BEGIN { FS = : }
{ printf "%-3s %.4d %.4d %-35s %s\n", $1, $3, $4, $5, $6 }
```

"$1" represents the first field in each line of the passwd file; "$2", the second; and so on. The format shown following the **printf** statement uses the same conventions of the C language **printf** statement. The command to print the file would be:

```
awk -f passwdprnt /etc/passwd
```

Awk uses the passwdprnt file as the program to process the file /etc/passwd. The resulting output would be:

```
lja    1    1    Jay Arthur x9999 /unix1/lja
pgm    2    2    Paula Martin x9999 /unix1/pgm
```

Awk, **pr**, and **nroff** give the user a variety of ways of printing information that has been selected and sorted by the commands already described in this chapter. These formatted reports simplify human interaction with UNIX and are desirable. Human effectiveness is only as good as the information given and the format in which it is presented.

SECURITY

Security is an important feature of UNIX and the Shell. You can create files and, by setting the permissions, allow people to read, write, or execute your files. The permissions are established in binary as shown in Figure 3.9. Two commands affect the accessibility of a file: **umask** and **chmod**. The long form of the list command (**ls -l**) will display the accessibility of any file or directory that the user can read.

There are three levels of security: what the owner of the file can do, what his or her related group can do, and what the world can do. The different levels or modes are also shown in Figure 3.9.

The **umask** command sets up the default security for any file or directory created. The default security for a file is 666 (read and write permission for everyone). The default security for a directory is 777 (read, write, and execute). Without the execute bit, directories cannot be searched. The **umask** command tells the operating system which permissions to exclude when creating a new file or directory. The **umask** command is executed at login time by either /etc/profile,

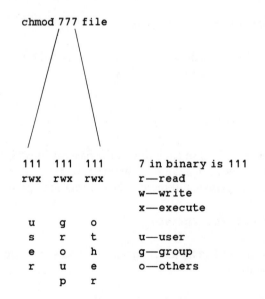

Figure 3.9   File security

$HOME/.profile, $HOME/.cshrc, or $HOME/.login. The most common **umask** command is:

```
umask 022
```

which says to omit write permission for the user's group and the world. Everyone can read your files or directories, but no one can write in or over them. If you want to keep the world out of your files, put the following command in your .profile or .cshrc:

```
umask 027
```

This lets your group read your files or directories but prohibits any other user from accessing your files in any way.

Once the file or directory has been created with default security, you will occasionally need to change the permissions on individual files or directories. The change mode command (**chmod**) allows you to do so:

```
chmod 755 shellcommand
chmod +x shellcommand
```

When you write a Shell command with one of the editors, the file is normally created with read and write permissions, but not execute permission. To make the file executable, you must change the permissions as shown above. To let your group and yourself execute the command, you would enter:

```
chmod 750 shellcommand
chmod ug+x,o-rwx shellcommand
```

Sometimes you will create an important file that you do not want to delete. The remove command **rm** will remove anything for which you have write permission. To get **rm** to ask you before it removes the important file, you can change the file's mode:

```
chmod 444 importantfile
chmod -w importantfile
rm *
rm: importantfile mode 444 ?
```

The **umask** and **chmod** commands allow control of file and directory access. Changing permissions is necessary and continuous in a UNIX environment. Knowing how to make files accessible and executable is an important part of creating Shell commands, but now we need to understand how the Shell finds commands.

BUILT-IN COMMANDS

The Shell, for efficiency, includes several built-in commands. The Bourne Shell has the fewest, relying on existing commands to do the work. For this reason, it is the smallest and fastest of the three shells. The Korn and C Shell have the most built-in commands, so they are noticeably larger and but not noticeably slower. The Shell built-in commands are shown in Table 3.4. They will be discussed in more detail in future sections.

TABLE 3.4 Shell Built-in Commands

Bourne/Korn Shell	C Shell	Purpose
:	:	null command
	alias	create a command name alias
	bg	run current command in background
break	break	exit enclosing `for` or `while` loop
	breaksw	break out of a `switch`
cd		change directory
continue		continue next iteration of `for` or `while` loop
	default	default case in `switch`
	dirs	print directory stack
	echo	write arguments on *stdout*
eval		evaluate and execute arguments
exec		execute the arguments
exit	exit	exit shell program
export		create a global variable
	fg	bring a command into foreground
for	foreach	execute `foreach` loop
	glob	perform file name expansion
	goto	go to label within shell program
	history	display history list
if	if	if-then-else decision
	jobs	list active jobs
	kill	kill a job
	limit	limit a job's resource usage
	login	terminate login shell and invoke `login`
	logout	terminate a login shell
newgrp		change to a new user group
	nice	change priority of a command
	nohup	ignore hang ups
	notify	notify user when job status changes
	onintr	control shell processing on interrupt
	popd	pop the directory stack
	pushd	push a directory onto the stack

TABLE 3.4 *(Continued)*

Bourne/Korn Shell	C Shell	Purpose
`read`		read a line from *stdin*
`readonly`		change a variable to read only
	`repeat`	repeat a command *n* times
`set`		set shell environment variables
	`set`	set a local C Shell variable
	`setenv`	set a global C Shell variable
`shift`	`shift`	shift the shell parameters $* or $argv
	`source`	read and execute a file
	`stop`	stop a background process
	`suspend`	stop the shell
	`switch`	CASE decision
`test`		evaluate conditional expressions
`times`	`time`	display execution times
`trap`		manage execution `signals`
`ulimit`		limit file sizes written by child processes
`umask`		set default security for files and directories
	`unalias`	discard aliases
	`unlimit`	remove limitations on resources
	`unset`	unset a local variable
	`unsetenv`	unset a global variable
`until`		UNTIL loop
`wait`		wait for a background process to complete
`while`	`while`	WHILE loop
	`% job`	bring a background job to foreground
`expr`	`@`	display or set shell variables

HOW THE SHELL FINDS COMMANDS

Most Shell commands reside in directories called "bins": /bin and /usr/bin. Others, important only to the system administrator, reside in /etc, /usr/rje, and /usr/adm. Users can create their own bin directories (more on this in Chapter Four). For the majority of users, the commands available in /bin and /usr/bin will be of most importance. The /usr/ucb/bin contains the Berkeley BSD 4.3 commands. On Berkeley systems, System V commands can be found in /usr/5bin.

When a user logs in, the Shell sets up a standard environment using several variables (see Table 3.5). The Shell uses the PATH (sh, ksh) or path (csh) variable to find each bin that a user can access. The PATH variable is initialized at login time. To find out the default paths available, try the following command:

```
echo $PATH     echo $path
:/bin:/usr/bin:    . /bin /usr/bin
```

TABLE 3.5   Shell Variables

Bourne/Korn Shell	C Shell	Purpose
`CDPATH`	`cdpath`	search path for `cd`
		`cwd` full path name of current directory
`HOME`	`home`	path name of the user's login directory
`MAIL`	`mail`	name of user's mail file
`PATH`	`path`	the Shell's search path for commands
`PS1`	`prompt`	the primary prompt string
		`"$"` for Bourne/Korn Shell systems
		`"hostname%"` for C Shell systems
		`"#"` for superuser
`PS2`		the secondary prompt string: ">"
`IFS`		internal field separators (space, tab, newline)
	`history`	number of commands remembered by history
	`ignoreeof`	ignore end of file
	`noclobber`	don't overwrite existing files
	`noglob`	inhibit file name expansion

The response means that you have all of the standard Shell commands available for execution. The Shell uses the PATH variable to determine where to search for commands and in what order you want to search the bins. The current value of PATH indicates that the Shell will search first the current directory, then /bin, and finally /usr/bin. The current directory is represented by a null name, followed by a colon. You can change the order of the search by redefining the value of PATH as follows:

```
PATH=/usr/bin:/bin::      set path=( . /usr/bin /bin )
```

which reverses the order of the search.

If you had a user bin under your home directory, you might add it to the search path using another Shell variable, HOME:

```
PATH=${PATH}:${HOME}/bin   set path=( ${path} ${HOME}/bin )
```

Using my login as an example, this would change the value of PATH to:

```
/usr/bin:/bin::/enduser/lja/bin
```

Whenever I execute a command, the Shell will look first in /usr/bin, then in /bin and the current directory, and finally in my user bin. This means that I can type a command name and the Shell will find it; I do not have to type in the full path name to use a command I have created. This is an important feature of the Shell that helps improve productivity; bins full of user commands can be placed anywhere in the system and accessed directly via the PATH variable.

The system administrator can redefine PATH to include common user bins by inserting the following lines into /etc/profile or a C Shell user's .cshrc:

```
        PATH=:/bin:/usr/bin:/local/bin
        export PATH
csh: set path=( . /bin /usr/bin /local/bin )
```

The export command makes the PATH variable available to all subsequent processes initiated by the user.

Because users would rather not change the PATH variable during every session, they may further modify the PATH variable automatically at login time. The PATH variable can be modified using either /etc/profile or the .profile in the users' home directory. In a C Shell system, the path variable can be modified in the users' .login or .cshrc files, which reside in the users' home directory. You can create the .profile (csh: .login/.cshrc) file in your HOME directory and add the following two lines to include your own command bin:

```
PATH=${PATH}:${HOME}/bin      setenv path=( $path ${HOME}/bin )
export PATH
```

These two lines will add your bin to the Shell's search path. The Shell will then be able to look automatically in all command bins to find any command you request. Problems can occur, however, if there are two commands with the same name in different bin directories; the Shell will execute the first one it finds. This is especially important in systems that have all three shells: Bourne, Korn, and C. Not all System V commands behave like Berkeley commands. To obtain System V commands, put them first in the PATH variable. On Berkeley UNIX systems, reverse the positions of /usr/5bin and /usr/ucb:

```
        PATH=:/bin:/usr/bin:/usr/5bin:/usr/ucb
csh: set path=(. /bin /usr/bin /usr/ucb /usr/5bin)
```

That's about all you need to know about the PATH variable. If you execute a command but it doesn't behave like the documentation, you might suspect the PATH variable is pointing to libraries in the wrong order.

The Bourne and Korn Shells also use an environment variable, CDPATH, with the **cd** command, to reduce typing. The users can set up CDPATH in their .profile to include any of their major directories. Then, no matter where they are in the directory structure, all they have to do is **cd** to the directory name and the Shell remembers where those directories are and changes to them without extensive typing. For example, if there was an entry in the .profile as follows:

```
CDPATH=$HOME/doc
export CDPATH
```

and you were already in the /usr/bin directory, you could change into the doc directory by typing:

```
cd doc
```

The directories can also be listed like the PATH variable to give immediate access to any of the major directories:

```
CDPATH=$HOME/bin:$HOME/doc:$HOME/src
export CDPATH
```

Using the **cd** command, users can change from one directory to another without typing long path names. The Shell will print the path name of the directory it has changed into:

```
cd doc
/unix1/lja/doc
```

SUMMARY

Shell commands are usually found in directories called bin. The two most frequently used directories are /bin and /usr/bin. As a user or toolsmith develops new Shell tools, they can be placed in local bins that can be directly addressed via the PATH variable.

The most commonly used file and directory commands are **ls**, **cd**, **cat**, and **grep**. The output of these commands has been structured to maximize their utility when combined with other commands, like **cut**, **paste**, **uniq**, and **pr**, that select portions of their output and report the information required.

Ordering the output in a meaningful way is the job of **sort , which handles both sorting and merging information. The join** command also can be used to integrate information from two different files.

Once output files have been created, the information they contain can be translated by **sed** or **tr**. **Sed** operates on strings of information; **tr** operates on characters.

More complex transformations that require operator intervention can be handled by using the UNIX editors. These can be invoked directly from the Shell or Shell procedures.

The output of these commands can be formatted for ease of use with the **awk**, **pr**, and **nroff** commands. Each of these commands can work on files of lines and the fields within those lines. **Awk** and **pr**, in particular, are good for prototyping report programs. **Awk** allows the user to create detailed reports that are not easily possible with the other two commands.

These basic commands are the roots of more advanced usage of the Shell.

Understanding how they interact with each other via the pipe or by input/output redirection is essential to advanced Shell usage.

EXERCISES

1. Describe the importance of PATH and CDPATH.

2. Describe the use of the Shell metacharacters:
   a. *
   b. ?
   c. [...]
   d. \

3. Given a directory containing the following files,

   Abel, Cain, George, Gorth, Greg, Sam, Ted, Trod

   use the **ls** command to list only those files:

   a. consisting of three letters
   b. consisting of four letters
   c. that begin with a "G" followed by "e" or "o"
   d. that begin with "T" and end with "d"

4. Describe the **ls**, **pwd**, and **cat** commands.

5. Describe the **grep**, **cut**, and **paste** commands.

6. Describe the use of **sort**, **join**, and **uniq**.

7. Name the different Shell translation commands and the type of data (strings, characters, delimiters) they are best designed to handle.

8. Write a Shell to extract, sort, and print all users in the global file system. (Use the /etc/passwd file as input.)

9. Using the Shell from exercise 8, extract only those users with multiple entries in the /etc/passwd file.

10. Write a Shell to translate the /etc/passwd file into upper case and translate the colon (:) delimiters into tab characters.

11. Describe the usage of **umask** and **chmod**. How do they offer security in a UNIX file system?

12. Write the **umask** command to prohibit all other users (except for the owner) from accessing files created by the owner.
    Write the **chmod** commands to make Shell programs executable by:

    a. the owner
    b. the owner and his or her group
    c. the world

13. Write the **pr** command to print the /etc/group file on the user's screen and printer.

14. Write a simple **awk** command to print the same information from the /etc/group file as in exercise 12.

Chapter Four

Shell Control Structures

Who can control his fate?

Shakespeare

The chapters to this point have provided information about using simple Shell commands. To make full use of the Shell, however, you will need a special set of Shell commands that control what happens and when. These commands will allow you to decide among:

- two different actions (IF-THEN-ELSE)
- many actions (CASE)
- looping through an action many times (FOR, REPEAT, WHILE, and UNTIL).

All third generation programming languages have these basic control structures: IF-THEN-ELSE, CASE, DO WHILE, and DO UNTIL.

The Bourne, Korn, and C Shells all provide these control structures, although the C Shell differs in many respects (Table 4.1). The Bourne Shell relies on the **test** command to handle the evaluation of all conditions. In the C Shell, evaluations of conditions are performed directly by the Shell. The Shell also provides mechanisms for executing repetitive commands interactively: **xargs, repeat** (csh), and **find**. Each of these control structures permits loops and decisions to be made by Shell procedures. There is a way to handle interruptions—breaks, deletes, rubouts, and hangups—named **trap**. Properly written, Shell procedures need never fail because they can always take a reasonable default action using **trap**. The ability to test conditions and take actions is the most important feature of the Shell command language.

TABLE 4.1   Shell Control Structures

Structure	Bourne	Korn	C Shell
IF	`if [...]`	`if [...]`	`if (...) then`
THEN	`then`	`then`	
ELSE-IF	`elif`	`elif`	`else if`
ELSE	`else`	`else`	`else`
ENDIF	`fi`	`fi`	`endif`
CASE	`case`	`case`	`switch`
	`value)`	`value)`	`case value:`
	`;;`	`;;`	`breaksw`
	`*)`	`*)`	`default:`
	`esac`	`esac`	`endsw`
FOR	`for`	`for`	`foreach`
	`do`	`do`	
	`done`	`done`	`end`
REPEAT	`xargs -1`	`xargs -1`	`xargs -1`
			`repeat`
UNTIL	`until`	`until`	
	`do`	`do`	
	`done`	`done`	
WHILE	`while`	`while`	`while`
	`do`	`do`	
	`done`	`done`	`end`

SHELL VARIABLES

The Shell lets you establish variables to hold values while you process them. It provides several standard variables (Table 3.5 and Table 4.2) that are always accessible. Variable names can be of any reasonable length and must begin with an alphabetic character or '_' followed by any of the characters: (_ a-z A-Z 0-9).

You can establish your own variables by simply assigning values to variable names:

```
temp_name=/usr/tmp          set temp_name=/usr/tmp
month=01                    set month=01
```

To access these variables, you can insert the variable name (preceded by a dollar sign) wherever you need it:

```
cp file $temp_name
echo "Current month is $month"
```

TABLE 4.2 Shell Variables

Bourne/Korn Shell	C Shell	Purpose
`$#`	`$#argv`	number of positional arguments
`$0`	`$0`	command name
`$1, $2 ...`	`$1, $2 ...`	positional arguments
	`$argv[n]`	positional arguments $1 ...
`$*`	`$*, $argv[*]`	$1 $2 ...
`$@`		$1 $2 ...
`$-`		shell options from **set** command
`$?`	`$status`	return code from last command
`$$`	`$$`	process number of current command
`$!`		process number of last background command

To be perfectly accurate and prevent errors, you should enclose the name in braces:

```
cp file ${temp_name}
echo "Current month is ${month}"
```

Otherwise, establishing other variable names can lead to problems when the Shell tries to interpret your commands:

```
temp=/tmp/              set temp=/tmp/
echo $temp_name         echo $temp_name
/usr/tmp                /usr/tmp
echo ${temp}_name       echo ${temp}_name
/tmp/_name              /tmp/_name
echo ${temp_name}       echo ${temp_name}
/usr/tmp                /usr/tmp
```

You can assign values to variables directly or from the output of various Shell programs. For example, to create a variable called current_month and assign the system's value for month, we could use the date command:

```
current_month=`date +'%m'`    set current_month=`date +'%m'`
```

The characters surrounding the date command (`) are called accent graves or back quotes. They tell the Shell to execute the command in a sub-Shell and to substitute the resulting value in place of the command. So, the date command returns only the month (%m), a value between 01 and 12. This powerful capability will be explored in more detail as the book progresses.

Because variables can be changed throughout the execution of a Shell program, looping and testing can be done without repeating the logic many times. The examples in the following sections will expand and clarify the benefits and usage of Shell variables.

TEST

At the heart of each control structure is a conditional test. The **test** command can determine whether a given name is a file or directory; whether it is readable, writable, or executable; and whether two strings or integers are greater than, less than, or equal to each other. Features of **test** also allow AND, OR, and NOT logic. Table 4.3 shows most of the basic comparisons available with **test**.

Test, like any other Shell command, always returns a true (0) or false (1) value in the Shell variable $?. All Shell commands should return a zero (0) when successful and a nonzero value (usually 1 or -1) when they fail.

If a file exists and it is readable the result is true (0):

```
test -r filename          test -r filename
echo $?                   echo $status
0                         0
```

Similarly, if two strings are not equal, **test** returns a false (nonzero) value:

```
test "myname" = "lja"     test "myname" = "lja"
echo $?                   echo $status
1                         1
```

When comparing two strings or a variable and a string, it is best to put both strings in quotes. That way, if one is null, the **test** command will still know how to evaluate the comparison:

```
test "$variable" = "lja"
```

Using the Bourne Shell, **test** can be written by enclosing the conditions in square brackets. The C Shell uses parentheses:

```
if [ -r file_name ]        if ( -r file_name ) then
```

These two versions are preferable because they make the control structures easier to read. The readability becomes apparent when looking at any of the control structures: IF-THEN-ELSE, CASE, DO WHILE, or DO UNTIL. More on using these with **test** will appear in the following sections.

Most tests will be performed on variable names created in the Shell. Use of the control structures will also depend on the use of variables.

TABLE 4.3 Common Test Operators

Bourne/Korn Condition	C Shell Condition	True if . . .
-r *file*	-r *file*	readable *file* exists
-w *file*	-w *file*	writable *file* exists
-x *file*	-x *file*	executable *file* exists
-d *dir*	-d *dir*	directory exists
-s *file*	! -z *file*	*file* exists and contains data
	-z *file*	file exists but contains no data
-z *string*		*string* length = 0
-n *string*		*string* length > 0
str1 = str2	==	*string* 1 equal to *string* 2
str1 != str2	!=	not equal
"*string*"		*string* not null
Numerical Comparisons		
-eq	==	equal
-ne	!=	not equal
-gt	>	greater than
-ge	>=	greater than or equal
-lt	<	less than
-le	<=	less than or equal
!	!	Not
-a	&&	And
-o	||	Or
(...)	(...)	grouping for precedence

EXPR

Like **test**, **expr** evaluates arguments and returns true (0) or false (1) for comparisons. Otherwise, **expr** returns a numerical value from an arithmetic evaluation. **Expr** uses the essentially the same numerical evaluators as the C Shell:

```
if expr $a = $b                    if ($a == $b) then
```

Expr will also work for string comparisons:

```
if expr "$my_name" = "Jay Arthur"  if ("$my_name" == "Jay Arthur")
```

Expr can also perform numerical evaluations, which are more straightforward in C Shell:

```
a=`expr $a + 1`                    @ a += 1
```

SEQUENTIAL CONTROL STRUCTURES

Several devices control execution of sequential commands. They are the following:

;   command delimiter
()   command grouping
``"``   command substitution
&& test for true return code and execute
|| test for false return code and execute

The command delimiter ';' allows for more than one sequential command on one line:

```
cmd1; cmd2; cmd3
```

The grouping parentheses '()' combine the *stdout* and *stderr* of multiple commands into one stream for ease of processing:

```
(cmd1; cmd2 | grep) | wc
```

Note that this cannot be accomplished in C Shell. The output of each command must be placed in a temporary file and then processed by later commands:

```
cmd1 > /tmp/tmp$$; cmd2 | grep >> /tmp/tmp$$
wc /tmp/tmp$$
```

The command substitution allows for the nesting of commands and their application to variables:

```
var=`grep "line" chapter? | line`
```

The two **test** operators '&&' and '||' test the previous command's return code to decide whether to execute the next command:

```
command1 && command2  # execute command2 if command1 returns true
command1 || command2  # execute command2 if command1 returns false
```

These commands control simple sequential execution of commands. To gain further control and the ability to turn information into knowledge, we will need decisions.

IF-THEN-ELSE

You will often want to **test** whether a file exists before attempting to modify it. The simplest way to make a true/false test is with IF-THEN-ELSE (Figure 4.1).

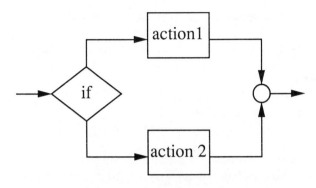

Figure 4.1   IF-THEN-ELSE

Bourne and C Shell versions of the IF-THEN-ELSE are almost identical. The two forms are:

```
if [ test conditions ]      if ( test conditions ) then
then
  process1                          process1
else                        else
  process2                          process2
fi                          endif
```

In most cases, you will want to take one of two actions. If a file exists, for example, you may want to print it on the screen. If not, you may want to create it. A simple test to do so would look like this:

```
if [ -r filename ]          if ( -r filename ) then
then                              ...
  cat filename
else
  echo "Enter the data for filename"
  cat > filename
fi                          endif
```

Some Shell commands will run in the background, without user interaction. They may also be run interactively. To test whether to send messages to the terminal or to mail them to the user (rather than interrupt what the user is currently doing), you could include the following logic in your Shell:

```
if [ -t 0 ] # (if the standard input is a terminal)
then
  echo "Error Message"
else       # (the command is running in background)
  echo "Error Message" | mail ${LOGNAME}
fi
```

You may also test whether a parameter has a value and take an action:

```
if [ "$PATH" ]                  if ( "$?path" ) then
then                            ...
  echo $PATH
else
  echo "No path is specified"
fi                              endif
```

Test automatically assumes that if there are no parameters it should return a false exit status. This test is particularly useful when applied to user-created variables and parameters.

The Bourne Shell offers a feature that the C Shell does not—an operator to nest IF-THEN-ELSE constructs, **elif**, which is useful for implementing CASE control structures.

```
if [ -d ${variable} ]
then
  process-the-directory ${variable}
elif [ -f ${variable} ]
then
  process file ${variable}
else
  error
fi
```

The IF-THEN-ELSE is useful for two-path decisions and nested tests of the form shown above, but to test a single variable for more than one value, use the CASE construct.

CASE AND SWITCH

A Shell command will often create variables or receive parameters that can have many different values. Although the IF-THEN-ELSE can be used to test each of these values and take action, the CASE control structure (Figure 4.2) is more convenient. It has the following forms:

```
case $variable in        switch ( $variable )
  value1)                   case value1:
    action1                   action1
    ;;                        breaksw
  value2)                   case value2:
    action2                   action2
    ;;                        breaksw
```

```
value3|value4)              case value3:
                            case value4:
   action3                     action3
   ;;                          breaksw
 *)                         default:
   default action             default action
   ;;                          breaksw
esac                        endsw
```

The last test '*)' is a default action; if no other value matches, then the default action is taken. Often, you will need to issue an error message and exit from the Shell without doing anything. CASE structures are particularly useful for processing parameters to the procedure. For example, the Shell variable $\#$ contains a count of the number of parameters passed to a Shell command. When working interactively, $\#$ is zero (0). When using a Shell command, the value can run from zero to several hundred. Most Shell commands require some parameters (at least a file to operate on) as information to begin processing. $\#$ should be greater than zero. To test for the number of parameters, use the CASE construct and $\#$ as shown on page 64.

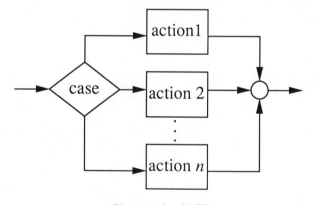

Figure 4.2   CASE

```
case $# in                              switch ($#argv)
  0)                                    case 0:
    echo "Enter file name:"              ...
    read argument1                       ...
    ;;                                  breaksw;
  1)                                    case 1:
    argument1=$1
    ;;
  *)                                    default:
    echo "Invalid number of arguments"   ...
    echo "Syntax: command filename"
    exit 1
    ;;
esac                                    endsw
# main processing begins here
```

Assume for a moment that you use Shell to create a monthly report and that the processing differs from month to month. To test and properly execute the command, you could use the **date** command and test for each of the months:

```
current_month=`date +'%m'`
case ${current_month} in
  01)
    January
    ;;
  02)
    February
    ;;
  .
  .
  .
  12)
    December
    ;;
  *)
    echo "Problems with the date command"
    ;;
esac
```

The Shell executes the command line:

```
case 01 in
```

January, February, and so on might be the actual names of commands that have to be executed.

The CASE control structure can also be used for character strings. Multiple character strings can be specified to default to the same action:

```
case $current_date in        switch ( $current_date )
   01|Jan|January)              case "01":
     January                    case "Jan":
     ;;                         case "January":
   02|Feb|February)                January
     February                       breaksw
     ;;                          ...
   ...
esac                         endsw
```

The CASE and SWITCH constructs are a powerful way of handling many comparisons and many different actions. Sometimes, however, an action needs to be repeated using different files or different information.

LOOPING COMMANDS

The commands to handle repetitive operations are **for**, **while**, and **until** (csh: **foreach**, **while**, and **repeat**).

For and Foreach

The **for** (Bourne Shell) and **foreach** (C Shell) commands (Figure 4.3) permit looping through a series of actions while changing a variable name specified on the command line. Both interactively and in a background mode, the use of Shell will require processing many different files the same way. The common forms of these control structures, as shown on page 66, are:

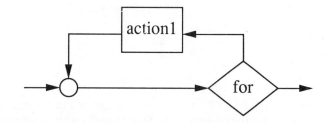

Figure 4.3   FOR (csh: FOREACH)

```
      for variable in value1 value2
      do
        action on $variable
      done

csh: foreach variable ( value1 value2 ... )
        action on $variable
      end
```

For example, to edit all of the files for this book, replacing 'shell' with 'Shell,' I could use the following commands:

```
for file in chapter*      foreach file ( chapter* )
do
ed - $file <<eof!
g/shell/s//Shell/g
w
q
eof!
done                      end
```

This could also be done for files with many different names:

```
for file in file1 filename xyz etc
```

FOR control structures, as well as any of the Shell control structures, can be nested inside of one another. For example, to process all of the files in the directories bin, doc, and src, I could use the following nested control structure:

```
for dir in bin doc src      foreach dir ( bin doc src )
do
  cd $dir                     cd $dir
  for file in *               foreach file ( * )
  do
    if [ -f $file ]             if ( -f $file ) then
    then
      process $file             process $file
    fi                          endif
  done                        end
  cd ..                       cd ..
done                        end
```

For each of the directories, the Shell would change into that directory; for each file it would test to ensure that the variable $file is really a file and not a directory. The Shell would then execute the command **process** on each file name. When the

Shell finished with all of the files under bin, it would change up to the parent directory and then start working on the doc directory. Nesting control structures is a convenient way to handle complex operations that would otherwise require extensive typing to accomplish the same ends.

The **for** and **foreach** commands are not the only way to handle looping through repetitive operations. The **while** and **until** commands provide another alternative.

While and Until

The **while** construct (Figure 4.4) takes a form similar to the **for** construct:

```
while command list        while ( expression )
do                          actions
  actions                 end
done
```

In the following example, let's use a variable, month, and the **while** loop to process every month's activity:

```
month=1                   set month=1
while [ ${month} -le 12 ]  while ($${month} < 12)
do
  process ${month}          process ${month}
  month=`expr $month + 1`    @ month += 1
done                      end
```

Using the Bourne Shell, you can do something you can't do in the C Shell—direct *stdout* into a conditional statement using the *pipe*:

```
for file in Chapter?
do
  cat $file | \
  while read line # read a line
  do
    process $line
  done
done
```

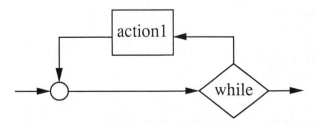

Figure 4.4   WHILE

This is a great way to process a file one line at a time. Or you may need to process the *stdout* from the command using a pipe:

```
for file in file1 file2        foreach file (file1 file2)
do
  line < $file                   line < $file >> /tmp/tmp$$
done | wc > header_count       end
                               wc < /tmp/tmp$$ > header_count
```

You may need, at some time, to start an infinite loop. The **test** command recognizes the existence of any value as true:

```
while [ 1 ]                    while ( 1 )
do
  process something              process something
done                           end
```

To prevent looping forever or forcing the user to break out of the loop by using one of the break or delete keys, you will need to break out of the loop. The **break** command, as shown in the following example, is the way to jump out of a loop without causing logic problems.

```
while [ 1 ]
do
  if [ end condition ]
  then
    break
  else
    process something
  fi
done
```

Sometimes the processing will need to continue without processing anything. The **continue** command handles these requirements:

```
while [ 1 ]
do
  echo "Enter file name"
  read filename
  if [ -r $filename ]
  then
    process $filename
  else
    continue
  fi
  echo "Processed file ${filename}"
done
```

The **while** command can also **test** variable names and files, processing them accordingly:

```
while [ "$variable" = something ]
do
  process $variable
done

ls |\
while read file
do
  process $file
done
```

The **until** form of the loop (Figure 4.5), only available with the Bourne Shell, is used less often. It executes the processing at least once and then tests the conditions.

```
until [ end conditions ]
do
  processing
done
```

For example:

```
until [ "`who | grep lja`" ]
do
  sleep 60
done
```

The **until** example shown above is useful when watching for known hackers to enter the system under a specific ID. A generalized hacker check could watch for the user ID to appear on the system and then send mail and call the system administrator as shown on page 70:

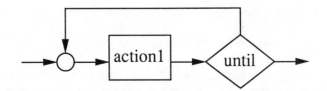

Figure 4.5   UNTIL

```
# Hacker Check
until [ "`who | grep $1`" ]
do
  sleep 60
done
echo `date` there's a hacker in the machine | mail lja
# call my office phone (or home phone)
cu 5551234
```

The C Shell also includes the **repeat** form of loop, which executes a command a specified number of times:

```
repeat 10 command
```

Aside from the **for**, **foreach**, **while**, **until**, and **repeat** commands, there are two other ways of handling loops and processing many files: **xargs** and **find**.

Xargs, Repeat, and Find

Xargs simplifies the implementation of loops when you need to execute only one command with a list of files. The problem is more complicated when every file under a user's ID must be examined or when entire file systems must be changed. The **find** command has the ability to look through entire directory trees for specific files or directories and then execute commands on those file or directory names.

Xargs takes lines of input and executes commands, substituting the input lines wherever specified. **Repeat**, in the C Shell, executes a command a specified number of times (**xargs** performs this function for the Bourne and Korn Shells). **Find** searches downward from a specified directory and executes user-specified commands, substituting file or directory names into the commands. **Xargs** is useful when interactively executing the same command on many files in a directory. **Find** is more useful for examining entire directory structures and executing commands.

Some Shell commands, like remove (**rm**), only work on a maximum number of files (100). Since the command **rm *** results in an error message when there are more than 100 files, **xargs** can be used to execute the **rm** command with the first 100 and then the remaining files:

```
ls | xargs -n100 rm -f
```

Similarly, a series of existing files can be copied to other names:

```
ls chapter* | xargs -i cp {} old{}
```

This command creates a duplicate set of the chapters from a book, named old-chapter1, and so on. Instead of creating duplicate copies, however, it would be better to store each of the chapters in the Source Code Control System (SCCS):

```
ls chapter* | xargs -i admin -n -i{} $HOME/doc/sccs/book/s.{}
```

This command stores the chapters in the directory $HOME/doc/sccs/book for later retrieval and update.

Users often change from one work group to another. To allow other members of their group to access a file, they can either change each file and directory, one at a time, or they can use **find**:

```
cd $HOME
find . -exec chgrp newgrp {} \;
```

which says find all of the files and directories under my login and change the group ownership of each one to the new group. The braces indicate where the **find** command should substitute the name of each file and directory found during its search. The same ability can be used to change the mode on all of the files or to copy the files from one place to another:

```
cd $HOME/bin
find . -exec chmod 775 {} \;
find . -print | cpio -pd new_place
```

Find can also test each name and take action. To change the mode on all of the directories under the login directory you could use:

```
cd $HOME
find . -type d -exec chmod 770 {} \;
```

Find can even ask you if it is okay to execute the command:

```
find . -type d -ok chmod 770 {} \;
```

The option -ok works just like -exec except that **find** will prompt you before executing the command.

Rules of Thumb:

1. Use **xargs** when working on a list of files.
2. Use **find** to operate on all of the directories and files under a specific directory.
3. Use **repeat** (csh) to execute a command many times.

They all work well when using the Shell interactively.

TRAP

Certain kinds of actions by the user and the system can interrupt a Shell program. The **trap** command handles virtually any interrupts: phone lines hanging up, breaks, deletes, kill commands. Each of these is a *signal* described in section 2 of the UNIX User's Manual under signal(2). The available signals are described in Table 4.4.

> Never test for an error condition you don't know how to handle.

Most often, when the Shell receives an interrupt, you will want to remove all temporary files and exit gracefully with a return code. This is accomplished by executing the following command:

```
trap (rm tmp*;exit 1) 1 2 3 14 15
```

When the Shell receives a hangup (1), interrupt (2), quit (3), alarm (14), or software termination (15) signal, it will remove the temporary files (**rm tmp***) and exit with a false value (**exit 1**). In other cases, the command may be working on many files and you may want to know where to restart the command:

TABLE 4.4   Signals

Signal	Interrupt
0	Normal completion
1	Hangup
2	Interrupt (break)
3	Quit
4	Illegal instruction
5	Trace trap
6	IOT instruction
7	EMT instruction
8	Floating point exception
9	Noncatchable kill
10	Bus error
11	Segmentation violation
12	System call error
13	Non-terminated pipe
14	Alarm clock
15	Kill (from `kill` command)
16	User-defined
17	User-defined
18	Death of a child process
19	Power failure

```
trap (echo ${filename} > stopfile; exit 0) 1 2 3 14 15
```

Stopfile will contain the name of the last file used by the command.

These are simple examples, but every Shell command should clean up after itself and take some meaningful action when interrupted. **Trap** encourages the active rather than passive handling of signals.

Trap is not available in the C Shell, but a similar command **onintr** handles trapping signals and taking remedial action.

SUMMARY

The Shell provides many facilities for controlling actions. The use of repetitive commands like **for**, **foreach**, **repeat**, **until**, **while**, **xargs**, and **find** will improve your productivity. The **test**, **if-then-else**, **case**, and **trap** commands help to improve the reliability and usability of your commands. The Shell control structures are the foundation of good Shell programming. Use them wisely and productively.

They can be used productively in two ways: interactively at the terminal, and as the basis for interactive and batch commands that automate much of a UNIX user's work. These subjects will be more fully explored in the next two chapters.

EXERCISES

1. Name the control structures in the Bourne and C Shells and describe their use.

2. What Shell facility handles all conditional tests for the Shell control structures? Which Shell variable contains the return code from a conditional test?

3. What other Shell commands can be used to handle repetitive processes?

4. What Shell facility handles errors and interrupts?

5. Write the IF-THEN-ELSE statement to test whether a variable name is a directory. Write the same test for file names.

6. Write a CASE statement to test a variable name for the values: "data," "source," "comments," or anything else.

7. Write a FOR loop to process all of the files in a directory.

8. Write an infinite loop to prompt the terminal user for file names to be removed; then remove them. Use **trap** to exit gracefully when finished.

9. Write an infinite loop to check a directory for files, print them using **pr** if any are found, remove them after printing, and then sleep for 15 minutes (900 seconds).

10. Use **xargs** to process all of the files in a directory.

11. Use **find** to locate all of the files in a user's ID named *.c (C language source code) and print them with **pr**.

12. Write the **trap** statements to handle:

    a. ignoring hangup signals.
    b. removing temporary files when QUIT or INTERRUPT is received.
    c. removing temporary files when the command ends normally.

Chapter Five

Shell Programming

Shell programming is little more than combining the commands and control structures you have learned up to this point. You can program interactively or by combining shell commands in a program that you and others can execute. Shell procedures are simple ways to automate complex processes as well as simple, everyday ones.

INTERACTIVE SHELL USAGE

One of the most productive ways to use the Shell is interactively at the terminal. People familiar with the Macintosh or any other WIMP (windows, icon, mouse, and pointer) interface will ask: Why bother? As an avid Macintosh user, I agree, for some applications. If you want to start up a single application program and just do one thing to one file, icons and mice are a great way to go. If, however, you want to start up many commands and do many things to many files, you'll need the Shell. The commands to do this are shown in Table 5.1.

When creating a Shell program (as described in the next chapter), you will often use the Shell interactively to *prototype* or test out how the command will ultimately work. So, interactive use of the Shell will also serve the development of Shell programs.

Shell Setup

As a user logs into and out of UNIX, several files come into play to set up the environment for the user and the Shell (Table 5.2). You can put any Shell commands in these files that you would use elsewhere, but each file has a specific use.

TABLE 5.1   Uses of Control Commands

Command	Actions	Files	Variables
case	many	*	one
for	many	many	one
foreach	many	many	one
find	one	many	none
if-else	two	*	one or more
repeat	many	*	none
switch	many	*	one
until	many	*	one or more
while	many	*	one or more
xargs	one	many	one

In the Bourne and Korn Shells, /etc/profile is defined by the system adminis-trator to set up the common shell environment for all users. To override this, you can place any commands you want in ${HOME}/.profile. As you login, UNIX executes /etc/profile and then ${HOME}/.profile before creating a Shell for you. ${HOME}/.profile is an excellent place to create specific global variables like PATH, or to send yourself a good morning message, or to change the default system prompts:

```
PATH=${PATH}:${HOME}/bin  # add bin to PATH
PS1="/unix1> "
PS2="More Input!> "
export PATH PS1 PS2
echo "G'day mate!"
```

${HOME}/.profile is also an excellent place to define *shell functions,* which will be discussed in the advanced material. For a simple example, however, let's take the **dir** command of MS-DOS:

```
dir( )
{
  ls -l
}
```

In the C Shell, ${HOME}/.cshrc performs similar functions. It is the perfect place to set key shell variables:

```
set noclobber  # don't let I/O redirection clobber files
set history=20  # keep track of 20 previous commands
set prompt="/unix1> "
set path=${path}:${HOME}/bin
echo "G'day Mate!"
```

TABLE 5.2   Setup Files

Bourne/Korn Shell	C Shell	Purpose
`/etc/profile`		system-wide setup procedure
`.profile`		user-specific setup for `sh` or `ksh`
	`.cshrc`	user-specific setup for `csh`
	`.login`	commands executed at *login*
	`.logout`	command executed at *logout*
`.exrc`	`.exrc`	`vi` setup commands

${HOME}/.cshrc is also an excellent place to put aliases for commands:

```
alias dir 'ls -l'
```

The ${HOME}/.login file executes after .cshrc. It is an excellent place to set terminal characteristics with **stty** and to set environment variables with **setenv**:

```
stty erase '^H'  # set erase to a backspace
setenv PRINTER MYroom  # set PRINTER default to MYroom
```

In a Sun workstation, you can also use .login to start up the window manager:

```
sunview
```

The ${HOME}/.logout file runs just before a user logs out of UNIX, so it's best to have only background processing in this file. It can say goodbye and then clean up junk files or whatever:

```
clear    # clear screen
echo "G'bye Mate!"
nohup nice find -name 'junk*' -exec \rm '{}' \; &
```

The final setup file, ${HOME}/.exrc, sets up the environment for the **vi** editor and allows you to define macros for use in the **vi** editor. For example, to maintain the same indentation as the previous line, a user could set **autoindent**. The program would then automatically follow the current indentation:

```
set autoindent
```

Or, for documentation, you can set **wrapmargin** to insert a *line-feed* automatically whenever you get close to the right-hand margin:

```
set wrapmargin=10
```

I have rarely used .exrc, but it's a handy feature for gung-ho power users and programmers.

Using the Shell Interactively

Any time you execute any command—**ls**, **cat**, or **who**, for example—you are using the Shell interactively: *stdin, stdout,* and *stderr* are all directed to the terminal. Combining commands via a *pipe* or executing existing Shell programs contributes to productive interactive use of the Shell.

You should use the Shell interactively whenever you need:

- to get immediate results (list a directory with **ls**),
- to interact with the command (it asks you questions),
- to perform a repetitive operation on a one-shot basis (look for and operate on specific files in a directory).

Simple commands, like the editors, represent an effective but less productive use of the Shell than joining Shell commands together to perform complex operations. Learning effective use of **grep**, **cut**, **paste**, and numerous other tools is the essence of productivity improvement. The Shell provides a consistent environment of reusable tools that can be joined together to manipulate virtually any text into some required form. The hard part is developing the mental focus to understand this flexibility and use it in everyday activities. The Shell can quickly extract and format information or it can handle more complex, recursive procedures.

In-Line Procedures

Selecting and reporting information is one way in which the Shell can really improve your productivity. Files consisting of fields and delimiters, like /etc/passwd, can be inspected and printed:

```
cut -f1,5 -d: /etc/passwd | pr
```

```
lja   Jay Arthur
pgm   Paula Martin
```

Or, you can print a document and mail it to many users:

```
nroff document_file | mail user_id user_id user_id
```

Using data selection commands like **grep, cut,** and **uniq** can quickly eliminate extraneous information. Reporting commands like **awk, cat, pr,** and **nroff** can then format the remaining information. For further information on these commands, refer to Chapter Three. Another good way to use the Shell interactively is with looping procedures.

Looping Procedures

In everyday usage, you will need to perform many operations on many files. The main Shell commands to help you are **find, for, foreach,** and **xargs. While** and **until** are also occasionally useful. **Find** is invaluable when you have left a file somewhere under your login, but have no idea where. To find the file from your HOME directory, type:

```
find . -name lostfile -print
./doc/unix/lostfile
```

Once you have identified that **find** is locating the proper file names, you can execute commands on those files. I would not, however, recommend executing commands that remove or change files before you have determined that **find** is obtaining only the file names you require. Otherwise, you could lose or corrupt a large number of files and never know it was done. If you are in doubt, use the -ok feature of **find** to check each file name before executing the command:

```
find . -name s\* -ok rm -f {} \;
./doc/unix/book/s.chapter1? n
./doc/unix/book/s.chapter2? n
./src? n
./src/slop? y
./src/sludge? y
```

Without these checks, **find** would have removed the SCCS files containing chapters 1 and 2. Recreating them would not be fun unless the system administrator could restore them from backup. A simple command to remove all junk files, however, would be:

```
find . -name junk\* -exec rm -f {} \;
```

Find is useful for any task that requires looking down through directory structures, finding files, and executing commands to modify or delete the files. It does not work well, however, when you want to work on just the files in the current directory. For these looping processes, you need **for** and **xargs.**

For and **foreach** (csh) let you perform multiple operations on numbers, strings, files, and output from other commands (e.g., **echo** and **cat**). **Xargs,** on the other hand, can only execute one command per file. One of the most frequent uses of the **for** loop involves editing files in the current directory to change an old word to a new one:

```
for file in chapter?        foreach file ( chapter? )
do
ed $file <<!                ed $file<<!
g/shell/s//Shell/g          ...
w
q
!
done                        end
```

The **for** command substitutes chapter0 through chapter9 for the variable file and executes the editor commands that follow.

Similarly, **for** could calculate the average length of each word in each chapter:

```
for file in chapter?
do
    totalchar=`wc -c ${file} | cut -c1-7`
    totalwords=`wc -w ${file} | cut -c1-7`
    average=`expr ${totalchar}/${totalwords}`
    echo ${file} ${average}
done
```

These are fairly simple examples, but they show the basic interactive uses of **for**. The other command for operating on files in a directory is **xargs**.

Xargs works well on files in a directory when you want to execute only one command:

```
ls junk* | xargs -i rm -f {}
```

Adding, getting, or creating deltas of files in SCCS is another application of **xargs**. In the following example, all of the chapters can be added to SCCS with one command line:

```
ls chapter? | xargs -i admin -i{} -y"First draft" s.{}
```

Xargs is a handy way to process many files at one time. For more complex loops, the Shell user will need **while** and **until**.

The **while** loop can be used interactively when you want to set a variable to a value and loop until it reaches some other value. The following simple example calculates the sine of all angles between 1° and 90°:

```
angle=1
while [ ${angle} -le 90 ]
do
  sine=`echo "scale=2;s(${angle})" | bc -l`
  echo "Sine of ${angle}=${sine}"
  angle=`expr ${angle} + 1`
done
```

All of the values would print out on the terminal. These values could also be directed into a file or printed with **pr**.

Note that the **while** loop simplifies interactive commands that change variables other than file names. **For** and **xargs** are more effective with files.

All of these commands—**find**, **for**, **foreach**, **until**, **while**, and **xargs**—allow the user to execute repetitive actions on files and directories. When the user needs to interact with these commands, the process should be run in foreground. Whenever possible, however, these commands should be run in background so that the user can continue working.

History

Once startup processing completes, the Shell begins reading commands from the terminal. Both the C Shell and the Korn Shell keep track of commands as they are entered from the terminal. The Shell stores these commands in memory and allows them to be recalled, modified, and executed.

History substitution, in the C Shell, begins by typing the character '!' (Table 5.3). There are many exotic ways to modify or execute previous commands in C Shell. The simplest way is to directly execute a previous command:

```
!!          execute last command
!n          execute previous command line n
!-n         execute current command line minus n
!str        execute the previous command line beginning with str
!?str?      execute the previous command line containing str
```

You can also select specific words from a previous command, using these as a prefix:

```
!!:1  !!:3    select words 1 & 3 from the last command
!!:2-4        select words 2-4 from the last command
```

You can also substitute words:

```
!?gerp?:gs/gerp/grep/   replace 'gerp' with 'grep' and execute
```

There are more exotic substitutions than this, and if you use the C Shell, I suggest you explore them. They can speed your effort at the terminal. The Korn Shell handles history somewhat differently (see Table 5.3).

Foreground and Background Procedures

Whenever you need immediate answers, execute Shell commands in foreground at the terminal. When you can afford to wait (the command takes a long time and will tie up a terminal that you could be using for other productive work), you can submit the command in background. The Shell facility to handle this is simple

TABLE 5.3 History Commands

Korn Shell	C Shell	Purpose
r	!!	execute last command
r n	!n	execute previous command line *n*
r -n	!-n	execute current command line minus *n*
r cmd	!cmd	execute the previous command line beginning with *cmd*
	!?str?	execute the previous command line containing *str*
r str = str2 cmd!cmd:s/str1/str2/		substitute and execute last *cmd*

and easy to remember: &. The ampersand at the end of a command line tells the Shell to run the command in background. Initiating background processes can be very productive; everyone should learn how to do it. In a previous example:

```
ls chapter? | xargs -i junkproc {} &
2304
```

The Shell started up a background process and printed out the process number (2304). This number is used to reference the process. The Shell variable $! contains the number of the last background process initiated.

You can also ask a command to **sleep** for a number of seconds and then execute:

```
(sleep 900 ; ls chapter? | xargs -i junkproc {} )&
2717
```

Processes may also be submitted to background so that you can hang up and let the process continue (all processes are killed otherwise). The facility that allows this is called **nohup**:

```
nohup nightlyprocess&
15342
```

Nohup stands for no hangup. It prevents the process from terminating when a user logs off. Any output generated by the command on either *stdout* or *stderr* is placed into a file called nohup.out, which can be examined later to determine the success or failure of the processing.

To be kind to your fellow UNIX users, the priority of any background processes should be lowered, to speed up terminal response time. The Shell facility to lower priorities is called **nice**. It should be used as follows:

```
nice command arg1 arg2 arg3 ... &
nohup nice command arg1 ... &
```

Note that both **find** and **xargs** lend themselves to background execution. **For**, **while**, and **until** are more easily initiated in foreground. But they can be executed in background by use of parentheses:

```
( for file in *
do
    cp $file newdir
done
) &
2413
```

While and **until** loops can be initiated in background in the same fashion.

Some systems have a command that allows execution of commands a specified time. The **at** command allows a UNIX user to execute commands at night, on weekends, or on holidays, without ever logging in to UNIX. It takes the following forms:

```
at 6pm nightlyprocess
at 6pm
nightlyprocess1
nightlyprocess2
cntl(d)
```

Nightlyprocess[12] will be executed at 6 P.M. with all of the user's characteristics. The **at** command is an excellent way to off-load CPU and I/O intensive activities to the evenings or weekends. When you begin to experience degraded response time on a UNIX system, consider using **at** to reduce prime time system load.

Bourne and Korn Shell Job Control These Shells use **kill** and **wait** to control background jobs. There are times when you will need to kill the most recently started background process:

```
kill $!
2717 killed
```

or you will need to wait for a process to complete:

```
wait 2304
```

C Shell Job Control The C Shell offers some additional *job control* features that can suspend background processes (**stop**) or switch them into and out of foreground: **bg** and **fg**. To stop a foreground process, type either **stop** or cntl(z). To stop a background job, type:

```
stop  %job
kill  <PID>
kill  %1
```

To pull a job back into foreground in csh, list the jobs using **jobs** and then select the job using **%** or **fg**:

```
jobs
1 find...
3 nohup...


%1
fg %1
```

Then you can send the job back with **%** or **bg**:

```
%1
bg %1
```

Interactive Shell Summary

Interactive Shell usage can be highly productive for extracting and reporting useful information. It can repetitively perform complex processes on files, directories, or whatever. Use of repetitive procedures and background processing promotes productivity. Processing can even be delayed into nonprime time with commands like **at**.

Interactive Shell helps test prototypes of new shells. It can also be used to prototype C language programs to eliminate bugs before coding the commands in a more efficient form.

Once you begin using the Shell interactively and discover that many interactive processes require too much typing, it is time to learn about Shell programming—putting those interactive commands into an executable file that you can reuse to further improve your productivity.

Complex commands should be created as Shell procedures. Trying to perform complex activities interactively is usually frustrating because syntax errors can easily negate all of your typing. If you try an interactive command a couple of times without success, consider putting the whole thing in a Shell procedure that can be edited and corrected as errors are uncovered.

WHEN TO CREATE SHELL PROGRAMS

You gain the most power from the Shell when you create Shell programs, commonly called Shell procedures, Shell scripts, or just plain "shells" for brevity. Create Shell programs (Figure 5.1) any time you need to perform:

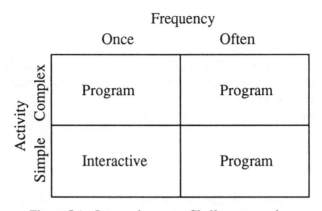

Figure 5.1   Interactive use or Shell programming

- a complex procedure using many command lines,
- a procedure from which all users can benefit,
- a simple command used over and over again.

An advantage of Shell is that it has access to many small functional commands. These reusable commands can be combined to automate increasingly complex functions that you would normally do manually.

CREATING SHELL PROGRAMS

To create a Shell program, Shell commands are combined in various ways to accomplish users' needs. This is the fun part. Users create procedures by entering Shell commands into a file via any of the available editors. To make the Shell file executable, all you have to do is change its mode:

```
chmod 755 shellproc
```

Rule of Thumb

1. Try each command line interactively, to make sure it works correctly.

2. Build the program using one of the editors interactively, one line at time, testing as you go.

Here are a few tips for creating a shell of any complexity. First, try each command line interactively, making sure that it works as expected. The following simple example extracts a user's name from the password file by login name and reports it:

```
grep lja /etc/passwd | cut -f5 -d:
Jay Arthur
```

If the field displacement or delimiter of the **cut** command had been wrong, I would have known it immediately. I can now include this command in a Shell procedure with faith that it works as I want it to.

You can execute commands directly from the **vi** editor as you create programs by typing:

```
:! shell_command
```

Then as you write your Shell program, you can test it right from **vi** by first writing using the following:

```
:w
:!your_shell_program -options argument(s)
```

To make commands reusable, however, you will need to know about argument lists.

Option and Argument Lists

Most Shell programs will need to have options and arguments on the command line, just like a typical Shell command:

command -options argument1 argument2 . . . .

When creating a Shell procedure, you will probably want to pass it the name of one or more files or you will need to give it some special information to affect its processing. This can be done easily with options and arguments:

```
shell_program -a file1 file3 file5
shell_program -k "Jay Arthur" "lja"
```

The Shell recognizes each of these arguments and assigns them names that can be accessed within the program—$1, $2, $3:

```
shell_program  -a     file1  file3  file5
   $0          $1     $2     $3     $4
```

To verify each of these options and arguments, we can use much of what we have already learned about looping in the Shell:

```
edit_status=TRUE
for arg in $*  #loop through arguments
do
  case $arg  #process options
   -a)
    process option -a
    ;;
   -k)
    process option -k
    ;;
   *)
    if [ `echo $arg  cut -c1` = '-' ]
    then
      echo "Option: $arg, invalid"
      edit_status=FALSE
    elif [ -f $arg ]
    then
      process $arg
    else
      echo "Invalid File Name $arg"
      edit_status=FALSE
    fi
    ;;
  esac
done
exit ${edit_status}
```

In this example, I verified all of the arguments to the command (rather than edit until I found one problem and then exit). Then, at the end, I checked for a valid status to decide whether to exit or continue processing the program.

The Shell variables—$1, $2, $3, etc.—can be changed as they are used, by using the **shift** command. **Shift** moves each argument, **$1** through **$#**, to the left, changing the previous argument list as follows:

```
shell_program  file3  file5
  $0             $1     $2
```

Shift is used with **while** loops to process arguments:

```
while [ "$1" ]      while ( "$1" != "" )
do                  ...
  process $1
  shift
done                end
```

This example processes each argument and then shifts the remaining arguments. When there are no more arguments, **test** will return a false value to the **while** loop and the command will exit successfully. **Shift** makes looping through arguments simple and straightforward. **Shift** is also useful when processing two or more arguments at a time:

```
while [ "$1" -a "$2" ]      while ( "$1" != "" && "$2" !="" )
do
  process $1 $2
  shift;shift
done                        end
```

Two other Shell variables reference the arguments $1 through $#: use $* and $@ when one Shell procedure invokes another with the argument list. The two are almost identical except in how they pass the arguments when they are quoted. $* passes all of the arguments to the receiving command as a single argument:

```
shell_program file?

#shell_program
rm "$*"
```

is the same as

```
rm "file1 file3 file5"
```

$@ passes the arguments as they were originally specified so that the command can work properly:

```
rm "$@"
```

is the same as

```
rm "file1" "file3" "file5"
```

If the executed command had been another Shell procedure instead of a re-move command, that procedure's arguments would have varied as follows:

```
subshell "$*"
(subshell `file1 file3 file5`)

$1 = `file1 file3 file5`
```

The following substitution would have occurred using $@:

```
subshell "$@"
```
(subshell `file1` `file3` `file5`)

$1 = file1 $2 = file3 $3 = file5

The $* form is useful with **echo** to display all of the arguments:

```
echo "$*"
file1 file3 file5
```


Without the double quotes, $* and $@ are equivalent, but these two can cause confusion and problems, so be careful.

Arguments to a Shell program should be edited using either the IF-THEN-ELSE construct for single arguments or the CASE construct for programs with more than one argument. Validating the arguments helps to improve a program's reliability.

A Shell program that expects a single argument, perhaps a file name, should test for too many arguments and for a valid file name:

```
if [ $# -eq 1 ]                         if ( $#argv = 1 ) then
then
  if [ -f $1 ]                            if ( -f $1 ) then
  then
    process $1                              process $1
else                                    else
    echo "$1 invalid file name"           ...
  fi                                      endif
else                                    else
  echo "$0 syntax: $0 filename"           ...
fi                                      endif
```

Most Shell programs, however, will have many options and files. One special command, **getopt**, can parse $* and separate flags when they have been clumped together by a user (e.g., -abct is actually -a -b -c -t). Some utility programs work this way, so it can be useful to design commands to handle users this way. To use **getopt**, simply reset the Shell's positional parameters, $*, by supplying a string of options:

```
set `getopt abct $*`
```

Once the positional parameters have been reset using **getopt**, a program with more than one argument can use the CASE construct to handle the argument edits:

```
case $# in                        switch ($#argv)
  0) # oops no arguments            case 0:
    echo enter argument1              ...
    read arg1
    echo enter argument2
    read arg2
    ;;                              breaksw
  2)                                case 2:
    arg1=$1                           ...
    arg2=$2
    ;;                              breaksw
  *)                                default:
    echo "$0 syntax: $0 arg1 arg2"
    ;;                              breaksw
esac                              endsw
```

A program may expect a series of options as well as file names or whatever. Options should be separated from the remaining arguments:

```
while [ `echo $1 | cut -c1` = "-" ]
do
 case $1 in
  -a|-b|-c)
   options="${options} $1"
   ;;
  *)
   echo "$1 is not a valid option"
   ;;
 esac
 shift
done
```

Then, the tests for the remaining arguments can be performed using the CASE construct or IF-THEN-ELSE. Editing arguments is an important part of building reliable Shell programs.

Variables

Assigning values to variables is an important feature of creating Shell procedures. Previous chapters showed how variables work with control structures (IF-THEN-ELSE, CASE, FOR, UNTIL, and WHILE). The Bourne/Korn and C Shells assign variables differently. The C Shell requires the user to **set** variables, while the Bourne Shell allows simple assignment:

```
variable=value    set variable=value
```

Shell users can also create variables to improve maintainability and reusability of the procedure. A simple example involves keeping all of the boilerplate for documents—letters, memos, forms, whatever—in a unique directory. To allow for future changes in the directory name on various systems, you might create a variable that points to the boilerplate directory:

```
docdir="/unixfs/boilerplate"
```

Then, create a Bourne shell (!sh) called **getdoc** that selectively retrieves boilerplate from the directory:

```
#!sh getdoc
docdir="/unixfs/boilerplate"
if [ -r ${docdir}/$1 ]
then
  cp ${docdir}/$1 $2
  echo "$1 boilerplate created as $2"
else
  echo "$1 boilerplate not found in ${docdir}"
  echo "Valid templates are:"
  ls ${docdir}
fi
```

Setting and using the variable docdir insures that the command can later be changed to point to other directories on other machines by changing only the variable assignment, not the entire procedure. Using variables for path names is definitely desirable: they are easily maintained and more reliable.

A common problem with new shells is that variables are referenced before they are assigned a value. To counter the effects of this problem, the Shell can be told to treat unset variables as fatal errors:

```
set -u
```

Or, you can specify a default value for a variable:

```
if [ -d ${docdir:=/unixfs/boilerplate} ]
```

The Shell checks to see if docdir has a value. If so, it uses it; otherwise, it uses /unixfs/boilerplate. Having meaningful defaults for variables means never having to say you're sorry. They prevent improper operation of the shell. For example, suppose that you had a command that did the following:

```
cd $temp
rm -rf *
```

If $temp has no value, the Shell will change to $HOME and remove all of your files. This could have been avoided by using a default value of /tmp:

```
cd ${temp:=/tmp}
rm -rf *
```

which would remove only those files in /tmp that belong to your user ID.

Variables can be set to the output of Shell commands by use of the accent grave characters. For example:

```
cmdpath=/usr/bin/nroff           set cmdpath=/usr/bin/nroff
dirname=`basename ${cmdpath}`    set dirname=`basename ${cmdpath}`
echo $dirname                    echo $dirname
/usr/bin                         /usr/bin
```

The **set** command can be used to set the command variables: $1, $2, $3, ... To set these variables to all of the file names in the current directory, use the following command:

```
set - *
```

To set $1 to a new value, **set** can also be used as follows:

```
set - "new value for $1" "new value for $2" . . .
```

Another ability of the Shell involves setting variables *before* execution, using the command line:

```
var1=value var2=value command -options argument1 argument2 . . .
```

Although this may not sound exciting at first, we can use it to act like a mail merge, adding names and addresses to a letter before printing (see Figure 5.2):

```
name="Jay Arthur" address="Radio Free Denver CO" \
l_print query_letter

#l_print
sed -e "s/name/${name}/g" -e "s/address/${address}/g" $1 | nroff
```

In this example, I set the variables name and address before executing the command **l_print**. Within **l_print**, I then had access to these two variables, used them with **sed** to change query_letter, and then formatted and printed the letter with **nroff**. This is one of the many ways in which presetting variables can be used in the Shell.

Variables are an important part of writing good Shell procedures. They can be assigned both string and numeric values from any source including the output of

Before:

July 1, 1990

name
address

Dear name,

    Thank you for your letter of ...
Sincerely,

After:

July 1, 1990

Mr. Jay Arthur
Radio Free Denver CO

Dear Mr. Jay Arthur,

    Thank you for your letter of ...
Sincerely,

Figure 5.2   Mail merge letter

other Shell commands. Put them all together with arguments, commands, and control structures, and you have the ability to manipulate files into any required format.

Built-In Commands

The Shell uses certain commands that are built in. The Bourne, Korn, and C Shell built-in commands were shown in Table 3.4. The commands **break**, **cd**, **exit**, **export**, **set**, **shift**, and **test** have been demonstrated in prior examples. Of equal importance are the **eval**, **exec**, **read**, and **wait** commands.

The **eval** command lets the user build command strings and then use them as if they were part of the Shell program. For example, a complicated Shell command might have to determine the proper input and output filters for a given command. Rather than execute the command many different ways, the Shell could create a variable containing the correct input filters and one containing the proper output filters. The complete command could be evaluated and executed as follows:

```
inputfilter="cmd1 | cmd2"
outputfilter="cmd3 | cmd4"
eval "$inputfilter | command | $outputfilter"
```

which would be the equivalent of executing the commands:

```
cmd1 | cmd2 | command | cmd3 | cmd4
```

Using **eval** can increase the flexibility of many Shell programs.

The **exec** command will execute a command in place of the current command without creating a new process. This is occasionally useful if control need never return to the parent shell. A more useful form reads a Shell program as input and executes the commands as if they were part of the current Shell program:

```
. shell_module        source shell_module
```

This facility encourages modularity (a key quality design goal of all software) and helps to encourage reuse of Shell programs. The Shell code in **shell_module** is reusable by any Shell program that needs it. Reusability, in turn, can reduce maintenance costs: rather than fixing 10 versions of the same code, only one module needs to be changed.

The System V **read** command gets a line from standard input. In most cases, *stdin* will be a terminal. In most Shell programs, if the user does not enter the correct number of arguments, it is better to ask for them than to exit and demand that they be entered on the command line. A combination of **echo** and **read** handles the job nicely:

```
if [ $# -eq 0 ]
then
  echo "Enter filename"
  read filename
else
  filename=$1
fi
```

Read can also get a line of input from a file or pipe used as standard input:

```
shellcommand < file
```

or

```
command | shellcommand

#shellcommand
while read inputline
do
  process inputline
done
```

This could also be handled by the System V **line** command, although **read**, because it is built-in, is faster:

```
while inputline=`line`
etc.
```

The **read** command is a handy built-in function to get information from the standard input and assign the result to a variable that can then be handled like any other.

The **wait** command, as its name implies, waits for a background process to complete before continuing. A Shell program might start a background process, do some other processing, and then have to wait for the background process (or processes) to complete before it can continue. **Wait** is a patient command:

```
command&        # put the command in background
```

other shell commands

```
wait $-         # wait for the last background command to finish
wait            # wait for all background commands to finish
```

continue processing

Wait, like the rest of these built-in commands, meets special needs of the Shell programmer. Built-in commands help make it simple to build useful Shell procedures.

SHELL PROGRAMMING

To illustrate the prior facilities and concepts, let's develop a few shells, ranging from simple to complex.

The **who** command tells who is logged on to the system at any time, but it only tells the person's login ID, not his or her name. This information is in the password file, but not in a form that can be easily used. Let's develop a command, called **whois**, to extract the user from the password file and print only the relevant information.

First, we need to extract the user ID from the /etc/passwd file and then extract only the person's name. **Whois** will have the following form:

```
# whois userid
if [ $# -eq 0 ]                                    if( $# == 0) then
then
# no user ids supplied
  echo "Enter userid"                                echo "Enter userid"
  read userid                                        set userid=$<
else                                               else
  userid=$1                                          userid=$1
fi                                                 endif
grep $userid /etc/passwd | cut -f5 -d:    ...

whois lja
Jay Arthur
```

To make this command work on more than one user ID, it could be modified as follows:

```
# whois userid(s)
if [ $# -eq 0 ]
then
# no user ids supplied
  echo "Enter userid"
  read userid
  grep $userid /etc/passwd | cut -f5 -d:
else
  while [ "$1" ]
do
    grep $1 /etc/passwd | cut -f5 -d:
  done
fi
```

The command could be made more efficient by using **egrep** and pasting all of the arguments together as follows:

```
# whois userid(s)
if [ $# -eq 0 ]
then
# no user ids supplied
  echo "Enter userid"
  read userid
else
  userid=`echo $* | sed -e "s/ /\|/g"`
fi
egrep $userid /etc/passwd | cut -f5 -d:
```

Another simple Shell procedure might need to look through all directories under the current one and execute commands entered by the user. This command should also trap interrupts and allow processing to continue:

```
# dirsearch [ directory name ]
# search the specified directory for other directories
# in each one, prompt the user for commands to be executed.
if [ -d "$1" ]
then
  cd $1                                    # change directory to $1
else
  dir=`pwd`                                # dir=current directory
for file in *                              # all files in directory
  do
    if [ -d $file ]                        # Directory ?
    then
      cd ${dir}/${file}
      while echo "${file} ?"
        trap "exit 0" 1 2 3
        read cmd  # read command
      do
        trap "" 1 2 3
        eval $cmd $file  #execute command
      done
      cd ..
    fi
  done
fi
```

Another simple but useful command displays information on the screen a page at a time. Using **cat** to display a file often causes the important information to disappear before the user can hit the no scroll key. Simple commands to display pages on 25 line terminals are **more** and **pg**. The same can be accomplished with **pr**:

```
pr -p -t -123 filename  # pause every 23 lines

more filename

pg filename
```

But on other occasions, it would be nice to page through the output of another command:

```
nroff -cm document | more
```

These can be combined into a single Shell that handles whatever it is given:

```
# page [files]
case $# in
  0)
          # if the terminal is standard input and
          # there are no arguments
          # prompt for a file name
    if [ -t 0 ]  # standard input is a terminal
    then
      echo "What file? "
      read filename
      more ${filename:=/dev/null}
    else    # read from standard input
      more <&0
    fi
    ;;
  *)
    while [ "$1" ]
    do
      clear
      more $1
      shift
    done
    ;;
esac
```

Another example involves a directory that contains files or commands spooled by another command. If the first line of each file contains a header line with the user's ID and other information, the user can check the status of those jobs as follows:

```
# status
spooldir=/usr/spool/whatever
cd ${spooldir}
( for files in *  # all files in spool directory
  do
  line < ${files} # read first line
  done
) | grep ${LOGNAME} #grep userid from first lines
```

In this example, **line** will extract the first line of each file in /usr/spool/whatever. Because the **for** loop is enclosed in parentheses, all of the output from each of the line commands is placed on *stdout*. Instead of many separate streams of information, the Shell combines the output of each of the line commands into a single stream that can be piped into **grep**. **Grep** then looks through the stream for header lines that match the user's login name, ${LOGNAME}.

Another simple need of a Shell user would be to execute a series of commands, but execute them at intervals so that the system's users would notice little degradation. The program, **today**, to read a command from an input file and execute it at 15-minute intervals, would look like this:

```
# nohup today commandfile&
exec 0< $1    #open commandfile as stdin
while
  read cmd    # get line from commandfile
  test -n "${cmd}"
do
  eval ${cmd}   # execute command
  sleep 900    # sleep 15 minutes
done
```

The possibilities for creating useful commands are endless. It requires some ingenuity to pick the best combination of commands, pipes, redirection, and Shell constructs to build a new shell, but with a little experience it is easy. One of the best ways to get new ideas is to study the shells that come with UNIX: those in /bin, /usr/bin, and /usr/ucb/bin.

TESTING SHELL PROGRAMS

Before subjecting the rest of the user community to your new Shell program, it is a good idea to test the shell thoroughly. The Shell provides a couple of interactive debugging facilities in the form of parameters (**-vx**).

You can execute a procedure and the Shell will display every command line as it reads it:

```
sh -v shell_program
```

Similarly, the Shell will display each command executed and the values substituted for variables:

```
sh -x shell_program
```

There are several other options that can aid in debugging a new procedure (Table 5.4). Any of these commands can be set at the beginning or anywhere within the procedure by use of the **set** command:

```
set -x
```

TABLE 5.4   Shell Debugging Options

Bourne/Korn Shell	C Shell	Purpose
-	-	turn option on
+	+	turn option off
	b	stop processing options
e	e	exit immediately on false return code
k		eliminate key words from environment
n	p	syntax check the program
t	t	read and execute first command
u		unset variables are an error
v	v	verbose
x	x	output executed statements

Any of the currently set options are contained in the Shell variable $-:

```
echo $-
x
```

To increase your speed, you can use **vi** and test the command interactively as you develop it. Once you're in **vi** and you've created the first few lines of the Shell program, write the file (:w). Then you can execute it without leaving **vi**:

```
:w                      :w
:!sh -vx %              :!csh -vx %
```

    :   gets you to the **vi** command line,
    !   tells **vi** to execute the following Shell command,
    %   tells **vi** to fill in the current file name.

If you use the **vi** editor (or other full screen editors with an *escape,* '!', facility), you won't believe how fast you can develop and test Shell programs.

These are the basic things a user needs to know to write and test Shell procedures.

SUMMARY

Shell procedures are simple to create—put a group of commands into a file and make the file executable. Shells should be created whenever too much typing is required to enter the commands interactively or when the series of commands can be reused by many users.

Arguments, variables, pipes, input/output redirection, Shell control constructs, and all of the existing commands are available for command construction.

Because of the simplicity of command interfaces, one Shell program can interface with another Shell or a native command. Increasingly complex processes can be automated with groups of Shell programs. Whole systems can be built with Shell. Once the system has been shaken out and the user's requests for changes decrease, Shell programs can be rewritten in C language for efficiency. But writing in C language before all of the requirements are known is often a burden. Use Shell to design a working model of what is needed. If it becomes too complex or slow, it can be rewritten in C. Otherwise, Shell is more maintainable and the Shell program should be used.

Subsequent chapters will give further examples of Shell programs. Examples are the best way to learn Shell concepts. Then, trying your own shells will help cement an understanding of how Shell programming can automate much of the routine, daily work of a user, programmer, analyst, or manager.

EXERCISES

1. Describe the two types of interactive Shell procedures.

2. Describe the difference between foreground and background processes. What is the Shell character that puts commands into background?

3. What command allows the Shell user to run commands in background and hangup?

4. In what other ways can interactive Shell usage serve the development of Shell programs?

5. Write an interactive command to search through your directories, removing junk files. Make sure the command runs after 10 P.M. to reduce system load.

6. Write a background command to edit all of the files in the current directory, replacing the word "while" with "until."

7. How are Shell programs created? How are they made executable?

8. What Shell options allow for "verbose" testing of Shell programs?

9. Which Shell variables contain the arguments to a Shell?

10. What Shell command changes the values of these variables?

11. Describe the difference between $* and $@.

12. What are the Shell built-in commands?

13. Write a Shell program to test for arguments: arg1, arg2, and arg3. If they are not present, prompt the user for them.

14. Write a Shell program to test for arguments of the form: -c, -d, -e, and so forth. Set arguments by the same names (c, d, e) to true (1) or false (0) depending on whether the argument exists on the command line.

15. Write a Shell program to loop through the arguments on the command line and process them if they are files.

16. Combine exercises 14 and 15 into one program to loop through the dashed arguments like -c, shifting the Shell variables; then loop through the remaining arguments, processing them if they are files.

17. Expand exercise 16 to prompt the user for file names if none are specified. Multiple file names are possible, so loop through the prompt sequence until the user enters a return without any file name.

18. Describe and write a program to use accent grave characters to assign values to variables in a Shell program.

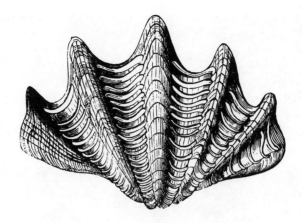

PART TWO

Shell Programming
for the User

Great is the art of beginning, but greater is the art of ending.

Longfellow

Chapter Six

Personal Computer Shell Programming

UNIX is possibly the only operating system to be ported up, down, and across hardware lines: from minicomputers into microprocessors, mainframes, and supercomputer systems; from DEC to IBM and AT&T to Apple. In 1989, personal computer installations of UNIX made up 42 percent of all UNIX installations and 9 percent of all 80386 operating systems (ComputerWorld, 1989). Virtually all major personal computer and workstation vendors offer UNIX and Shell with their hardware platforms. One of the first successful ports to microcomputers was XENIX. Later, when IBM brought out its personal computer, Microsoft developed the operating system—MS-DOS, which showed a remarkably UNIX-like bias. MS-DOS has evolved from a simple microcomputer operating system into progressively more UNIX-like versions, with a hierarchical file system, paths, and input/output redirection. Future versions will have additional UNIX-like facilities, including multitasking and multiuser capabilities. If you already know MS-DOS, UNIX preserves your investment and builds on what you've learned. The Shell, however, offers you much more. MS-DOS users ask; UNIX users *know*.

Again, Shell programming is an important part of productivity in a microcomputer environment. Each of the forthcoming UNIX operating systems for personal computers will use the Shell. MS-DOS, A/UX, XENIX, and UNIX will each provide users with doors of opportunity. The Shell is the key to unlock those doors.

MS-DOS

Microsoft's Disk Operating System (MS-DOS) was the first overwhelmingly successful personal computer operating system. It was fairly simple, allowing users to operate one program at a time.

MS-DOS followed most of the concepts of UNIX quite closely. Command names were changed to be more meaningful. Path names were specified with the backslash (\) instead of the slash (/). Standard output (*stdout*) could be redirected into files. Argument lists could be addressed by thinly veiled Shell variables like %1, %2, and so on. MS-DOS became little more than a simplified, single-user version of UNIX for the personal computer.

MS-DOS, unlike UNIX, does not care whether command names are upper or lower case characters. Like most IBM systems, it doesn't differentiate.

MS-DOS Commands

Many MS-DOS commands perform functions similar to those of UNIX (see Table 6.1). As you will see in Chapter Seven, User Friendly Interfaces, it is fairly straightforward to turn these UNIX commands into MS-DOS imitators, to make MS-DOS users more comfortable and productive in a UNIX environment.

.BAT Files

In all versions of MS-DOS, PC users could put commands into files and execute them. These command files are similar to Shell procedures. The only difference is that they all have a suffix to the command name (**.bat**), which stands for batch. From working with batch (**.bat**) files, every MS-DOS user should have some concept of how Shell works and how it can help get work done more easily.

Like Shell, the MS-DOS command processor uses variables %1, %2, ... to represent the arguments on the command line:

```
        %1    %2   ...
command  arg1  arg2  ...
```

The following example will compile and link a C language program using the C compiler and the Microsoft linkage editor:

```
rem cc.bat — cc file compiles file.c
if exist %1.c msc %1.c
if exist %1 msc %1
```

To compile and link a program named **prog.c**, the DOS user would enter the following command:

```
cc prog
```

The **cc.bat** command would substitute "prog" for every occurrence of %1, causing the compiler to generate an object file called prog.obj and an executable file called prog.exe. The **cc.bat** command acts like any Shell command, substituting arguments and executing commands under DOS instead of under UNIX. As

TABLE 6.1   MS-DOS and Shell Commands

MS-DOS	Bourne/Korn Shell	C Shell
ASSIGN	mount	mount
BACKUP	ar, cpio, tar	ar, cpio, tar
BREAK	break	break
CD, CHDIR	cd, pwd	cd, pwd
CHKDSK	fsck, df	fsck, df
CLS	clear	clear
COMP	diff, comm	diff, comm
COPY	cp	cp
DATE	date	date
DEBUG	adb, sdb	adb, sdb
DEL	rm	rm
DISKCOMP		
DISKCOPY	find . –cpio /dev/rmt?	
	volcopy	
DIR	ls –l	ls –l
ECHO	set, echo	set, echo
EDLIN	ed, ex	ed, ex
ERASE	rm	rm
FIND	grep	grep
FOR	for	foreach
FORMAT	mkfs	mkfs
GOTO		goto
IF	if	if
MKDIR, MD	mkdir	mkdir
MODE	stty	stty
MORE	more, pg	more, pg
PAUSE	echo, read	echo, read
PRINT	pr	pr
PROMPT	PS1 =	set prompt =
RECOVER	fsck	fsck
REM	echo	echo
RENAME	mv	mv
RESTORE	ar, cpio, tar	ar, cpio, tar
SET *var=val*	*var=val*	set *var=val*
SHIFT	shift	shift
SORT	sort	sort
SYS	ldtape, volcopy	
TIME	date	date
TREE	find	find
TYPE	cat	cat
VER	uname	uname
VERIFY		
VOL	labelit	

in Shell, you can also use **shift** to operate on a long list of arguments, taking them one at a time.

You could also use a **.bat** file to clear the screen and print a menu:

```
rem menu
cls
copy menufile.txt con:
```

    1. Edit a file
    2. Update a file
    3. Select data from a file
    4. Report from a file

You would then have various **.bat** files (1.bat, 2.bat, 3.bat, 4.bat) that handle the user's response.

Keeping in mind that the least flexible component of any computer system is the user, you could also use a **.bat** file to create imitation UNIX commands. For example, the following will imitate the **ls** command:

```
echo off
rem ls.bat
dir %1 | sort
```

Similarly, you could use **.bat** files to create the following Shell commands:

```
cat.bat:    if exist %1 type %1
            if not exist %1 echo %1 file not found
cp.bat:     if not exist %2 copy %1 %2
            if exist %2 echo File %2 exists
mv.bat:     if not exist %2 ren %1 %2
pr.bat:     for %%f in (%1 %2 %3 %4 %5 %6 %7 %8 %9) do print %%f
pwd.bat:    cd
rm.bat:     for %%f in (%1 %2 %3 %4 %5 %6 %7 %8 %9) do rm %%f
```

To execute other **.bat** files from the current **.bat** file is easy, but you will need to use **command** to do so. Normally, if you execute a **.bat** file from within another, it will not return control. **Command**, however, acts like a subroutine call (sh:. or csh:**source**). In the following example, we can use **command** to set up the laser printer before calling the word processor:

```
echo off
cls
command/c laser
wp
```

For more exotic processing, you can call the **basic** interpreter from the **.bat** file. You can create **basic** programs and then execute them within the **.bat** command:

```
echo off
cls
basica print.prg
```

Well, enough of simple **.bat** commands. Now let's take a look at the MS-DOS control structures.

Control Structures

The MS-DOS command interpreter offers three control structures: **for**, **if**, and **break**. To do something to more than one file at a time, you could use **for** interactively to print the book:

```
MS-DOS:    for %a in (1 2 3 4 5) do print chapter%a.doc

sh:        for ch in chapter[1-5]
           do
           pr $ch
           done
```

Or, use it in a **.bat** file to backup the chapters:

```
rem bookbkup.bat
for %%a in (1 2 3 4 5) do copy chapter%%a.doc a:
```

As you can see, some of the Shell's power is available in the MS-DOS command processor. To gain more of the power of Shell you can purchase an MS-DOS Shell.

MS-DOS Shells

A number of companies have created UNIX look-alike commands for MS-DOS. These give you the power of UNIX tools, but not the power of the Shell. Some companies (e.g., Mortice Kern Systems—MKS) have taken on the task of porting the UNIX Shell to MS-DOS. So, if you are a die-hard UNIX user, you can now purchase the Korn Shell for your MS-DOS machine. MKS gives you the look and feel of UNIX on your MS-DOS platform, but I'm not sure that I would recommend this for the average MS-DOS user at this time. The MS-DOS versions don't seem to have the robustness of the System V or BSD 4.2 UNIX Shells, but if you're willing to put up with some minor glitches, these MS-DOS versions can give you the flavor of Shell for only a few hundred dollars.

Or, if you would like the power of UNIX in your personal computer, then you can run XENIX. It is a *real* port of UNIX that supports the various UNIX Shells and offers commands to interface with MS-DOS. The commands—**doscat, doscp, dosdir, dosls, dosrm, dosmkdir,** and **dosrmdir**—allow XENIX to operate with DOS files. If you have a large hard disk, you can have both XENIX and MS-DOS, and run either based on your needs.

PCs can coexist with UNIX: they can be networked with UNIX servers, act as X-Window workstations, or act as asynchronous terminals.

UNIX WORKSTATIONS

UNIX is the de facto operating system standard for workstations; you will get the Bourne and either the Korn or the C Shell with your purchase. Any user logging on to a UNIX workstation will have a hard time discerning the difference between workstation and minicomputer UNIX. The commands, Shell, and processing are all the same. Shell programs written in one environment can be ported to the other with little or no change. Productivity and quality benefit from using the same shells in each environment. Maintenance costs are low, because shells can be centrally maintained and installed on whatever machine needs them. This means that a workstation UNIX-user will be able to learn in a small environment and then move into larger systems as the need arises, without retraining or other common problems.

MS-DOS users will find the transition relatively easy as well. In one case (Unger 1989), John Unger found that his computer usage shifted dramatically from MS-DOS to UNIX:

	MS-DOS	UNIX
Initial	80%	20%
One year later	5%	95%

Once the domain of CAD/CAM (computer-aided design and computer-aided manufacturing), UNIX workstations are coming down in price and up in popularity. UNIX workstations provide many advantages:

1. Single point of contact for all terminal interactions

2. Multiple interactions: more than one host processor can be accessed at a time allowing data-sharing among applications

3. One look and feel (windows, icons, mouse, and pointer)

4. All Shell tools available for custom needs

5. Quick response through local processing of data

Most workstation UNIX systems come with several different Shells: **sh**, **csh**, **ksh**, and **vsh** (the XENIX visual Shell—a simple interface for occasional users). Workstations offer a wide diversity of Shells for different applications.

SUMMARY

Since MS-DOS seems to be evolving toward UNIX, it seems logical to assume that most business-oriented personal computers will ultimately run some form of the UNIX multitasking operating system. So, intuitively, much of the content of this book will be usable by MS-DOS users. They will ultimately require a multi-tasking operating system as they become more sophisticated.

Because of its portability and multitasking capabilities, UNIX has quickly risen as a major competitor for the microcomputer operating system market. Both IBM and AT&T have a significant investment in UNIX for personal computers. In the workstation market, SUN, HP, DEC, and IBM are all embracing UNIX and the Shell. Standards battles should rage for a while, but the Shell will always be at the center of UNIX's popularity. This book should help all personal computer users understand the philosophy and use of the Shell.

EXERCISES

1. Name some currently available UNIX-like personal computer operating systems.

2. Name three Shells available on the various personal computers.

3. Describe the similarities between MS-DOS and UNIX.

4. Describe the benefits of UNIX as a microcomputer operating system.

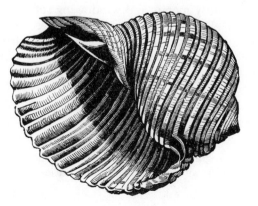

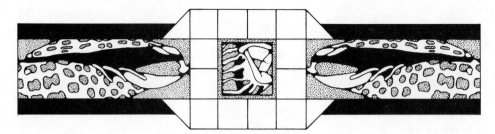

Chapter Seven

User Friendly Interfaces

The least flexible component of any system is the user. For the novice, using UNIX and the Shell may seem like an unnatural act. Invariably, novice UNIX users come with some excess baggage. They know how to use some other system, whether it's IBM's TSO, VAX/VMS, MS-DOS, or whatever. The UNIX Shell will seem foreign to them; its concepts will seem awkward and unwieldy. What we need are user seductive interfaces. Lawn mowers don't push people around and neither should computers. Creating user friendly interfaces, mimes, mimics, and master imitators is the easiest way to shorten a new user's learning curve.

> Software stands between the user and the machine.
>
> *Harlan D. Mills*

A variety of user friendly menus and windowing software packages are becoming available for UNIX. These should be acquired and implemented to encourage users to learn UNIX. Later, as they gain familiarity, they will begin to use more of the native commands. But what else can be done to encourage rapid learning?

CREATING MASTER IMITATORS

> The program should always respond to the user
> in the way that astonishes him the least.
>
> *Geoffrey James*

The Shell environment can be tailored to any individual's or group's needs by simply creating Shell programs that mimic their existing environment. The link (**ln**) and **alias** commands, and Shell *functions* and *programs* provide opportunities to make life easier for the new UNIX user. UNIX gurus who may feel that these crutches are unnecessary, should consider that the learning curve for a new UNIX user may extend for a year or more. It makes sense to shorten this curve in any way possible.

The link (**ln**) command can be used to link a UNIX command to a command name that the user already knows. For example, an IBM TSO user knows the list command as **listc**, the line editor as **edit**, and the full screen editor as **spf**. To make it easy on them initially, the system administrator can link the UNIX list (**ls**), line editor (**ed**), and full screen editor (**vi**) to the TSO command names **listc**, **edit**, or **spf**:

```
cd /bin
ln ls listc      alias listc /bin/ls
ln ed edit       alias edit /bin/ex
ln vi spf        alias spf /bin/vi
```

Similarly, an MS-DOS user could learn more easily with the following changes:

```
ln ls dir        alias dir ls -l
ln ed edlin      alias edlin ex
```

For a more friendly interface, shells can be created to inform users of what the system is doing for them when they execute a command:

```
# edlin
echo "edlin is a DOS command."
echo "initiating the UNIX editor—ed"
ed $*
```

Creating these look-alikes can also be handled by two special facilities of the C Shell and Bourne Shell: **alias** and *functions*. As we've seen in the last few examples, the C Shell **alias** command lets the user create an alias for any command. The same can be done with the Bourne Shell (UNIX System V Release 2 and later versions) using Shell *functions*.

The C Shell **alias** command takes the form:

```
alias command-name command(s)
```

The previous examples using the **link** command could have been handled equally well using **alias**:

```
alias edlin "echo Initiating UNIX editor \(ed\);ed"
```

The **alias** can also rename more complex commands that are contained in external C Shell files. The C Shell command to read and execute a Shell command is **source**. Use it with **alias** to include external files:

```
alias command-name "source external-shell-command "

alias trash "source cleanup"
```

These **alias** commands should be included in the user's *.cshrc* file. When the user logs in, the C Shell will automatically evaluate the **alias** commands and make them available to the user.

Similarly, the Bourne Shell allows the user to establish an alias, but the means are different. The user must create a Shell *function*. Shell functions should be included in the user's *.profile* for automatic invocation by the Shell. The previous examples are implemented as follows:

```
dir( ) {
ls $*
return
}


edlin( ) {
ed $1
return
}
```

Functions, unlike **alias** commands, are not restricted to a single line. They can include loops, IF-THEN-ELSE decisions, or whatever. But the **alias** command can include Shell source code from anywhere in the system, so it can effectively implement anything that the Bourne Shell can.

Functions are *executed directly* by the Shell: if the **exit** function is used instead of the **return**, the Shell will exit, logging the user off.

```
oops( ) {                  okay( ) {
  shell commands . . .       shell commands . . .
  exit 0                     return
}                          }
```

As shown in these examples, the C Shell's **alias** command and the Bourne Shell's *functions* give the user a flexible way to define user friendly names for any system commands.

The C Shell and the Bourne Shell also let users build specialized commands to make their jobs both easier and more ergonomic. Shell commands should be written to automate most of the commands that users are familiar with on other systems. Additional Shell commands should be written to simplify human-machine interfaces. For example, error messages could be standardized and a standard error routine developed:

```
# error error_code additional information
error_msg=`grep $1 /usr/local/error_messages`
shift      # shift the error code
echo $error_msg $*     # standard error message and information


error 1 filename
File not found: filename
```

Another simple example involves clearing the screen and painting lines on the screen from the top down. This is much easier on the eyes than watching each new line scroll up from the bottom of the screen. Stationary lines at the top of the screen are easier to read than lines jumping up from the bottom every split second.

```
# clear terminal screen     clear
tput clear
```

Many systems already have the **clear** command without the need to execute the System V **tput** command. **Clear** can be executed from any other Shell command that needs it:

```
# anyother shell
   shell commands . . .
   clear                    # clear the screen
   display information
```

To extend the concept of friendly commands, the more exotic commands available on systems other than UNIX can be implemented in Shell.

SUMMARY

The Shell is a powerful environment for building user friendly interfaces to the facilities of UNIX. Because all new UNIX users come with some excess baggage from previous systems they have used, it makes sense to use the Shell to shorten their learning process.

There are many ways of creating user friendly interfaces, from simple **ln** and **alias** commands to more complex Shell programs to handle almost any command on any other system. Some careful planning and development of user friendly interfaces can reduce training costs and complaints as new users begin using the system. Users are the heart of any system. Keeping them happy is of paramount importance.

EXERCISE

Use the facilities of the Shell to create user friendly imitations of the MS-DOS commands listed in Table 6.1.

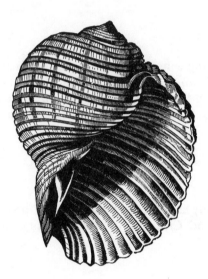

Chapter Eight

User Shell Programming

Up to this point, we have looked at Shell and all of its facilities to gain a foundation of understanding. For Shell to benefit us in the real world, however, we need to know how to compose application systems using Shell and its supporting tools. This chapter will help most users experience ways to build entire systems using Shell. These systems will ultimately result in enhanced effectiveness and efficiency.

In Shell, we compose systems from various programs written in Shell. In the world of software, five basic program designs (Figure 8.1) make up virtually all systems:

1. *Data input:* Users enter data and information.

2. *Information queries:* Users request specific information and it is displayed.

3. *Information output:* Screens and reports condense the data into useful views of the information contained in the data base.

4. *Data base update:* Data input by users or data passed in from other systems changes the information in the data base. The three key actions against the data base are *add, change,* and *delete.*

5. *System interfaces:* Input from and output to other systems is exchanged, since all systems interrelate in some fashion.

As we discovered in Chapter Three, virtually all Shell utilities will support one of these categories. Shell programs may consist of one or more of these designs.

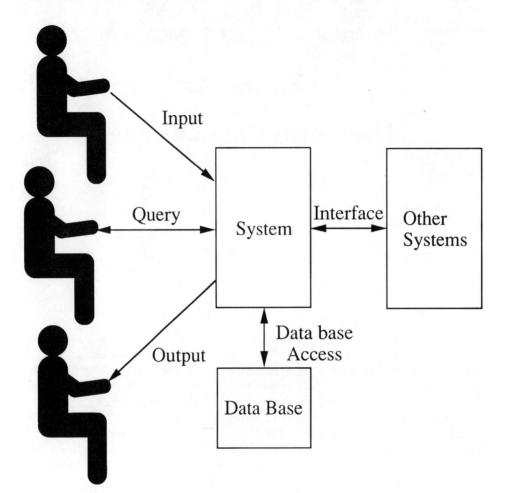

Figure 8.1   Program types

The *input* process, which creates information, may consist of:

• displaying a menu
• getting the user's selection
• displaying the input fields
• reading and validating the input

Once valid, up-to-date data is in the data base, the user may want to *query* the data base to extract information. Queries are both an input and an output process. Outputs may be either screen displays or reports. To create an output, the steps are:

- *select* information
- *organize* it
- *format* it, and finally
- *display* or *report* the desired information.

Getting the data into the data base is a trick in itself. The *update* process adds, changes, or deletes data from the data base. Finally, all systems interact with each other, sharing data. *System interfaces* link application with application and machine with machine.

Having introduced the basic kinds of programs, the following sections will delve into each of the five program designs and ways to implement each in Shell. First, however, we need to look at the data and how to manage it for maximum effectiveness.

THE SHELL RELATIONAL DATA BASE

One of the keys to Shell power is the ability to use UNIX files and Shell commands to form an elementary relational data base management system (RDBMS). Data bases are the primary problem-solving tools of industry; where else can you find everything there is to know about your business in an automated form that can be easily analyzed? The *relational table*—a table much like a spreadsheet—stores data and information in the simplest usable form: rows and columns. A *relational model* of a user's system consists of a collection of interrelated tables.

Traditional relational data bases use lots of resources, require complicated setup and lots of training, and use proprietary data storage formats. Using the Shell and relational files, on the other hand, gives you the power to use all of the existing Shell tools to massage your data into any shape or form. The simplicity of implementing an RDBMS in Shell, added to the straightforward file formats it uses, gives you a powerful tool for data processing and information gathering. Let's begin to harness this power, by looking at the design and use of relational data bases.

Relational Data Base Design

All applications require some kind of data base. The relational data base is the current *hot* one. Before we begin examining how to implement this data model in Shell, I'd like to give you *the key* to successful software system development: **Design the data first.**

More than anything else I've said in this book, remember that well designed data will: minimize the amount of effort you spend to build and maintain a software system, maximize the flexibility of the resulting system, reduce duplication of data, and build a safe foundation for the future. Relational data bases will accent this power and flexibility.

Relational data bases store the data in tables. Within a table there are *rows* and *columns*. In Shell, we use lines in plain files to represent rows and fields separated by delimiters to represent columns. Together, they implement relational tables. The most common delimiter character is the *tab* (\t). Since the *tab* character is "invisible," it is also common to choose characters like the colon (:) as a delimiter. (The /etc/passwd file is a good example of an online data base.) The format of these tables is:

	column 1		column 2		column 3
row 1	*index/key*	*delimiter*	data_item	*delimiter*	data_item...

The first field is the index or key to what's in the rest of the record. The key should *uniquely* identify all subsequent data items. To begin to illustrate the nature of data base design and the relational model, let's use the simple model of a payroll system shown in Figure 8.2. There are three data base tables:

- Employee
- Time Worked
- Tax Tables

The employee number (Figure 8.3)—the Social Security number (SSN), for example—could be the key to an *employee* record:

SSN		Last		First		Middle		Sex		Birthday		Salary
527964942	\t	Arthur	\t	Lowell	\t	Jay	\t	M	\t	1951/12/18	\t	35000 ...

In this example, I used my SSN, last name, first name, middle name, sex, birthday, and salary to define a row in a table. I used a tab character (\t) as the delimiter between fields. *SSN* is the primary key; *last name* could be a secondary key. This will simplify sorting, organizing, and retrieving the information later. *Birthday* contains three other subfields: year, month, and day. Subfields can be created by using a different delimiter character—in this case the slash (/). You could also use the colon (:), semicolon (;), blank ( ), or any other character between fields and subfields. A word of caution, however: Do not use a delimiter character that might commonly appear within the row, record, or field. Errors will result when the Shell attempts to separate fields based on such a character.

Notice also that I ordered the data items in the sequences that we most often like to use in organizing information: alphabetical by last name and chronologically by year/month/day. The *query* and *reporting* tools can handle putting the data back in user friendly order.

In a well designed relational table, there are rarely more than five to nine (7 ± 2) data items. If your table wants to be larger, it's probably because there should be more than one table.

There are *many-to-one* relationships that require additional tables. For example, I might represent the second data base table, days and time worked, in a different way (Figure 8.2):

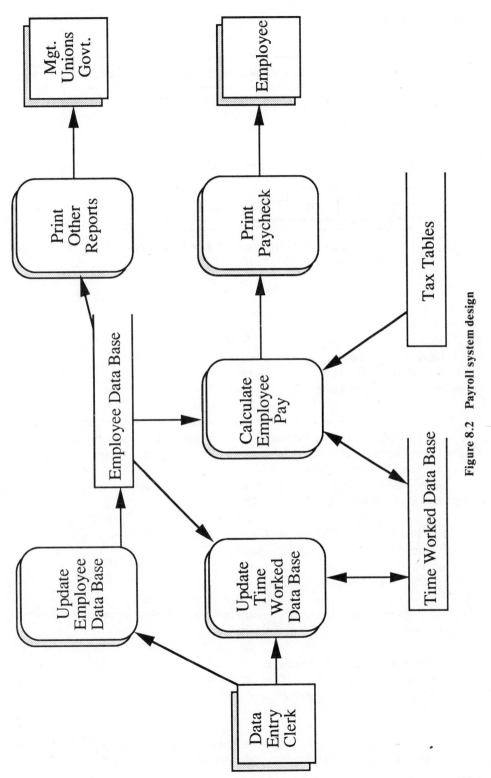

Figure 8.2   Payroll system design

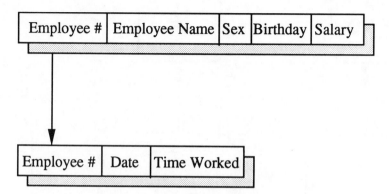

Figure 8.3   Partial payroll data base design

SSN	Day	Time Worked
527964942 \t	1990/01/02 \t	9.5
527964942 \t	1990/01/03 \t	7.0
527964942 \t	1990/01/04 \t	8.5

These separate tables, **employee** and **time_worked**, can then be processed independently, merged, or joined based on their primary keys. Scrubbing tables together often creates the greatest insights and knowledge about your system, your customers, and your company.

Finally, we might have to show relationships between tables. Suppose we define the company's department table as follows:

Department Number	Department Name
1 \t	Corporate Headquarters
47 \t	Information Systems

We could then define the relationship between employees and departments (*many-to-one*) in another table as follows:

Department Number	(has an)	Employee SSN
47	\t	527964942
47	\t	513234567

There are also *many-to-many* relationships. In today's corporate culture, with matrix management, an employee could work for multiple departments:

Department Number	(has an)	Employee SSN
47	\t	527964942
12	\t	527964942

Another command, **join**, combines existing tables by matching on specific fields. **Join** does not merge lines. When it finds matching records in the two input files, it creates a single output record containing any or all of the fields in both records. Imagine two files with the following lines in each file:

File1	File2
Arthur:555-1234	Arthur:123 Main:Denver:CO:80202
Martin:555-2345	Martin:245 Juniper:Denver:CO:80202
Smith:555-3456	

The command **join -t: file1 file2** will produce:

```
Arthur:555-1234:123 Main:Denver:CO:80202
Martin:555-2345:245 Juniper:Denver:CO:80202
```

Only the matched lines are joined to create an output line. To generate an output line for all lines in file1, the command could be changed to:

```
join -a1 -t: file1 file2
```

```
Arthur:555-1234:123 Main:Denver:CO:80202
Martin:555-2345:245 Juniper:Denver:CO:80202
Smith:555-3456
```

To get only the name, phone number, and zip code from these files, **join** would be invoked as:

```
join -a1 -o 1.1 1.2 2.5 -t: file1 file2
```

```
Arthur:555-1234:80202
Martin:555-2345:80202
Smith:555-3456
```

The -o option specifies that only fields one and two in file1 (1.1 and 1.2) and the fifth field of file2 (2.5) should be output.

Join, as shown in these examples, creates new files by adding fields to an existing file or by assembling whole new files from subsets of the fields in the original files. It is another weapon in the arsenal for updating files.

Paste is similar to **join**: it puts two files together regardless of their order:

```
paste -d: file1 file2
```

Arthur:555-1234:Arthur:123 Main:Denver:CO:80202
Martin:555-2345:Martin:245 Juniper:Denver:CO:80202
Smith:555-3456

Paste, in this form, gives the user another way to create tables. It is more primitive than **join**, but it often serves a useful purpose in Shell programming.

You now have a brief overview of the various kinds of relational table designs using UNIX files. To summarize, here are a few key rules for tables:

1. Use a single unique delimiter (\t) between columns.

2. Use a different unique delimiter (/:;) between subfields.

3. Organize the data for machine efficiency: *Primary* keys first, *secondary* keys next, then data items.

4. Restrict the number of fields per table to fewer than ten data items or redesign the table.

5. Create additional tables for multiple occurrences of data items (*one-to-many, many-to-one,* or *many-to-many* relationships).

6. Small tables—under 50 rows/records—are more efficient than larger tables. They are faster to sort and faster to access sequentially.

Now let's take a look at how to use this foundation to construct the inputs, queries, outputs, updates, and interfaces to an application system.

SCREEN HANDLING

The screen is the window to your user's soul. The screen can help the user navigate through the system using menus, enter data on screens, formulate queries, and display the resulting information. For the moment, however, let's focus on menus and data input.

Screen Input

Through the use of the terminal description files */etc/termcap* and */etc/terminfo* the Shell supports a huge array of terminal types—everything from the old vt100 to Sun workstations. To use these files to simplify screen handling:

1. The TERM variable must be set to the appropriate terminal type.

2. The System V **tput** command must be available on your system. If not, you can get by on the **clear** and **echo** commands.

Table 8.1 shows the various capabilities of **tput**. Since most of these capabilities are simple character sequences, you can store most of them in variables and then use the variables to improve efficiency:

```
term_bel=`tput bel`
term_blink=`tput blink`
term_bold=`tput bold`
term_clear=`tput clear`
max_cols=`tput cols`
term_dim=`tput dim`
term_ed=`tput ed`
term_el=`tput el`
max_lines=`tput lines`
last_line=`expr $term_lines - 1`
term_so=`tput smso`
term_eso=`tput rmso`
term_su=`tput smul`
term_eul=`tput rmul`
term_rev=`tput rev`
```

TABLE 8.1   Tput Capabilities

Option	Action
bel	echo the terminal's "bell" character
blink	blinking display
bold	bold display
clear	clear the screen
cols	echo number of columns on the screen
cup *r c*	move cursor to row *r* and column *c*
dim	dim the display
ed	clear to end of the display
el	clear to end of the line
lines	echo number of lines on the screen
smso	start stand out mode
rmso	end stand out mode
smul	start mode underline
rmul	end underline mode
rev	reverse video (black on white) display

Once these are set, you can proceed to set up the screen any way you please, using variables and **tput** cursor movements. For example, let's create a Shell to center one or more text lines, beginning on a given row:

```
#center_text row_number input_text_file
max_cols=`tput cols`
max_lines=`tput lines`
row_number=$1
shift
cat $* | \               # read from stdin
while read input_text
do
  line_length=`echo $input_text | wc -c`
  tput cup $row_number `expr \( $term_cols - $line_length \) / 2`
  echo $input_text
  row_number=`expr $row_number + 1`
  if [ $row_number -ge $max_lines ]
  then
    echo "Too many lines for the screen"
    break
  fi
done
```

We could also center rows on the screen, beginning at a certain column:

```
#center_lines col_number input_lines
max_lines=`tput lines`
col_number=$1
shift
cat $* > /tmp/tmp$$  # create temporary file
number_of_lines=`wc -l < /tmp/tmp$$`
row_number=`expr \( $max_lines - $number_of_lines \) / 2`
cat /tmp/tmp$$ | \
while read input_line
do
  tput cup $row_number $col_number
  echo $input_line
  row_number=`expr $row_number + 1`
  if [ $row_number -ge $max_lines ]
  then
    echo "Too many lines for the screen"
    break
  fi
done
```

Using these two tools, variables and **tput**, we can now create a menu screen for the Time Reporting System. First, we can create a header file (trs_header) and a menu file (trs_menu) containing the menu of choices:

trs_header	trs_menu
Time Reporting System	1. Add Time Worked
Time Worked Data	2. Change Time Worked
	3. Delete Time Worked
	x. Exit

Then, using these two files, we'll print the header on the screen and then center and indent the menu choices. Finally, we'll then print and ask the user to input a choice:

```
term_clear=`tput clear`
max_lines=`tput lines`
last_line=`expr $max_lines - 3`
echo $term_clear                                  clear
trs_prompt="Please enter your choice> "           set trs_prompt=...
trs_indent=15
center_text 0 trs_header                          cat trs_header
center_lines $trs_indent trs_menu                 cat trs_menu
tput cup $trs_indent $last_line
echo $trs_prompt                                  echo $trs_prompt
read reply                                        set reply=$<
case $reply                                       switch ($reply)
  1)                                                case: 1
    add_time                                          add_time
    ;;                                                breaksw
  2)                                                . . .
    change_time
    ;;
  3)
    delete_time
    ;;
  'x'|'X')
    exit TRUE
    ;;
  *)
    echo "Invalid choice"
    ;;
esac                                              endsw
```

Once the user selects an action, we can have a series of screens to add, change, or delete the data. Since the basic screen *mask* will be used by all of these Shell programs, we can create the command **time_screen** as follows:

```
# time_screen
center_text 0 trs_header
tput cup 4 0; echo "SSN:"
tput cup 6 0; echo "Date:"
tput cup 8 0; echo "Time Worked:"
```

We can then add time reporting data by first displaying the field names and their default values, and then getting the data for each field. (As you read through the example, notice how to edit each field, especially the SSN, and how to add the record to the data base.)

```
term_clear=`tput clear`
max_lines=`tput lines`
last_line=`expr $max_lines - 3`
echo $term_clear
text_indent=15


time_screen          # display time worked screen mask


Date=`date %y/%m/%d`  # set date
tput cup 6 $text_indent; echo $Date
tput cup 8 $text_indent; echo "8.0"


while [ TRUE ]
do
  tput cup 4 $text_indent; read SSN
  if [ -z "`grep $SSN employee.db`" ]  # check for SSN
  then
    tput cup $last_line 0; echo "$SSN not in Employee Data Base"
  else
    break
  fi
done


tput cup 6 $text_indent; read tmp_date
  if [ ! -z "$tmp_date" ]  # not default date
  then
    Date=$tmp_date
  fi
tput cup 8 $text_indent; read time_worked
```

```
if [ -z "$time_worked" ] # default time worked 8hrs
then
  time_worked=8.0
fi


echo "${SSN}\t${Date}\t${time_worked} >> time_worked.db
```

Getting valid file or directory names, correct string and numeric variables, and so on, is essential to having a Shell program execute correctly and reliably. To ensure that all variables, files, and special files are valid, you must verify the data and names. Is the file name correct and is the file readable? Writable? Executable? Is the name a directory, block special, or character special file? Is a variable equal to a specified value or another variable? Each of these questions is answered by editing the data within the Shell procedure (see Figure 8.4). The primary commands for editing data are **test** and **awk**.

Test combined with the **if-then-else** handles most edits on arguments or data in a Shell program. The **case** statement handles the rest of the edits normally required.

Expr can be used to edit the content of fields. **Expr** will compare a variable to a regular expression and return a count of characters matched. So, for example, we can evaluate alphabetic and numeric variables as shown on page 132:

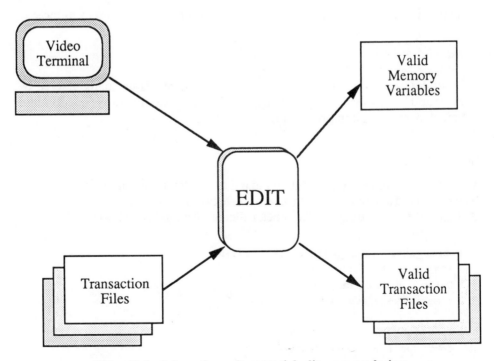

Figure 8.4   Interactive and sequential edit program design

```
expr $var : '[a-zA-Z]*'  # count alphabetic characters
expr $var : '[-+]*[0-9.]*'  # count numeric characters
```

To ensure that we got only what we expected, we could compare the returned length to the total length of $var:

```
if [ `expr $var : '[-+]*[0-9.]*'` -eq `expr $var : '.*'` ]
then
  # its numeric all the way through
else
  # its not
fi
```

Another useful editing program is **awk**, which can edit fields using the matching operator (~). In the following examples, we can test each field of the time_worked table for validity and numeric input:

```
$0 ~ /[0-9]+/
$1 ~ /[0-9][0-9]\/[0-9][0-9]\/[0-9][0-9]/
$2 ~ /[0-9]+/
```

Similarly, we can edit the *last name* field from the employee record as follows:

```
$2 ~ /(A-Z)(a-z-)+/
```

Input data, including Shell command-line arguments, is normally entered by humans and is therefore most prone to error. The data should always be edited for validity before using it in processing.

Screen Output

We can modify the existing input command to display information from the data base one record at a time. To do this, let's create two commands, one, called **trs_view**, to display the screen mask, and another, called **time_data**, to display the data:

```
# time_data  input_record  text_indent
  SSN=`echo $1 | cut -f1`
  Date=`echo $1 | cut -f2`
  time_worked=`echo $1 | cut -f3`

  tput cup 4 $2; echo $SSN
  tput cup 6 $2; echo $Date
  tput cup 8 $2; echo $time_worked
```

```
# trs_view time_worked.db    or trs_view 3< file
term_clear=`tput clear`
max_lines=`tput lines`
last_line=`expr $max_lines - 1`

echo $term_clear
text_indent=15

if [ "$1" ]  # file specified
then
  exec 3< $1  # open fd 3
# else the command must be executed with 3< file
fi

time_screen    # display time worked screen mask

while
  input_record=`line <&3`  # read record from stdin
  test ! -\ "$input_record"
do
  # display time worked data
  time_data "$input_record" $text_indent

  if [ -t 0 ]  # terminal is stdin?
  then
    tput cup $last_line 0; echo "Press Return for Next Record"
    read next
  fi
done
```

Using the **trs_view** command, we could display the whole data base one record at a time:

```
trs_view time_worked.db
```

Or we could sort it first:

```
sort time_worked.db > /tmp/tmp$$
trs_view /tmp/tmp$$
rm /tmp/tmp$$
```

This command will be useful for updating existing records as well as displaying the results of queries.

Screen Query

We can use essentially the same chunk of code to query the data base by painting
the screen, getting the user's selection criteria, and then searching the data base
and displaying the results:

```
# trs_query
term_clear=`tput clear`
max_lines=`tput lines`
last_line=`expr $max_lines - 1`

echo $term_clear
text_indent=15

if [ "$1" ]  # file specified
then
  exec 3< $1  # open fd 3
  # else the command must be executed with 3< file
fi

trs_screen    # display time worked screen mask

while [ TRUE ]
do
  tput cup 4 $text_indent; read SSN
  if [ -z "$SSN" ]  # not selecting by SSN
  then
    break
  elif [ -z "`grep $SSN employee.db`" ]  # check for SSN
  then
    tput cup $last_line 0; echo "SSN not in Employee Data Base"
  else
    break  # valid SSN
  fi
done
tput cup 6 $text_indent; read Date
tput cup 8 $text_indent; read time_worked

if [ "$SSN" -a "$Date" -a "$time_worked" ]
then
  grepstr="$SSN\t$Date\t$time_worked"
elif [ "$SSN" -a "$Date" ]
then
  grepstr="$SSN\t$Date"
elif [ "$Date" -a "$time_worked" ]
```

```
then
  grepstr="$Date\t$time_worked"
elif [ "$SSN" ]
then
  grepstr="${SSN}"
elif [ "$Date" ]
then
  grepstr="${Date}"
elif [ "${time_worked}" ]
then
  grepstr=$time_worked
else
  exit FALSE
fi
grep "$grepstr" time_worked.db > /tmp/tmp$$
trs_view /tmp/tmp$$
rm /tmp/tmp$$
```

This would show one record per page (Figure 8.5). If, instead, we would like to see multiple records per page (Figure 8.6), we could substitute the following for the display portion of the previous program:

```
echo " SSN    Date    Time Worked"
grep "$grepstr" time_worked.db
```

```
            Time Reporting System
              Time Worked Data

            SSN:  527964942

            Date:  1990/01/02

            Time Worked:  8.0
```

Figure 8.5   Time_Worked output screen

```
            Time Reporting System
              Time Worked Data

    SSN:          Date:        Time Worked:

    527964942    1990/01/02        8.0
    527964942    1990/01/03        9.5
    527964942    1990/01/04       10.0
```

Figure 8.6   Multiple record output screen

```
                      Time Reporting System
                       Time Worked Data

      SSN:              Date:        Time Worked:

      527-96-4942     01/02/1990         8.0
      527-96-4942     01/03/1990         9.5
      527-96-4942     01/04/1990        10.0
```

Figure 8.7   Formatted output screen using awk

This Shell program is a simple example of how we can query the time_worked data base for information by SSN, date worked, or time_worked. More exotic queries can be handled using **awk**.

The output from the previous example was fairly crunched together. Instead of using **more**, we can use the advanced formatting features of **awk** to beautify the output (Figure 8.7):

```
echo " SSN    Date    Time Worked"
awk 'BEGIN { FS=OFS=~\t" } \
  { split($2, Date, "/") \
  printf(" %3d-%2d-%4d %2d/%2d/%4d %4.1f\n", \
    substr($1,1,3), substr($1,4,2), substr($1,6,4), \
    Date[2], Date[3], Date[1], \
    $3) }'
```

These are just a few of the ways in which you can gather input from a screen, query a data base, and output to the screen. Later in this chapter we'll look at more exotic ways to use **awk** for selecting and formatting information for reports. Next, however, let's look at what it takes to update a data base.

DATA BASE UPDATE

Updating a file or data base means adding, changing, or deleting data. Earlier in this chapter we learned some ways to take input data from a screen and *add* a record to the data base by appending the record to a table. Now let's consider ways to *change* the data base and *delete* records from it.

The design of a simple sequential update program is shown in Figure 8.8. There are one or more possible transaction files or screens that affect the original or master file. The master (or old) file is used as input and a new file is created as output. Any errors are directed onto *stderr*.

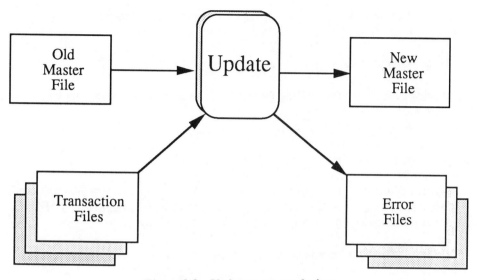

Figure 8.8   Update program design

The Shell commands that handle most of the common updates to UNIX files are **awk**, **cat**, **echo**, **grep**, **join**, **merge**, **paste**, **sed**, and **tr**. The UNIX editors also update files, but they do so manually rather than mechanically. This section will deal with the automated forms of file update.

The simplest update program is **cat**, which can create new files, concatenate several files into one new file, or append one file to an existing file. Each of these forms of update is shown in the following examples:

```
cat > file              # enter data from the terminal
cat file1 file2 > file3 # create a new file from two
cat file3 >> file4      # append file3 to file4
```

In each of these examples, **cat** adds data to a new or existing file. Similarly, **echo** can combine fields and add a single record to a data base:

```
echo "$field1 $field2 $field3" >> table.db
```

Cat and **echo** work well for creating or adding lines to a file, as long as there is no concern about the order of the information. When the information should be in order, however, either **sort** or merge (**sort -m**) serves as a better update program.

Sort can put one or more files into a specified order. This form of update is best used on unsorted files:

```
sort file1 file2 > file3
```

When the transaction and master files are already in order, however, it is more efficient to merge them:

```
sort -m table.db trans1 trans2 > newtable.db
```

A simple example involves listing two directories and merging the files found:

```
ls /bin > binlist
ls /usr/bin > usrbinlist
sort -m binlist usrbinlist > combinedlist
```

When updating files in this way, duplicate entries may cause problems. There should not be two records exactly the same in the resulting new master file. To eliminate duplicates, the output can be passed through **uniq**:

```
sort -m table.db trans1 | uniq > newtable.db
```

or

```
sort -mu table.db trans1 > newtable.db
```

Each of these examples using **sort** assumed that the first field in each file was the sort key. Other keys can be specified with positional parameters.

To update tables safely using these tools, we will need to create a temporary copy of the revised file, rename the old one as backup (bak), and give the temporary file the data base name:

```
update employee.db > tmp$$
mv employee.db employee.bak
mv tmp$$ employee.db
```

The commands that actually change information within a file or table are **sed** and **tr**. **Tr** translates characters within a file. **Sed** can also be used to delete records from the table. To change the text in the file to upper case would require the following command:

```
tr "[a-z]" "[A-Z]" < file2 > tmp$$
cat tmp$$
```

ARTHUR\t123 MAIN\tDENVER\tCO\t80202
MARTIN\t245 JUNIPER\tDENVER\tCO\t80202

Sed lets the user update fields within the file. For example, assume that everyone moved to San Francisco, California. **Sed** could handle all updates as follows:

```
sed -e "s/Denver\tCO/San Francisco\tCA/" file2 > tmp$$
cat tmp$$
```

Arthur\t123 Main\tSan Francisco\tCA\t80202
Martin\t245 Juniper\tSan Francisco\tCA\t80202

Or the edit commands, including the zip code change, could have been placed in a file called city_state:

```
s/Denver/San Francisco/
s/CO/CA/
s/80202/74539/
```

Then **sed** could be invoked as follows:

```
sed -f city_state file2 > tmp$$
```

To delete information from files, **sed** can selectively delete lines or parts of fields from files. To delete all of the records for people on Juniper Street and the word "Denver" from file2, the following command would be required:

```
sed -e "/Juniper/d" -e "s/Denver//g" file2 > tmp$$
cat tmp$$
```

Arthur\t123 Main\t\tCO\t80202

"/Juniper/d" is a line editor command to delete lines containing the word "Juniper." **"s/Denver//g"** is the line editor command to substitute nothing (//) for each occurrence of the word "Denver." Using these editor commands, **sed** acts like a program that updates fields or deletes lines. We could encapsulate the *update* capability into the following command:

```
trs_screen    # paint the screen
tput cup 4 $text_indent; read SSN
tput cup 6 $text_indent; read Date
if [ "$SSN" -a "$DATE"]
then
  search_string="${SSN}\t${Date}"
elif [ "$SSN" ]
then
  search_string="$SSN"
elif [ "$Date" ]
then
  search_string="$Date"
```

```
else
  echo "You must supply either the SSN or the Date"
  search_string="999999999"
fi
cp time_worked.db time_worked.bak    # create backup of data base

grep "$search_string" time_worked.db | \
while
  read record
do
  echo $record | trs_view
  sed_string=`echo $record | cut -f1,2 -d' '`
  tput cup 8 $text_indent; read time_worked
sed -e "/${sed_string}/s/[0-9.]*\$/$time_worked/" \
                                        time_worked.db > tmp$$
  mv tmp$$ time_worked.db
fi
```

It would then be simple to apply this same technique to display a given record and ask for confirmation before deleting the record.

Each of the commands presented in this section serves a specific purpose when updating UNIX files. Once the files have been updated and put in correct order, the data will need to be retrieved and printed. The commands to do so will be described in the next two sections.

DATA SELECTION

Both queries and reports require selection of select data (Figure 8.9). Selecting information from files can be handled in a number of ways with the Shell. Information can be selected row by row, field by field, or both. The primary commands that perform data selection are **awk**, **cut**, **grep**, and **uniq**.

Uniq is perhaps the simplest. It works on a line-by-line basis, eliminating duplicate lines or every line except for the duplicate lines. **Uniq** assumes that its input is sorted. Given the following sorted file, called names, note how **uniq** selects the various lines in the file:

Original File	uniq names	uniq -u names	uniq -d names
Arthur	Arthur	Arthur	Martin
Martin	Martin	Smith	
Martin	Smith		
Smith			

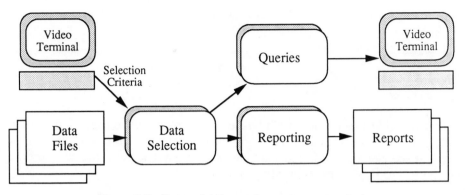

Figure 8.9   Data selection and report program design

The first selection removed the duplicated name "Martin" from the original file. The second eliminated "Martin" entirely. The final example eliminated all names except the duplicated "Martin." **Uniq** provides an efficient tool for extracting duplicated information from files.

Grep also operates on a line-by-line, row-by-row basis. It looks through a file for lines that contain the regular expression specified. Any matching records are selected. The extended grep (**egrep**) and fast grep (**fgrep**) commands provide for selecting on more than one regular expression at a time or by matching entire lines.

Given the following file, **grep** and its cousins can extract information and place it on *stdout*:

```
Arthur Denver CO
Martin Denver CO
Smith Colorado Springs CO

grep "Denver" file

Arthur Denver CO
Martin Denver CO

egrep "Martin\|Smith" file

Martin Denver CO
Smith Colorado Springs CO

fgrep "Martin Denver CO" file

Martin Denver CO
```

Grep can also select everything except certain lines by using the -v option:

```
grep -v "Arthur" file
```

Martin Denver CO
Smith Colorado Springs CO

To select information on a field-by-field basis requires the use of **cut** or **awk**. **Cut** can select fields from a file based on the character positions or on the delimiters that separate the fields. An example of selecting fields uses the time_worked data base. The fields selected are the SSN (f1) and time worked (f3):

```
cut -f1,3 time_worked.db    awk -F"\t" 'print $1, $3' time_worked.db
```

527964942 8.0
527964942 9.5
527964942 10.0

Fields can also be selected by their character position within a file. Consider a long listing of a directory:

```
ls -l
```

drwxrwx---	3	lja	adm	992	Dec 1 05:39 bin
drwx------	28	lja	adm	496	Dec 4 12:28 doc
drwxr-x---	2	lja	adm	192	Sep 5 17:55 jcl
drwx------	2	lja	adm	816	Sep 5 16:15 job
drwxrwxrwx	2	lja	adm	3760	Dec 3 09:37 rje
drwxrwxrwx	32	lja	adm	1008	Dec 3 18:22 src

```
          1         2         3         4         5         6
12345678901234567890123456789012345678901234567890123456789 0
```

Fields can be selected by column:

```
ls -l | cut -c16-24,55-
```

lja   bin
lja   doc
lja   jcl
lja   job
lja   rje
lja   src

In the directory example, **cut** selected only the information contained in columns 16-24 and 55 through the end of each line. In both of the time_worked and the directory examples, **cut** shows its ability to select specific information for future reporting.

Grep and **cut** can be combined to extract information line by line and field by field. The output of **grep** can be piped into **cut**. In the following example, the commands extract the SSN 527964942 from the time_worked data base, cut the time_worked column, and print the result on *stdout*:

```
grep "527964942" time_worked.db | cut -f3
```

```
8.0
9.5
10.0
```

Grep and **cut** are good for quick work, but do not handle formatting of the information. **Awk**, however, handles both row-by-row and field-by-field data selection (see Figure 8.10) as well as formatting data for reports or screens. Why not use it all of the time, instead of **grep** and **cut**? **Awk** has to interpret a data selection and reporting program and then process the file. For less sophisticated processing, **grep** and **cut** are optimized to do their job more efficiently. When more exotic data selection criteria are applied to a file, however, **awk** gives the user more flexibility.

Awk Syntax

awk *'program' files* —interactive use
awk **-f** *program_file files* —programming

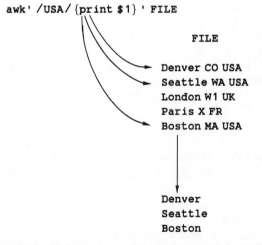

Figure 8.10   Using awk to select and report information

The previous time_worked example using **cut** could have been written in **awk** and summed as follows:

```
BEGIN { FS=OFS="\t" } # field separator is a colon
/527964942/ { print $3; sum += $3 }
END { print sum }
```

This program sets the file separator (FS) to a tab (\t) and then in the processing section looks for all records that match the string 527964942 and prints the third field in the records matched. Assuming that this **awk** program were stored in a file called Arthur_time, the command could be executed as follows:

```
awk -f Arthur_time time_worked.db
```

```
9.5
7.0
8.5
8.0
33
```

As data selection criteria become more complex, **awk** can greatly enhance the user's ability to get at the information stored in files. In another example using the previous long listing of a directory, **awk** can extract the lines containing files last updated in September and print just the owner, group, and file name as follows:

```
ls -l | awk '/Sep/ { print $3, $4, $8 }'
```

Without a specified field separator (FS), **awk** assumes that a blank delimits fields. The following lines show how **awk** would pick up the fields from each record:

```
 $1         $2   $3   $4     $5 $6   $7     $8
drwxr-x---  2    lja  adm    192 Sep 5 17:55  jcl
```

The resulting output would be:

```
lja adm jcl
lja adm job
```

Awk can also select information from fields within each line. In the following portion of an **awk** program, the hours and minutes are selected from a long directory listing:

```
split( $8, hourmin, ":" )
print hourmin[0]; # print the hours first
print hourmin[1]; # print the minutes next
```

This particular example splits the hours and minutes field ($8) by use of the delimiter (":") and places the two resulting numbers into the two-dimensional array hourmin. The next two statements print the hours (hourmin[0]) on one line and the minutes (hourmin[1]) on the line below, producing two lines for each line from the long listing. The same processing using **grep** and **cut** would have been more complex. **Awk** handles the processing more clearly.

As shown in these examples, **awk** can handle the functions of **grep**, **cut**, **paste**, and **pr**. **Awk** also has the basic control structures **if-then-else**, **for**, and **while**. Almost any data selection or reporting need can be programmed in **awk**.

Once the information has been extracted from a file using **grep**, **cut**, **sed**, or **awk**, it needs to be reported in ways that humans can best use. There are many Shell commands that support clear concise reports. The following section will describe them in detail.

REPORTING

The design of a typical report program is shown in Figure 8.11. Notice that it is very similar to the design of a typical command, using *stdin* and *stdout*. Each of the standard Shell commands produces report-like output that is fairly legible. The **cat** command will reproduce files on either the terminal screen or a printer. Commands like **ls** and **who** generate readable listings. But when data selection commands like **grep**, **cut**, and **awk** have been used on files, a more specific reporting mechanism is often required to make the output readable.

There are two major facilities for reporting information: **pr** and **awk**. **Pr** produces paginated reports that fit the printed page or a terminal screen. **Awk** can handle more exacting report specifications with 'C'-like precision. **Lpr**, the print manager, handles the simple spooling and printing of output to a wide variety of printers.

Printing files or selected information on a printer is more useful when the output is indented (-i) by eight characters to allow room for a three-hole punch on the left-hand side:

```
pr -o file | lp                              pr file | lpr -i8
```

Files with field delimiters like the tab (\t) can be printed more legibly with **pr**:

Figure 8.11   Report generation program design

```
cut -f1,3 time_worked | pr -e20
```

```
527964942                8.0
527964942                8.5
527964942               10.0
```

Printing these two fields in reverse order would have been much more difficult using **cut**, **paste**, and **pr**. It is easier to use **awk** when manipulating fields. The **awk** program to reverse these fields and print them would be:

```
awk -F'\t' '{ print $3, $1 }' time_worked.db
```

```
 8.0    527964942
 8.5    527964942
10.0    527964942
```

To obtain a more readable version of this report, the program could have used **printf**, an **awk** function that is like the C language function by the same name:

```
BEGIN { FS="\t" }
{ printf "\t%-10.1f %-10s\n", $3, $1 }
```

```
 8.0    527964942
 8.5    527964942
10.0    527964942
```

The **printf** statement uses a *format* statement (enclosed in double quotes) to describe how the output should look. In this example, there is a tab character, a right-aligned floating point number of length 10 (%-10.1f), another (right-aligned) string (%-10s), and a newline character (\n). The first and third fields of the time_worked data base are formatted in reverse order using this format specification. Increasingly more complex formatting operations can be handled with **awk** and **printf**.

Awk is the best Shell tool for formatting detailed reports. For more information, see the **awk** reference in the Bibliography. Now, with all of the four key programs available for application use, let's look at ways to plug our system into the others around it.

SYSTEM INTERFACES

Other systems often provide input to or accept output from our system via disk, tape, or electronic transmission (Figure 8.12). The commands that interface with other systems are shown in Table 8.2.

Ar (archive) typically manages libraries of C object modules. If a file is on disk,

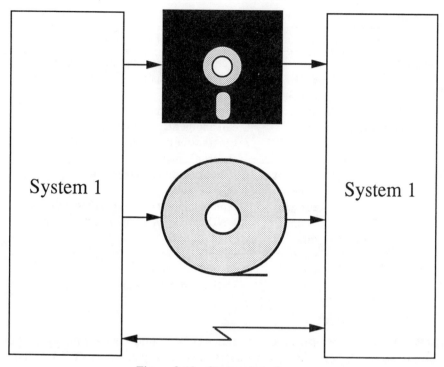

Figure 8.12   System interfaces

there is usually little problem getting the file into or out of the archive. To copy files from one disk to another, **cpio** is a useful mechanism. **Cpio** can be used with either a disk or a tape. **Tar**, like **cpio**, packages and compresses information for storage on tape:

```
Input Interface                      Output Interface
ar x archive.a                       ar q archive.a file1 file2 ...
cpio -i < /dev/mt0                   ls file* | cpio -o > /dev/mt0
ls olddir/file* | cpio -pdl  .       ls file* | cpio -pdl new_dir
tar xf - | application               tar u file*
```

Both disk and tape interfaces have their place, but are often cumbersome. (Trust the Postal Service with my tape? Never!) Nothing beats the immediacy of electronic transmission. Using a modem, we can call another UNIX system using **cu**:

```
cu 95551234
```

On a local area network, we can use **rlogin** to access another UNIX system, login, and accomplish file transfers. Over wider networks, we can use **ftp**

TABLE 8.2   System Interfaces

Interface	Command	Description
Disk	`ar`	archive and library maintenance
	`cpio`	copy input/output
Tape	`tar`	tape archive
	`cpio`	copy input/output
Transmission	`cu`	call another UNIX system
	`ftp`	file transfer program (network)
	`mail`	electronic mail
	`rjestat`	remote job entry (RJE) status
	`send`	RJE job submission
	`rlogin`	remote login to a system on the network
	`uucp`	UNIX-to-UNIX communication program
	`uustat`	status of uucp
	`uuto`	uucp file copy
	`uupick`	uucp file pickup
	`uux`	UNIX-to-UNIX command execution

(ARPANET file transfer protocol) to move files around the nation and the world. **Mail** allows for direct contact with users on virtually any system. **Uucp** handles file transfers with a greater degree of security. **Send** (System V) lets a little old UNIX system flog a big IBM mainframe with job requests, retrieve information, and hack it up for more exhaustive processing in Shell. And a host of other communication programs, like Kermit, wait in the public domain. Some examples of these commands follow:

```
rlogin network_system
ftp remote_hostname
mail system!system!username
uucp system!filenames destination_system!dir
uuto filenames system!user
uupick
```

For most application developers, intimate knowledge of these commands will be unnecessary. The UNIX wizard, however, will find them to be a vital tool in the worldwide quest for knowledge.

Working with Numbers

Every Shell programmer encounters the need to work with numbers: a sine here, a sum there, and an occasional graph. A significant part of UNIX is text, but the other part is numbers. Manipulating them and integrating them with the Shell is simple, because there are only a few commands that affect numbers: **bc**, **dc**, and **expr**.

Aside from handling various string comparisons and evaluations, **expr** also handles basic integer math: addition, subtraction, multiplication, and division. This facility is useful for simple mathematical processing and for controlling loops. Interactively, **expr** can handle simple calculations:

```
expr 327 + 431
758
expr 431 / 327
1
```

In loops, it can handle repetitious calculations. For example, the following command would sum all of the numbers from one to 100:

```
while [ ${i:=1} -le 100 ]
do
  total='expr ${total
  i='expr ${i} + 1`
done
echo $total
```

Expr can also control the number of times a loop executes. Since the Bourne Shell has no **repeat** control construct, **expr** and **while** handle the repetition of processing.

```
while [ ${i:=1} -le 10 ]  # repeat 10 times
do
  process something
  i='expr ${i} + 1`
done
```

The C Shell can handle simple integer arithmetic using standard C language operators: +, -, *, /, and %. When assigning values to parameters, the C Shell can use the integer operators of C: +=, -=, *=, /=, ++, and --. The following example demonstrates the use of integer arithmetic:

```
if ( $variable + 1 > $maximum ) then
  @ var1 += 5
  @ var2--
endif
```

Handling more complex mathematics and floating point numbers requires the use of **bc** or **dc**. The desk calculator **dc** works just like a desk calculator, but is not as flexible as the basic calculator **bc** for use with Shell programs. **Bc**, using a syntax not unlike C or the C Shell, provides for unlimited precision arithmetic. It can also work in bases other than base 10. **Bc** has at its command the IF, FOR, and WHILE control structures. It also has access to various functions: sqrt, length, scale, sine, cosine, exponential, log, arctangent, and Bessel functions. **Bc** also allows users to define functions that can be included to handle complex math operations.

When executed, **bc** first reads any files that were specified as arguments. User defined functions can be stored in these files. Then, **bc** begins to read the standard input, which can be a file, a device, or a terminal. The calculations at the start of this section could be accomplished with **bc**:

```
echo "327 + 431" | bc              # add 327 and 431
758
echo "scale=2;431 / 327" | bc      # divide 431 by 327
1.32
```

In the first calculation, the **echo** command creates an input string for **bc**, adding 327 and 431. The second calculation first sets the decimal accuracy (scale) to two; then the division of 431 by 327 is echoed into **bc**. Unless set to another value, the **scale** of every **bc** command defaults to zero decimal places.

For simple integer arithmetic, **expr** is the best choice. But when higher precision is required, **bc** handles the job nicely.

Bc can also use the math library functions to calculate various limited equations. To calculate the sine of all angles from 1°-90°, the basic calculator can be invoked in a **while** loop:

```
while [ ${angle:=1} -le 90 ]        # for angles < 90
do
  # calculate the sine to four decimal places
  sin=`echo "scale 4;s(${angle})" | bc -l`
  echo "Angle=${angle} Sine=${sin}"      # print the result
  i=`expr ${angle} + 1`                   # increment the angle
done
```

Bc can also handle functions stored in files to process more complex equations. The following functions handle converting Fahrenheit to Celsius:

```
scale=2
define f(c) {         /* convert celsius to fahrenheit */
  auto f              /* fahrenheit variable */
  f = ( c * 1.8 ) + 32    /* convert */
  return(f)               /* return value */
}
define c(f) {         /* convert fahrenheit to celsius */
  auto c              /* celsius variable */
  c = ( f - 32 ) / 1.8    /* convert */
  return(c)               /* return value */
}
```

Assuming that these functions were contained in a file called temp, conversions could be handled by invoking **bc**:

```
bc temp          # invoke bc with fahrenheit/celsius conversions
f(100)           # convert 100 degrees celsius to fahrenheit
212.00
c(32)            # convert 32 degrees fahrenheit to celsius
0.00
quit
```

Or the results could be stored in a variable:

```
fahrenheit=`echo "f(100)" | bc temp`
celsius=`echo "c(0)" | bc temp`
```

Although these are simple examples, **bc** can use functions to process significantly more complex arithmetic equations as the need arises. **Bc** can also handle other functions required by programmers, like conversion of numbers from one base into another.

Computers use base 2 for their calculations, but most of them display their information in octal (base 8) or hexadecimal (base 16). **Bc** can handle these conversions easily by assigning an input base and or an output base. An octal calculator would set both input base (*ibase*) and output base (*obase*) to 8:

```
bc
ibase=8     /* set input base to octal */
obase=8     /* set output base to octal */
11 + 7      /* octal 11 + 7 = 20 octal */
20
quit
```

The same facility is available for the hexadecimal environment; or hexadecimal or octal can be converted directly to decimal:

```
bc
ibase=8     /* input base is octal, output base is decimal /*
10          /* octal 10 is 8 decimal */
8
ibase=16    /* input base is hexadecimal output base is decimal */
10          /* hexadecimal 10 is 16 decimal */
16
quit
```

Here, an octal 10 is equal to a decimal 8 and a hexidecimal 10 is equal to a decimal 16. When reading octal or hexidecimal dumps of data or programs, these calculators can improve any programmer's productivity.

SUMMARY

As you have seen, you can construct complete application systems using the Shell as a fourth-generation language. You can create Shell systems whenever a simple system will serve many users. As your system grows and evolves, it may eventually need to be rewritten using an actual data base—Oracle, Ingres, Informix, Unity, Unify, or some other RDBMS, and a programming language like C. This leads us to one of the fundamental laws of software engineering:

> Any system that works has always evolved from a simple system that works.

In any situation, a Shell prototype will serve as an excellent model for the development of a needed system. The prototype system can then serve the needs of customers and clients until the final product is available. A prototype system is composed of the five common types of software programs: input, output, query, data base update, and interface. This chapter has demonstrated the key commands and Shell programs that support each of these types of program designs. Any Shell user who wants to maximize their effectiveness and efficiency should become familiar with the system-building capabilities described in this chapter.

EXERCISES

1. When should you use the Shell to create application systems?

2. Describe the format of a relational table.

3. What are the five basic program designs most often created in Shell?

4. Which Shell commands are used in each of the basic program designs?

5. Build the input, output, query, and data base update programs for:

   - the **employee** data base
   - the **tax** tables

6. Write the paycheck program for the payroll system.

7. Why are data modeling and design so important?

Chapter Nine

Handling User Documentation

Documentation is one of the major features of UNIX. Major word processing and desktop publishing packages such as WordPerfect, Interleaf, and Framemaker are now available on UNIX machines. Since these software tools are not part of UNIX, we'll focus on the documentation facilities that come with UNIX and how the Shell can aid their use.

> In any bureaucracy, paperwork increases as you spend more
> and more time reporting on the less and less you are doing.

In 1975, long before word processing and desktop publishing in personal computers, there lived two commands, **nroff** and **troff**, that could do virtually everything that modern packages could do. **Nroff** formats documentation for the existing ocean of dot-matrix and letter-quality printers; **troff** formats documents for Post-Script laser printers and phototypesetters. Using **nroff** and **troff** can be made much easier by use of Shell. The major documentation commands are shown in Table 9.1. Because of the number of commands and terminals that work with these two commands, it is often confusing to get all of the commands put together to generate the correct output. Shell helps eliminate those problems.

Otherwise, formatting documents with **nroff** would be as simple as:

```
nroff  document_file
```

Usually, however, it takes many parameters and a few input and output filters to format a document correctly. The most frequently used parameters invoke a macro package.

TABLE 9.1   Documentation Commands

Command	Description
checkeq	check a document's usage of equation macros
checkmm	check a document's usage of mm macros
col	process reverse line feeds
cw	prepare constant width text for troff
deroff	remove nroff/troff macros
diffmk	mark differences in two versions of a document
eqn	equation preprocessor for troff
gath	gather files
greek	prepare output for special terminals
lp	spool output to printers (System V)
lpr	spool output to printers (Berkeley)
man	format UNIX manual pages
mm	format documents using Memorandum Macros
mmt	typeset documents, view graphs, and slides
neqn	equation preprocessor for nroff
nroff	format documents for ASCII terminal
ptx	generate permuted index
spell	check spelling of documents
tbl	table preprocessor
troff	format documents for a phototypesetter

MACRO PACKAGES

There are a number of macro packages designed to handle most documentation problems. These packages are contained in /usr/lib/tmac and /usr/lib/macros. The most common ones are the memorandum macros (**mm** or csh:**ms**) and manual page macros (**man**). The available macro packages are shown in Table 9.2. Typically, a separate Shell command is necessary to invoke each different macro package:

```
nroff -mm document        nroff -ms document
nroff -man manpage
```

To speed up loading of the macros and to improve efficiency, use the compacted macros—a "compiled" version of the macros:

```
nroff -cm document        nroff -cs document
nroff -can manpage
```

Documentation problems that couldn't be solved easily with these macro packages required special preprocessors to prepare the input files for **nroff**. Commands were developed to handle tables and equations.

TABLE 9.2   Documentation Macro Libraries

Macros	Description
man	manual page macros
mm	memorandum macros
mosd	operations systems deliverable documentation macros
mptx	permuted index macros
ms	manuscript macros (Berkeley)
mv	view graph and slide macros
cm	compiled memorandum macros

INPUT FILTERS

The commands that preprocess **nroff** files are **eqn**, **tbl**, and **gath** (System V). **Eqn** processes equations for mathematical output. **Tbl** creates the **nroff** macros needed to format tables. And **gath**, which normally works with the remote job entry (RJE) facility, can be used to set keywords, include files, or execute commands and use their output as input to **nroff** or **troff**. Each of these commands expands the capability of **nroff** for text formatting.

Eqn

Eqn preprocesses mathematical equations for **troff**. Its twin, **neqn**, processes equations for **nroff**. They are useful for serious scientists, but hold little value for the average user.

They are invoked as input filters to **nroff** or **troff**:

```
eqn files | troff
neqn files | nroff
```

For the average documentation user, **tbl** and **gath** hold more interest.

Tbl

Tbl takes files of the form shown in Figure 9.1 and turns them into usable input for **nroff**. The resulting output from the following command is also shown in Figure 9.1.

```
tbl document | nroff
```

To build a command that accurately formats all documents regardless of content takes planning. On any system, **tbl** is a hog. It is more efficient to check the file for tables than it is to use **tbl** on all documents. We could use **grep** to check the file and only execute **tbl** if required:

```
center tab(:)
l c c c
l n n n.
Sales:January:February:March
_
Southwest:100:110:120
Northwest:230:150:170
.TE
```

Sales	*January*	*February*	*March*
Southwest	110	110	120
Northwest	230	150	170

Figure 9.1   Documentation example using `tbl` macros

```
# get the names of any files that have tables
if [ -z `grep -l "^.TS" $* | line` ]
then
  nroff -cm $*              # no tables in the file
else
  tbl $* | nroff -cm        # process tables and format file
fi
```

The **grep** takes less time than running **tbl** on every file. It also keeps the user from forgetting to invoke the table preprocessor when required. Both of these advantages make the cost of searching each file for tables an inexpensive proposition.

Gath

Gath gathers information together just like the **send** command, but it doesn't send the information over the RJE. Instead, it puts the output on *stdout*. Gath can preprocess text to prompt for keywords, include files, and execute commands.

Keywords are useful when the document doesn't change but certain key phrases do:

```
~=:FIRST
~=:LAST
~=:ADDRESS
~=:CITYSTZIP
.nf
FIRST LAST
ADDRESS
CITYSTZIP
```

```
.sp
Dear FIRST,
.sp
.fi
. . . letter
```

```
gath letter | nroff -cm
```

```
FIRST=Jay
LAST=Arthur
ADDRESS=123 Anystreet
CITYSTZIP=Anytown, AZ 12345
```

Gath will prompt for each keyword, as previously shown, and then substitute them for all occurrences. The keywords can also be supplied on the command line:

```
FIRST=Jay LAST=Arthur ADDRESS="123 Anystreet" \
CITYSTZIP="Anytown, AZ 12345" gath letter | nroff -cm
```

Gath can also include files in the text:

text...
~filename
text...

Gath will include filename at that point in the text. But **gath** can also execute commands. In the following example, **gath** retrieves a file from SCCS and runs it through **tbl** before inserting the text in the file.

text
~!get -p s.tablefile | tbl
text

Gath can even include the output from specific commands like **ls**:

text
~!cd;ls -l
text

These are trivial examples, but they illustrate the potential for preprocessing **nroff** and **troff** input to allow for more robust documentation. The presence of **gath** commands can also be detected with **grep**:

```
grep -n "ˆ~" $*
```

In cases where both **gath** and **tbl** are required as input filters, execute **gath** before **tbl** to ensure that all tables are included with the text before invoking **tbl**.

```
gath $* | tbl | nroff -cm
```

Once the input has been processed correctly, **nroff** or **troff** must be brought into play, to format the resulting text in a way that is suitable for the output device.

TERMINAL PREVIEWING OF DOCUMENTS

Because UNIX uses mainly asynchronous communications (you send UNIX a character and it echos it back), there are innumerable types of terminals that can be used with UNIX. Video display terminals (VDTs) vary from so-called "dumb" terminals to workstations. Hardcopy output devices range from dot-matrix and letter-quality printers through laser printers. These are all available to UNIX; they are connected as shown in Figure 9.2.

Because of the variety of output devices, **nroff** and **troff** use numerous parameters to control their output. (See Table 9.3.) **Nroff** and **troff** also extract a heavy toll

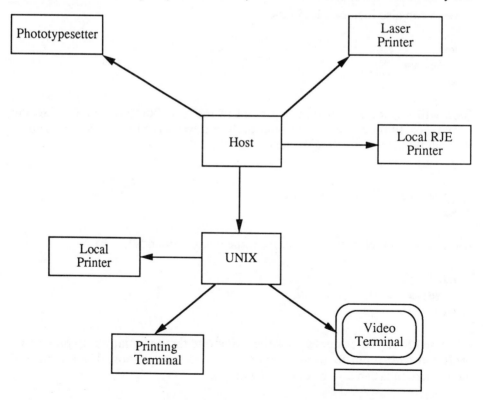

Figure 9.2   Printing options

TABLE 9.3   Nroff and Troff Formatting Options

Option	Descriptions
Nroff and **Troff**	
-i	read standard input
-nn	number first page as n
-o	print requested pages
-q	use input.output mode of .rd request
-rAn	set register A to n
-sn	stop every n pages
-z	print messages generated by .tm requests
-cm	include compacted macro library m
-km	compact the macros and store in the current directory
-mm	include macro library m
Nroff Only	
-e	invoke proportional spacing
-h	use tabs to speed output
-T$name$	format output for terminal type $name$
-un	set emboldening factor to n

from the system when they format a document. In many active UNIX systems, **nroff** and the screen editors will consume most of the system's resources. All too often, when users enter an **nroff** command, they will forget to enter all of the parameters needed. So, they try again and again to get everything "right" for their terminal. In the process they eat up huge chunks of system resources.

To circumvent this resource drain, it is usually wise to develop Shell commands to handle **nroff** or **troff** output to the various terminal types. The following sections will describe using **nroff** with each terminal type.

Video Display Terminals

VDTs come in two screen widths: 80 and 132 characters. To have **nroff** format the output correctly for comfortable viewing, the width and offset options must be set as follows:

```
nroff -rO0 -rW79 document
nroff -rO0 -rW131 document
```

Why are the line widths one character less than the maximum length? At the end of each line printed by **nroff** are a carriage return (CR) and line feed (LF). Most VDTs have what is called a wraparound feature—when a long line is not truncated at the edge of the screen, a line feed is automatically generated and the remainder of the line prints on the next line on the screen. If the lines are 80 in length, then a CR would generate a wraparound LF and the LF following would leave a blank line on the screen. Line widths of 79 and 131 seem to work best. Since what people see on the screen should not differ from what ultimately prints on a printer, these width options should be used for all printer output as well.

Emboldening—making text appear darker—is possible with **nroff** and **troff**. **Nroff** emboldens text by overstriking each character as many as four times. There are several ways to embolden text:

```
nroff        mm          nroff
.bd          .B text     \fBtext\fR
text
```

The result of using **nroff** on the following emboldened text is a series of characters and backspaces:

```
\fBuser\fR
u<u<u<us<s<s<se<e<e<er<r<r<r
```

Since most VDTs switch into enhanced print via a control character sequence, all of these backspaces and extra characters are unnecessary and require longer transmission times. Unless the administrators have developed an output filter to handle these special situations, suppress them by using the -u option to eliminate emboldening:

```
nroff -cm -u -rW79 -rO0 document
```

This helps speed up the transmission of the formatted document. Most other adjustments to the output are handled with output filters.

Printers

The type of printer can be specified with the -T parameter when printing directly on a given printer (i.e., when not using **lp** or **lpr**):

```
nroff -cm -T450 -rW79 -rO8 document
```

This command specifies a Diablo printer (-T450) and says the output is to be offset eight spaces to the right (-rO8).

Local line printers can receive output by I/O redirection of the **nroff** output into a device name or a spooler:

```
nroff -cm -rW79 -rO8 document > /dev/lp
sh: nroff -cm -rW79 -rO8 document | lp
csh: nroff -cm -rW79 -rO8 document | lpr
nroff -cm -rW79 -rO8 document | opr
```

OUTPUT FILTERS

The most common output filters for **nroff** are **col**, **pr**, **sed**, and **uniq**. All four are useful with VDTs. **Col** is also useful with some printers.

Col removes reverse line motions that are used to handle underlining, super-scripts, and subscripts. VDTs and a few line printers cannot handle reverse line motions, so **col** is used to convert reverse line motions into single-line combinations of backspaces and characters. **Col** removes super- and subscripts from **nroff**'s output. The output of any **nroff** command for a VDT should be run through **col**:

```
nroff -cm -rO8 -rW79 document | col
```

The output of **nroff** can be further optimized for screens by use of filters. The most obvious one is **uniq**, which suppresses duplicate lines. Duplicates are most often blank lines at the end of a page. At 1200 baud, a short last page can zip off the screen before the user can read it. To eliminate all but one occurrence of each blank line, use **uniq**:

```
nroff -cm document | col | sed -e "s/\b.//" | uniq
```

Another way to handle the problem is to present only 24 lines at a time and then allow the user to request more information with **pr**, **pg**, or **more**:

```
nroff -cm document | col | sed -e "s/\b.//" | pr -l24 -t -p
nroff -cm document | col | sed -e "s/\b.//" | pg
nroff -cm document | col | sed -e "s/\b.//" | more
```

Pr, **pg**, or **more** will sound the terminal bell and the user can hit return to view each new section of a formatted document.

PUTTING IT ALL TOGETHER

Customizing document output for a particular terminal can be handled with a variety of input and output filters. The command line for each terminal type looks like this:

```
input filters | nroff -macros parameters | output filters
```

To put all of these filters together requires changes to /etc/profile and the creation of a new command that we can all **output**. First, /etc/profile should ask for the terminal type and assign it to the variable TERM:

```
echo "Enter Terminal Type: "
read TERM
case $TERM in
    vt100|5420|tv970)
        tabs
        ;;
    lp|620|630|laser)
        ;;
    ti|700|745)
        tabs
        ;;
    *)
        echo "Setting up default terminal"
        ;;
esac
```

Users will be prompted for this information when they log in. The output command can then use $TERM to make intelligent default choices for **nroff**. It should check for tables, equations, and commands for **gath**. Next, it should invoke output filters for the terminal type:

```
# output file(s)
if [ $# -gt 1 ]      # check parameter count
then
    # save the parameters entered by the user
    while [ `echo $1 | cut -c1` -eq "-" ]      # flags
    do
        parameters="${parameters} $1"          # save flag
        shift                                  # delete flag
    done
    # check the files and save their names
    while [ "$1" ]                             # while more arguments
    do
        if [ -r $1 ]                           # readable file?
        then
            files="${files} $1"                # save file name
        else
            echo "file $1 not found"
        fi
        shift                                  # delete argument
    done
    # determine the input filters
    tblcnt=`grep -c "^.TS" $* | cut -f2 -d: | sort -nr | line`
    gathcnt=`grep -c "^~" $* | cut -f2 -d: | sort -nr | line`
    if [ $tblcnt -gt 0 ]
```

```
    then
        inputcnt=`expr ${inputcnt:=0} + 1`
    fi
    if [ $gathcnt -gt 0 ]
    then
        inputcnt=`expr ${inputcnt:=0} + 2`
    fi
    case $inputcnt in
      0)
        inputfilter="cat $files | "
        ;;
      1)
        inputfilter="tbl $files | "
        ;;
      2)
        inputfilter="gath $files | ""
        ;;
      3)
        inputfilter="gath $files | tbl | ""
        ;;
      *)
        echo "Error in output: filters $inputfilter"
    esac
    case $TERM in
      vt100|5420|tv970)
        parameters="$parameters -u -rO0 -rW79 "
        outputfilter=" | col | sed -e "s/\b.//g" | uniq"
        ;;
      lp|620|630)
        parameters="-rO8 -rW79 $parameters "
        outputfilter=""
        ;;
      ti|700|745)
        parameters="-rO0 -rW79 $parameters "
        outputfilter=" | col "
        ;;
    esac
    eval "${inputfilter} nroff ${macros:="-cm"} ${parameters} \
          {outputfilter}"
else
    echo "No files specified"
fi
```

The actual makeup of the **output** command will vary with the type of terminals in use. The advantages of typing the following simple command to print files should be obvious:

```
output document
```

Once formatted, documents can be spooled for output to any number of devices or line printers.

SPOOLING DOCUMENTS

A line printer (**lp** or csh: **lpr**) spooler was added to UNIX Version 4 and later versions. **Lp** allows the system administrator to define the types of printers on the system. Each user can spool files to a printer without actually logging on, and the printout can be picked up later at the user's convenience. **Lp** can even send the user mail when the file finishes printing.

To use **lp**, the printers have to be defined and labeled by the system administrator. Then, documents can be spooled easily by creating a command to make a few decisions. The spooler must decide whether to print an existing file or to execute a command and print its output. Using **lp** (sh) or **lpr** (csh), documents can be formatted with the **output** or **pr** command, and printed by the line printer:

```
output file | lp          output file | lpr
pr -o8 file | lp          pr file | lpr -i8
                          troff -t troff_file | lpr -t
```

In the first example, the **output** command will format the document file and spool the resulting file. In the second example, **pr** will format the text file and then print it, indented by eight spaces. The last **csh** example formats the document using **troff**; **lpr** then converts the **troff** (-t) input into PostScript for the receiving printer. Formatting requests that are more complex than those provided by the use of **output** and **pr** will require the use of other miscellaneous filters.

To check on the status of print jobs, just enter the command **lpstat** (csh: **lpq**). This command checks the queues and lets you know if your job has finished printing.

MISCELLANEOUS DOCUMENTATION FILTERS

Figures 9.3 and 9.4 show the various filters available for handling documents with **nroff** and **troff**.

Troff uses the same input filters as **nroff** with one exception: **cw**, the constant width preprocessor. **Cw** uses some additional macros to handle special output requirements. Each of these filters is handy for special circumstances, but most users will rarely need them.

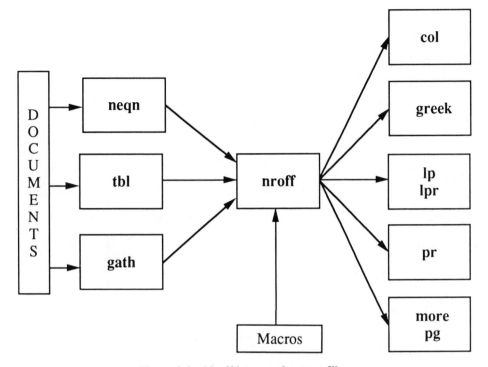

Figure 9.3   Nroff input and output filters

ˇ MISCELLANEOUS COMMANDS

A number of commands work with **nroff** text: **man, mm, mmt, deroff,** and **spell.**
Man formats manual pages using a unique set of macros. It executes **nroff** with a
variety of options to format the output.

Mm invokes **nroff** using the memorandum macros (System V). It can do many
of the things the previously developed Shell commands, like **output,** can do, but it
lacks the robustness available with the Shell.

Mmt typesets slides and viewgraphs (System V).

Deroff removes all **nroff** and **troff** macros from a file, which is occasionally
useful.

In Berkeley systems, the formatting commands are **ms** and **me. Ms** handles
standard text processing. **Me** provides multicolumn capabilities for formal papers
to academia or publications.

Document Analysis

Spell is one of the most useful document processing tools. It finds most of the
spelling errors in a document. **Spell** produces its list of errors one word per line. If

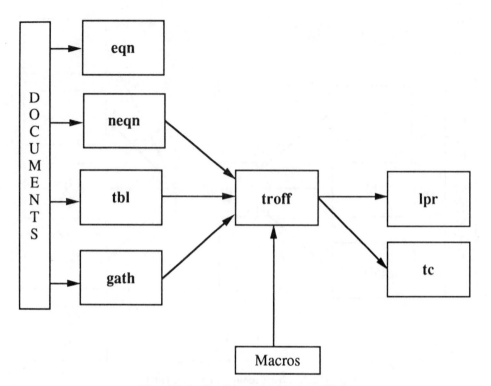

Figure 9.4   Troff input and output filters

there are extensive errors, the list will scroll off the screen quickly. A solution is to print the output of spell horizontally:

```
spell document | pr -4
```

The Writer's Workbench facility also provides some excellent tools for examining and improving documents. Commands like **style** and **prose** can be beneficial to writers. Shell commands can be created to run all of these commands against a document and print or store the results. These Shells should be created as needed.

Let's use Shell to build an analyzer of our own. One of the things I find most useful is to know what the keywords are in a document—those that are repeated most frequently. These words often capture the true content of a document. How could we do this using Shell? First, using **deroff**, we would want to remove all of the **nroff** or **troff** formatting commands:

```
deroff $1
```

Then, we would want to transform the file in the following ways:

- Convert upper case to lower case (so that **Troff** and **troff** would be counted as the same word).
- Convert blanks and tabs to newlines (to create one word per line).
- Convert all punctuation into newlines (so that "sentence." and "sentence" will be counted as the same word).

We can accomplish all of this using **tr**:

```
deroff $1 | \
tr [A-Z \t#',.;:()] [a-z\012\012\012\012\012\012\012\012\012\012]
```

Next, we can select just the words (using **grep**), **sort** the word list in descending numeric order, and then count words using **uniq**:

```
deroff $1 | \
tr [A-Z \t#',.;:()] [a-z\012\012\012\012\012\012\012\012\012\012] | \
grep [a-z] | sort -nr | uniq -c
```

If we executed this command, we'd get a listing of keywords that includes the following:

```
127    the
 86    a
 32    an
 31    shell
 27    programming
```

Words like "the" and "a" are the most common words in the English language. We might want to use **sed** to eliminate these words and to help illuminate the true keywords. Similarly, the numbers are only useful to get the file in order. We can use **cut** to eliminate them:

```
deroff $1 | \
tr [A-Z \t#',.;:()] [a-z\012\012\012\012\012\012\012\012\012\012] | \
grep [a-z] | sort -nr | uniq -c | \
cut -c6- | sed -f conjunctions
```

The file, conjunctions, would contain entries for all filler words—*a, an, and, but,* and *the*. It would tell **sed** to delete them as follows:

```
/^a$/d
/^an$/d
/^and$/d
/^but$/d
/^the$/d
. . .
```

With all of the filler words out of the way, we might want to capture just the first ten keywords. We could use **head** to do this for us:

```
deroff $1 | \
tr [A-Z \t#',.;:()] [a-z\012\012\012\012\012\012\012\012\012\012] | \
grep [a-z] | sort -nr | uniq -c | \
cut -c6- | sed -f conjunctions | \
head
```

Using this command on this chapter, we might get the following results:

```
document
documents
nroff
documentation
troff
shell
printer
terminal
```

From these results you'll notice that **keyword** cannot differentiate between the singular and plural words (*document* and *documents*). To overcome this, we could write another Shell program, **plural**, to extract words that end in "s:"

```
# plural
cat $* > /tmp/tmp$$
# find plurals
sed -e "s/s$//" /tmp/tmp$$ | sort | uniq -d > /tmp/tmp1$$
if [ -s /tmp/tmp1$$ ]    # plurals were found!
then                     # create sed file to delete them
  sed -e "s/^/\//" -e "s/$/s\/d/" /tmp/tmp1$$ > /tmp/tmp2$$
else
  cat /tmp/tmp$$
fi
rm -f /tmp/tmp*$$
```

These commands, **keyword** and **plural**, can dramatically aid the development of an index for a book or a reference index for an information archive. First you must figure out what items are most important and then combine them into a beginning table of contents:

```
for file in chapter*
do
  keyword $file >> /tmp/tmp$$
  sort /tmp/tmp$$ > index
  rm /tmp/tmp$$
done
```

This is just a simple example of the ways that documents can be examined and evaluated using Shell. I hope it has opened your eyes to the possibilities inherent in the flexibility of the Shell.

SUMMARY

Shell provides some excellent tools for handling documents and preparing them for output on the wide variety of devices available to UNIX. Connecting all of these tools can improve efficiency and reliability: users type one simple command and it determines how to format each document. Commands can be easily created for each set of **nroff** or **troff** macros.

Documentation is one of the strengths of UNIX. Full-screen word processors are available that are beginning to displace **nroff** and **troff**, but there are still hundreds of thousands of **nroff** users who need simple interfaces to its facilities. Use the Shell to fill their needs.

EXERCISES

1. Describe the various input and output filters for **nroff** and **troff.**

2. Describe the macro packages available for document preparation.

3. Write a **while** loop to use **gath** to enter names and addresses for inclusion in an **nroff** text file.

4. Use **spell** to check the correctness of any document in UNIX.

5. Write a Shell command to display the output of **nroff** on a terminal screen and pause between pages.

6. Use the commands in the Writer's Workbench to examine the style and prose contained in any UNIX document.

7. Extend the **plural** command to eliminate plural words that end in "es."

8. Extend the **keyword** command to handle phrases of two or three words (e.g., Shell programming) using **paste** or **awk**.

PART THREE

Shell Programming
for the Power User

Many men go fishing all of their lives without
knowing that it is not fish they are after.

Henry David Thoreau

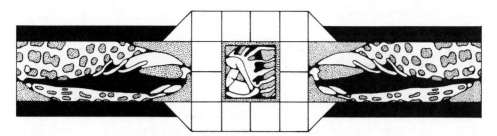

Chapter Ten

The Shell Innovator

The sole advantage of power is that you can do more good.

Baltasar Gracian

Over the past 40 years we have automated virtually all of the systems that support existing business needs. Unfortunately, automation has locked us into the way we did things 10, 20, or 30 years ago and the way we did things then was fairly inefficient and ineffective. Most of these automated systems are too inflexible to meet the challenges of the 1990s. Some of the concerns that face software professionals because of these dinosaurs include "manual" interfaces, redundant and inaccessible data, and the closed proprietary architectures of today's vendors. The Information Society is an economic reality, not an intellectual abstraction.

I know of no teachers so powerful and persuasive as a little army of specialists. They carry no banners, they beat no drums; but where they are men learn that bustle and push are not the equals of quiet genius and serene mastery.

Oliver Wendell Holmes, Jr.

The Shell power user will set the pace for other users and give them direction and inspiration. As a power user, you will need to lead by example. If you do things in a half-baked way, so will everyone else. The Shell innovator demonstrates the power of Shell.

Inventors and men of genius have almost always been regarded as fools at the beginning (and very often at the end) of their careers.

Dostoyevski

UNIX and Shell offer the promised land of application portability across all types of computers. The POSIX standard put UNIX in the hands of the user, not the vendor. The long reign of hardware tyranny is coming to an end. UNIX will be the software cockpit of the 1990s and Shell will be one of the weapons in your arsenal.

This ability to develop applications that run in UNIX but need no specific hardware environment gives users freedom of choice and a way to lower overall costs. It also gives connectivity to all existing applications via the communication tools, which will ultimately lead to increased vendor and hardware independence. This freedom will also:

- protect your application portfolio
- give you leverage with vendors
- increase organizational flexibility to use the same software everywhere
- simplify application maintenance
- reduce risk of technological change
- increase user control
- provide full suites of programming, text, interface, and support tools
- encourage continuity of user knowledge from MS-DOS
- enhance access to corporate data as needed.

Using UNIX and Shell to integrate existing systems and develop new strategic systems is a global solution that leads to:

- lower costs
- greater results
- reduced time-to-market
- empowered employees
- increased competitive advantage.

The winners of the future will need to:

1. Select the right opportunities and

2. Apply the appropriate methodology and technology.

The right opportunities for businesses in the 1990s include the integration of existing systems and the development of strategic information systems. The right methods and tools include rapid application development (RAD) and open systems architectures (OSA). Their absence causes entropy, illness, and the death of Information Systems (IS). IS death occurs when management retreats behind policies and procedures to preserve the status quo. Those who fail at these two key activities will fumble their future. The key issues at stake in this information revolution are:

- survival
- revenue
- reputation for quality, price, and service.

True simplicity is not easy.

The challenge facing all users and software developers is to *redesign existing processes* to be more effective and efficient, and *then* to automate them. While we're redesigning, however, we will have to continue to grow and evolve the old systems. This is no simple challenge. The systems we have today live lonely, separate lives. In today's business climate, they need to share data and information to meet the company's information needs (see System Interfaces, in Chapter Eight). Rather than build a whole new system to replace several others, we can use 80 percent of the existing system or systems to perform the core processing and use UNIX and Shell to integrate the user interfaces. With this strategy, we can integrate existing systems at 20 percent of the cost of building new ones.

SYSTEMS INTEGRATION

All "operating cost reduction" software was built in the 1960s and 1970s. These tactical systems are getting older every day, while vast hordes of programmers add new functions and patch bugs in the software. Unless someone is actively rejuvenating this software, entropy is moving it and your company closer to the software graveyard. Information managers keep waiting for some magic to appear that will redesign and rewrite these systems overnight. Alas, no such luck.

If the user is the least flexible element in any system, then existing software systems must be the second most inflexible element. Fortunately, however, we can use UNIX and the Shell to create user-seductive interfaces, integrate existing systems, and breathe a few more years of life into these dinosaurs (Figure 10.1). The data we need is available from existing screens or reports; all we need to do is extract it using Shell tools like **grep** or **awk**. Consider the following examples:

1. Two (or more) systems maintain the same data (e.g., an employee record, the area codes of phone numbers, or a state code table). Use Shell as a front-end preprocessor to build a single update screen (as we demonstrated in Chapter 8), manage the data, and update the data in both systems (Figure 10.2) using Shell communications.

2. Your company buys a smaller company with its own suite of systems and programs. Use Shell (Figure 10.3) to bridge the chasm between the two companies' systems until you can merge them.

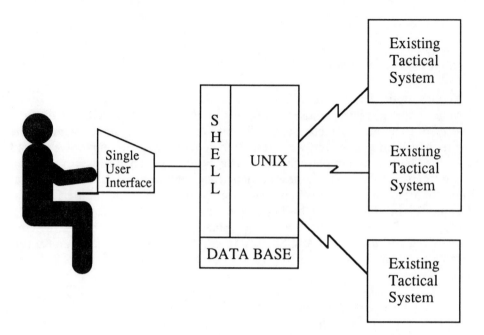

Figure 10.1   Systems integration

There are, however, a few drawbacks to this technique:

1. The response time of the integrated system is equal to the response time of the slowest system.

2. Functionality is impaired when one of the systems is down.

3. The integration is highly dependent on existing screen and report design. If these change, then the integration package must change as well.

Aside from these minor drawbacks, system integration is an excellent way to maximize the benefits of Shell. Most computer vendors specialize in certain areas—data management, real time transaction processing, or whatever. Unfortunately, their architecture is closed. Vendors are like a railroad: you have to stay on their line and only stop in certain places, which makes it difficult to share data among disparate systems. Connecting diverse vendor systems is like trying to connect short stretches of superhighway with long, narrow dirt roads that wind through mountains, deserts, and rolling plains. Using the open architecture of UNIX and the Shell you can build your own superhighway between these systems to help you access data, and then do what you want with it. This is the power and freedom of Shell.

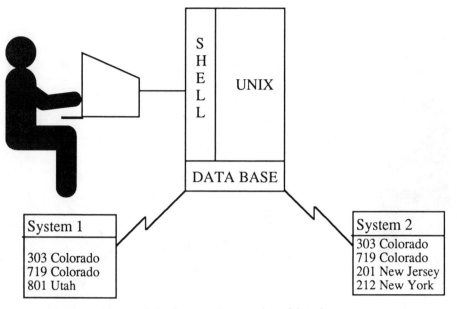

Figure 10.2   Systems integration of data bases

STRATEGIC INFORMATION SYSTEMS

The one that controls the software controls the war.

Katsuhide Hirai

Estimates project that the world software market will explode from $50 billion to $1 trillion during the 1990s. The United States consumes 52 percent of the world's software and controls 70 percent of the market (Rifkin and Savage, 1989). And yet, today's businesses are suffering from an advanced case of information starvation and indigestion. Marketing types hunger for the information to forge new markets. They need real-time customer information to find and develop new markets. Strategic information systems can help you identify markets and decide where you'll be in three to five years; tactical systems maintain the status quo. Existing systems feed a flood of data into the corporate hierarchy—far more information than can be digested. Using the power of Shell and UNIX to glue these systems together and scrub their combined outputs into meaningful information will accelerate the growth and power of your company.

Existing systems are tactical in nature: they keep the business running from day to day. Although they provide value by keeping the business going, they are rarely of strategic value (Figure 10.4). The future belongs to companies that can access information in new ways to identify strategic opportunities. Information technology is a competitive weapon. Most information systems managers are just

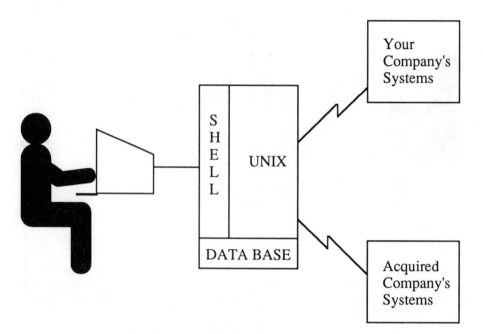

Figure 10.3   Systems integration of companies

beginning to hear of and see the potential of strategic information systems. With the power of UNIX and the Shell, you can create strategic systems today.

As an example of a strategic system, consider a frequent flyer system in an airline company. If you knew the 20 percent of the people who supply 80 percent of your business, would you be in a better position to target your marketing and sales to those people? You bet you would. If, in the case of a public service company, you knew that you could gather data from several different systems and provide service within an hour of when a customer calls in a request, would that generate more revenue? Of course. Or, if you could tell from some visual display that a customer's call came from an upscale neighborhood, wouldn't you try to sell more upscale services that appeal to that neighborhood? You bet. These are strategic uses of information.

> An information tool like an electronic
> mail system can have a tremendous effect.
>
> *Walter B. Winston*
> *CEO, Citibank*

In 1984, as the Bell System approached divestiture, U S WEST was formed from three existing Bell Operating Companies—Mountain Bell, Pacific Northwest Bell, and Northwestern Bell. Facsimile transmission didn't exist at the time

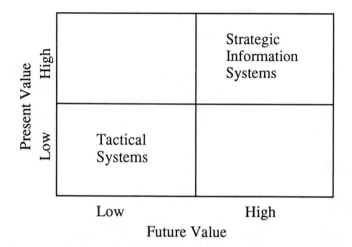

Figure 10.4   Information system value—tactical and strategic systems

and we needed a way to connect the presidents of the three companies. Of course there were three different kinds of office automation systems and they simply refused to talk to one another. There were, however, UNIX systems in all three companies. In less than three days from the announcement of divestiture, the system administrators in each company had connected the three presidential offices via UNIX **mail** and **uucp**. Did this have an impact on U S WEST's ability to cope with the change? Does UNIX speak binary?

Now there are more exotic possibilities for communication. The growth of information data bases like Dow Jones and networks like Usenet offer unlimited opportunity for information gathering. Unfortunately, it would take a herd of analysts to pull all of the information every day and then digest it. Using the Shell tools we've discussed so far you could automate this process (see Figure 10.5):

1. Access these services using dial-out facilities like **cu**.

2. Use a script to interact with the data base to retrieve any pertinent information.

3. Store the data in a simple UNIX data base or file.

4. Scrub the stored data against the other data collected.

5. Filter the information.

6. Compose it in some usable format.

7. Mail the information electronically to interested people.

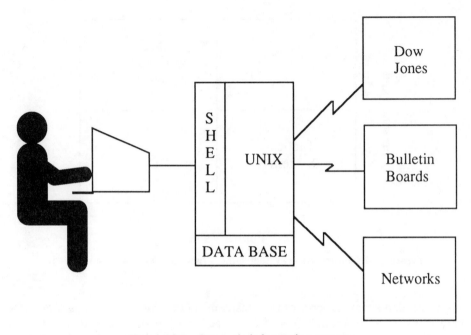

Figure 10.5   Strategic information system

With UNIX and the Shell, you can use the open communications facilities, bring in data, manipulate it with Shell, and present the information in any desired fashion.

That is power.

The Shell, coupled with the vast toolkit at its disposal and the simplicity of the UNIX file system, can accelerate the development and deployment of these strategic information systems. Some people have asked: "Why not buy an existing application system that provides this strategic ability?" Simple. Purchased systems only "level the playing field." If everyone else can buy it, there is no strategic advantage. Purchased systems, however, might be an extremely valuable way to deliver tactical systems—accounting, payroll, and so on. Strategic systems are not off-the-shelf.

Why not use existing mainframe computers? Mainframe computers are great for the centralized, tactical systems that require high transaction volumes and the like. They are terrible, however, for strategic applications. The centralized architecture of the past is inappropriate for strategic information systems, which draw their strength from putting the data and processing power close to the customer. A distributed systems architecture which is perfectly suited to UNIX and the Shell is essential to successful implementation of strategic information systems.

Strategic systems also require quick development, to maximize their benefit. To build a strategic system, therefore, you will require very different tools and techniques than those you have used in the past for conventional development.

You can't wait 18 months for a strategic system. You need to know *now* where you should be in 18 months. A few weeks, or a couple of months at the outside, is often all you will have. You must choose your weapons to match the war. To achieve their goals, strategic systems will rely on rapid prototyping, rapid evolutionary development methods and superior tools.

UNIX and Shell satisfy those needs.

RAPID PROTOTYPING

> A complex system that works is invariably found
> to have evolved from a simple system that works.

> A complex system designed from scratch never
> works and cannot be patched up to make it work.

Strategic information systems lend themselves to prototyping and rapid application development. Prototyping allows us to manage the expectations of our customers by involving them deeply in the project from the outset, and to construct a system quickly to meet the needs of the business.

Building the strategic and integration systems of the future will require a software attack team (SWAT) that is highly skilled in the application of the rapid development tool suite. To succeed at rapid prototyping and rapid development, we must shift from custom coding to composition of systems from libraries of existing tools (Figure 10.6). The Shell provides these capabilities. Using Shell and prototyping can dramatically reduce the time-to-market for a strategic system or the integration of existing systems. To give you an idea of how dramatically Shell can impact productivity, consider the following: Bruce Cox, the father of Objective-C—one of the object-oriented C languages—gave the following comparison of productivity when using Shell, object-oriented programming, and C language:

Shell	1 line of code
Object-oriented	10 lines of code
C language	100 lines of code

As you can see, Shell helps you quickly evaluate various design alternatives and then convert them into more rigid languages. Since requirements and design inject over 60 percent of all system defects, it is important to weed these out before the system is implemented. Shell programs play an important part in prototyping full-scale applications. Using the hundreds of tools in Shell, we don't have to start from scratch. We can compose, extend, and create whole systems, as we demonstrated in Chapter Eight. This gives us:

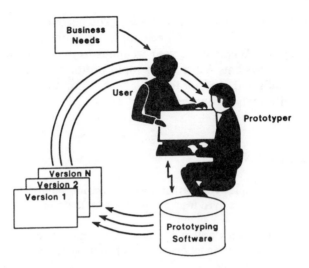

Figure 10.6   The prototyping life cycle (Reproduced with permission from John Wiley & Sons, New York, 1984. From *Application Prototyping* by Bernard Boar.)

1. the ability to build things quickly

2. the ability to rapidly identify a user's real requirements

3. portability at the system level (UNIX), not at the hardware level.

Given a prototype, users can always tell you what they don't like. That saves a tremendous amount of effort that might have been wasted developing the *wrong* system. Customers don't want data or information; they want knowledge they can act upon to create value for the corporation. More importantly, customers always want more of everything. Prototyping lets us add that functionality *before* we deliver the system, not during the two years after release.

The goal of prototyping is to deliver the 20 percent of a system's functionality that provides 80 percent of the customers' needs. Rapid iteration, as shown in Figure 10.6, can rapidly converge on the customers' key requirements. To deliver the full system, however, requires additional effort—typically to develop the other 80 percent of the functionality that satisfies the customers' remaining needs. Using the Shell as described in Chapter Eight, we can determine most of the customers' requirements for a system. A true relational data base management system (RDBMS) may then be needed to achieve the levels of security and response time required in the final system. With most of the clients' demands met by the Shell prototype, however, rapid implementation of the end product is much easier. And it's typically easy to integrate a relational data base into Shell programs using SQL, the structured query language:

```
echo "select first, middle, last, salary from employee" | sql
```
Lowell Jay Arthur 35000

Chapter Eight described the five basic types of program designs: input, output, query, data base update, and system interface. It also described the various tools available to a Shell programmer for implementing these designs. These tools can be used to develop a working version of any program design. The resulting Shell program is a prototype of the final working version that can be created in C language, or any other for that matter.

One of the best design tools for describing new programs is the data flow diagram (see Figure 8.2). Shell is one of the best tools for implementing a working model—a prototype—of a data flow. Because of facilities like pipes, tees, and input/output redirection, an idea can be prototyped in Shell, tested, changed as required, and then implemented in C. Many different designs can be tested, rejected, and accepted in a short time frame, using Shell. The triumphant design can then be created in C language for efficiency, but in many cases the Shell program will be sufficient. In the instances that require C programming, the program design evolved using the Shell will be more resilient and open to change.

Data flows have long been recognized as excellent methods of describing system, as well as program, designs (Stevens 1982). Shell helps implement those designs. Prototyping, in a UNIX environment, works best with a small design team that is experienced with Shell programming. The result of such a design process is a simple, economy-grade, working system.

C Shell provides an excellent pseudocode for C. The following example is a C Shell prototype of a C language main program:

Bourne	C Shell
`for file in *`	`foreach file ($argv[*])`
`do`	`    process $file`
`  process $file`	`end`
`done`	

C Language
```
main(argc,argv)
int argc;     /* number of args */
char **argv; /* argument array */
{
int i = 0;
   for(i=1;i<argc;i++) {
       process(argv[i]);
   } /* END FOR */
} /* END MAIN /*
```

The Shell takes the complexity of data definition out of the program and allows the designer to concentrate on *what* the program should do, not the intricacies of *how* it should be done. The Shell serves as a clear design definition as well. Shell prototypes can also be used to design and test enhancements to the program as they are required.

C Shell can also implement the use of tables and can access the elements of those tables more effectively than the Bourne Shell:

```
csh:  set table=(John Jerry Terry)
      foreach person table[*]
          process $person
      end
      mail $table[2] < letter

C:    static char **table = { "John", "Jerry", "Terry" };
      for(i=0;i<3;i++) {
          process(table[i]);
      }
      sprintf(cmd,"mail %s < letter", table[2]);
      system(cmd);
```

The Bourne Shell, unlike the C Shell, cannot directly access any item in the table. To obtain the last name, Terry, it would have to be cut out of the list or processed with **awk**:

```
lastperson=`echo $table | cut -f3 -d" "`
echo $table | awk '{ process $1; process $2; process $3 }' -
```

There are other advantages to the C Shell. The C Shell CASE construct, switch, is identical to the C language construct except that it will work with strings and the C language switch works only on characters. The IF-THEN-ELSE construct is also identical to the C language one. This parallel design allows quicker understanding and translation of designs into code.

The CASE construct translates into C language differently, depending on how it is used. If switch is used with characters or integers, the translation is identical:

```
switch $variable            switch(variable) {
   case 'a':                   case 'a':
     whatever                     whatever;
     breaksw                      break;
   case 10:                    case 10:
   case 11:                    case 11:
     whatever                     whatever;
     breaksw                      break;
   default:                    default:
     default action               default(action);
     breaksw                      break;
endsw                        } /* END SWITCH */
```

When the switch works on strings, however, the C language switch cannot be used. A series of IF-ELSEIF statements must be used along with the string comparison functions:

```
switch $variable          if(strcmp(var,"Jan")==0) {
   case "Jan":               January();
   January                } else if(strcmp(var,"Feb")==0) {
   breaksw                   February();
   case "Feb":            } else if ...
   February
   breaksw
   default:               } else {
   default action           default(action);
   breaksw                } /* END CASE */
endsw
```

Aside from the Shell constructs—IF-THEN-ELSE, CASE, FOR, and WHILE— just about anything else required of a C language program can be implemented in Shell. Writing to a terminal and reading a response are easy with **echo** and **read**:

```
echo "Enter filename"     printf("Enter filename");
read file                 gets(file);
```

More complex processes, involving pipes and several commands, often translate into submodules in C language. For example, the best way to process the following command in C language is to open /etc/passwd, match the name, and then print the required values:

```
grep lja /etc/passwd | cut -f1,5
```

Throughout the course of these examples you have seen the possibilities of using the Shell to prototype C language programs. A rudimentary working system can be constructed quickly and tested easily. Different design choices can be evaluated and accepted or rejected. Design changes can be accomplished quickly before coding begins. As much as 80 percent of the errors in developed systems can be traced to problems in the design phase. Using Shell to weed out those problems can keep a software development project on track and produce a higher quality product. Once coding begins, the Shell takes on other duties that aid in the development and maintenance of C language programs: coding, compiling, testing, debugging, configuration management, and release control.

UNIMAGINABLE SYSTEMS

From a negligible impact in 1980, personal computers multiplied to become an ominous presence in all walks of life by 1990. The 1990s will deliver completely unimaginable systems. Multimedia systems will stimulate the senses with graphics, text, sound, animation, and video. Computer animation houses have discovered that UNIX and Shell fit their needs. Specialized software coupled with UNIX and the Shell is winning animation awards all over the world. Animation tools are created in UNIX and C so that they can be picked from the toolbox and hooked together with pipes! The biggest advantage of UNIX and Shell for animators is that they can develop software today without knowing what machines they'll be running on tomorrow.

Technological innovation requires an open, loosely structured, risk-taking, forgiving environment. The Shell innovator will be at the core of this information revolution. The challenges lie in discovering creative ways to meet your company's information needs as these toolkits emerge.

SUMMARY

As a power user of Shell, your future and your company's future depend on your ability to create the information bridges and strategic information systems that will drive your company's success in the 1990s and beyond. Because of the diversity of options available for system integration and strategic information systems, this chapter discussed only possible opportunities. As you read this chapter, I hope you saw, heard, or felt the creative challenges that a power user can look forward to in the use of Shell.

EXERCISES

1. Build a rapid prototype of an airline reservation system, based on what you know about the airline industry.

2. Build a rapid prototype of a frequent flyer system, based on what you know about the airline industry.

3. Build a strategic system to capture data from both of these systems (exercises 1 and 2), to develop marketing data for the holiday and summer travel seasons.

4. Use a Macintosh running Hypercard, connected to a UNIX system, to deliver a button-driven interface to the Time Worked system described in Chapter Eight.

Chapter Eleven

The Shell Toolsmith

Most software managers and their clients will agree that the biggest problem facing business today is programmer productivity: how to get new systems more quickly and how to maintain those that already exist. Toward this end they seek "magic" solutions that will improve productivity from 100 percent to 1,000 percent. Is this unrealistic? Yes and no. Depending on a single tool, such as a fourth-generation language, to accomplish a 1,000 percent improvement is unrealistic. Using an integrated family of products and tools to achieve such an increase is not.

> In the universe, great acts are made up of small deeds.
>
> *Lao Tzu*

Many managers overlook quality improvements (from local tool construction) as the stepping stone to vast productivity improvements, but this is one of Tom Peters's lessons in *A Passion for Excellence*: 1,000 percent improvements are possible through small improvements in many aspects of the work. Part of the problem with software manufacturing is that much of the critical work is tedious or time-consuming. Fortunately the Shell offers a vast arsenal of tools to handle much of the effort. Toolsmithing can create pathways of information and automate day-to-day tasks. These small improvements attain the productivity goals, not the other way around.

> For better or worse, man is the tool-using animal,
> and as such he has become the lord of creation.
>
> *William Ralph Inge*

Many software managers and clients try to solve their problems by depending on a single hardware system and a group of unrelated software products to handle their programming needs. As evidence of this, one need only look at large mainframe development groups and stand-alone personal computer users. The PCs are excellent for word processing and graphics, but are deficient for sharing information, which is essential to successful software development and maintenance. Mainframes are excellent for compiling and testing products, but are clumsy for editing, word processing, and similar human intensive activities.

The productivity and quality solution should use an integrated network of mainframes, minis, and microcomputers for each task required of a programmer or analyst. Software for these hardware components (Figure 11.1) should:

- provide the strongest integrated tools for each programming or analysis need—development or maintenance

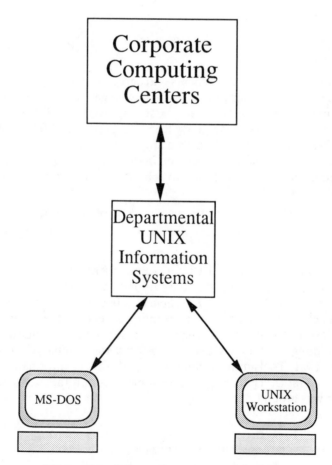

Figure 11.1   Information systems of the future

- allow for exchange of text and data among the machines and people
- minimize the training required to use each tool
- maximize product quality

UNIX fits all of these categories for virtually all types of software development and maintenance. If it is also the target machine for the developed software, it can be used for compilation and testing. UNIX is also used to simulate personal computer operating systems, thereby emulating the target machine for faster testing in more powerful machines.

UNIX, because of its communication facilities, can provide many of the development and maintenance activities for any host system. As such, programmers and analysts need learn only this one environment to develop and maintain programs for a wide array of host machines. This minimizes retraining costs when moving from one host to another.

Technology is a jealous god. It can demand more and more from people, but not serve them. Managers often ask: "Why isn't Sammy coding yet?" In the rush to deliver products, we often forget the keys to success: people, process, and, only then, technology (Figure 11.2). People are the most costly part of most software development efforts; finding out what they do and how they do it (the process) and then automating the process will lead to powerful improvements in productivity and quality for both development and maintenance.

DEVELOPMENT AND MAINTENANCE TOOLS

To maximize productivity and quality, we must automate the development and maintenance activities that are human-intensive. There are nine of these activities:

1. *Documentation.* Requirements, designs, plans, and all operational documentation or user guides are elements of documentation. Word processing facilities are essential to productivity improvements. Graphics tools that create pictorial representations of designs, such as data flow diagrams and hierarchy charts, are important as well. Admittedly, **nroff** and memorandum macros are not the most user friendly of word processing facilities, but micro-based packages written in C

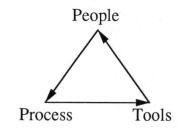

Figure 11.2   The three keys to productivity

are moving into the minicomputer environment. Productivity improvements using these tools vary from 3 percent to 25 percent for people whose major work products are written documentation.

2. *Communications.* Keeping users and programmers informed of changes in an ongoing maintenance or development effort improves productivity and quality. Programmers may be wasting up to 30 minutes per day playing telephone tag and leaving notes. Electronic mail can be sent anytime and read when time is available. Electronic mail, unlike its paper counterpart, cannot get lost on someone's desk. **Mail** and **uucp** are inexpensive methods of communicating in a UNIX environment. Electronic mail costs little (less than 1 percent of the machine usage), but will average 20,000 messages per month. In an environment with 100 users (AT&T 3B20), that means 200 messages per user per month. Most studies have found a 3 to 5 percent improvement in productivity with the use of **mail**.

3. *Editing.* Entering and editing source code is another human-intensive activity that is best performed in a highly responsive personal computer, not on larger machines with slower transmission rates. There are many sophisticated UNIX and PC full-screen editors that will meet this need. Editing is best performed in PCs and minicomputers. It is a waste of resources on a host machine. Programmers spend up to 75 percent of their time editing. Any improvement in their response time and effectiveness will significantly improve productivity.

4. *Project management.* Scheduling of work and resources needs to be updated as events finish. To keep software available for update and review by all project members, it should reside on a shared resource. Scheduling of work and resources is available on micros and UNIX minicomputers. It is best accomplished on a minicomputer where the information can be shared. With its existing graphics and documentation facilities, UNIX can exchange information among these tools easily. Project management keeps projects on schedule and therefore contributes to productivity.

5. *Configuration management.* All of the source code and documents should be controlled under a common configuration management system. The object and executable programs should be controlled on the target system. Configuration management improves the quality of the delivered software, and often of productivity, by reducing the chaos surrounding software evolution. UNIX has possibly the best configuration management systems—Source Code Control System (SCCS) and Revision Control System (RCS)—for controlling all of the source code and documents developed or maintained for a given software project. Control of software and documentation rarely appears to improve productivity, but it can reduce delivered errors in systems by 20 to 30 percent, which drastically reduces overtime costs for corrective maintenance.

6. *Change management.* Mechanizing change requests will improve communications with the client, improve the quality of information collected from maintenance, and automate much of the auditing and quality assurance processes. When coupled with the configuration management system, change management can secure the software from unauthorized modifications, a protection that is especially important in financial systems. The Change Management Tracking System (CMTS) mechanizes change request initiation and tracking. CMTS can be coupled with SCCS to prevent unauthorized changes, and ensures that changes are not lost, misplaced, or ignored. It can also feed the project management systems with information about project status. It automates the audit trail and the collection of quality assurance data, for example, programs or modules with reliability or maintainability problems that are candidates for restructuring or rewrites. By identifying and correcting these wayward programs, maintenance and downtime costs can be reduced by as much as 60 percent.

7. *Application generators.* The number of tools available for rapid prototyping has grown tremendously in recent years. The ability to use these tools to specify system requirements undoubtedly improves the quality of delivered systems by reducing requirements defects. It also improves productivity by speeding up the requirements process and providing a working system for the developers to expand upon. The Shell command language is an excellent tool for rapidly prototyping UNIX applications. Entire systems can be created with Shell and rewritten in C as the requirements settle down. Other tools like C English and data bases like Oracle can prototype UNIX and IBM DB2 systems respectively. These application generators improve development productivity by 50 percent or more.

8. *Tool kits.* The need for integrated tools and a Shell command language to encourage automation of mundane manual tasks should be recognized. Automating repetitive tasks eliminates defects and improves productivity. Programmers and analysts who understand how to use these tools consistently outperform their counterparts. Integrated tools and Shell command language encourage automation of mundane manual tasks. The author's studies and those of B. Boehm (1984) have shown that this tool kit improves productivity by a minimum of 15–25 percent. It often takes several years to learn all of the facilities of UNIX and the Shell, so these improvements occur not once but progressively over time.

9. *Data base management systems.* A portable relational DBMS that spans micro, mini, and mainframe lines would allow for development and prototyping to occur in any environment and would minimize training costs. Larger information-crunching data bases should remain in the host, while distributed relational data bases will serve the decision support needs of clients more readily. These systems will need to work with the office automation systems and virtually all of the other eight tools to provide business information. A host of data bases span the decision support system needs of most users. Oracle, Ingres, Informix, UNIFY, and a

variety of SQL compatible relational data bases span the micro and minicomputer environments. This vertical portability of applications enhances productivity and allows selection of hardware based on user needs.

There is a vast array of hardware and software that can be brought to bear on the existing productivity and quality problems. Selecting an integrated set of tools and an environment that will meet future requirements will insure continuous productivity and quality improvement.

SHELL TOOLS

Shell can automate activities for everyone, including the Shell toolsmith. For example, hundreds of tools lie waiting for discovery. How do apprentice, journeyman, and master Shell builders find these tools? In some systems, the **man** command has an option to search the documentation by keyword. We could create a Shell browser that searches by keyword:

```
# browser keyword
if [ "$1" ]
then
  while [ "$1" ]
  do
    echo $1
    man -k "$1"
    shift
  done
else
  clear
  while
    echo "Keyword: "
    read keyword
    test ! -z "$keyword"
  do
    man -k "$keyword"
  done
fi
```

What if we didn't have this extension to the **man** command? Could we create a data base of commands and keywords, and the commands to search it? Of course. Using **keyword** and **plural** from Chapter Nine, we could examine all of the **man** pages, extract their keywords, and create a data base. Using the query and reporting options we covered in Chapter Eight, we could compose commands to search the data base using the toolsmith's keyword choice. To do this, we would start by building the data base for the browser. First we could create a list of all of the commands in /bin, /usr/bin, /usr/5bin, and so on:

```
ls /bin /usr/*bin | sort | uniq > cmdlist
```

Next, we need a command that can build data base records for each command using **keyword** and **plural**:

```
# builder
cmd=$1
CMD=`echo $cmd | tr "[a-z]" "[A-Z]"`

# delete upper case headers
man $cmd | sed -e "/$CMD/d" > /tmp/$cmd

keyword -20 /tmp/$cmd | sed -e "/$cmd/d" | plural | \
head -14 | paste - - - - - - - - | sed -e "s/^/$cmd\t/" >> browse.db
rm /tmp/$cmd
```

This command will build records for the data base containing the 14 most common keywords in the document (after removing headers and references to the command itself, which can skew the results). Next, we need a simple command to execute this command on all of our commands:

```
# build_db cmdlist
while
  read cmd
do
  builder $cmd
done
```

Now we can run the whole thing overnight to create the data base:

```
nohup nice build_db cmdlist&
```

This will give us a data base like the following:

```
adb     print address value systems command names symbol
adb     source objectfile file default current subprocess
cp      copy directory file contents system subdirectories ls
grep    expression regular match string character line file
...
```

Now all we need is a command to search the data base for us. The **browser** we wrote before can be changed to meet our needs:

```
# browser keyword (s)
if [ "$1" ]
then
    clear
    while [ "$1" ]
    do
      echo $1
      grep $keyword browse.db | cut -f1 | sort | uniq | pr -7
      shift
    done
else
    clear
    while
      echo "Keyword: "
      read keyword
      test ! -z "$keyword"
    do
      grep $keyword browse.db | cut -f1 | sort | uniq | pr -7
    done
  fi
```

This is only one of the many tools that can be assembled to aid in the construction of systems. This type of browser would be effective for C language programs. Just extract the comments and build a data base from there. What I love about tool-smithing is that one idea leads to another and another. This ability drives high levels of productivity, all due to a little thing called portability.

PORTABILITY AND PRODUCTIVITY

UNIX is available in many sizes of hardware, from micros to mainframe computers. One of the most important factors in the productivity game is the availability of computer resources. With UNIX on micros and minis, resources can be purchased as required at far less cost than a replacement or additional mainframe. There is also a wide variety of hardware supporting UNIX, so that users have a choice of hardware to meet varying needs, thereby keeping the vendors on their best behavior.

C language programs are easily portable among UNIX systems. Since many micro-based systems are written in C language, these applications should migrate easily into the mini and mainframe environments. Many of the MS-DOS based packages have already begun this trek.

MS-DOS, in concept and implementation, is reminiscent of UNIX. Retraining MS-DOS users to use UNIX will be simple (as explained in earlier chapters).

Portability will improve productivity by reducing training costs; application programs should be available across the spectrum of UNIX and MS-DOS machines, which will reduce the cost of porting a developed application from one machine to another. The quality of software is improved because there is a common environment for the development and maintenance of software.

Shell, because of its design and implementation, works as a good example of structured programming and modular concepts. This example works its way into the minds of analysts and improves the quality of every system designed thereafter. I have seen its principles applied in a complex IBM IMS system development project, to the benefit of the resulting system. The way information flows over pipes is similar to the messaging concept of object-oriented programming. Shell will not only help you integrate elegance into your programming, it can also help you build tools to support everyday programming tasks.

C LANGUAGE PROGRAMMING

The Shell, especially the C Shell, is oriented to work with C language programming. The Shell can assist in all phases of C language development: prototyping, coding, compiling, and testing. The Shell provides the means to try out new ideas quickly and easily. C language is the vehicle to construct a program, once its design has been established and tested with Shell.

Chapter Eight described the five major types of program: input, output, query, update, and interface. Each can be prototyped easily with Shell. Then begins the important task of translating the shells into C language. One of the best ways to speed up the process of writing C language programs is to establish a directory containing skeletal programs of the five major program designs. These can be easily copied into the programmer's directory for expansion using Shell:

```
# proto skeleton newname.c
skeletondir=/global/C/skeletons
case $# in
    0|1)
            echo "Prototype List:\n"
            ls $skeletondir
            echo "Enter skeleton type"
            read skeleton
            echo "Enter newname.c"
            read cname
            ;;
    2)
            skeleton=$1
            cname=$2
            ;;
    *)
            echo "$0 syntax: $0 skeleton newname.c
esac
```

```
while [ ! -f ${skeletondir}/$skeleton ]
do        # prompt until they get a valid skeleton type
    echo "Skeleton $skeleton not found"
    echo "Enter skeleton type"
    read skeleton
    echo "Enter newname.c"
    read cname
done
cp $skeleton $cname          # copy skeleton to newname.c
echo "Skeleton module $cname has been created"
```

C or Bourne Shell skeletons of the five major program designs should be
created and maintained for the prototyping staff. Reusing designs and code is
much more productive than reinventing the wheel. So, let the Shell handle as
much of the typing and logic as possible. A simple C language skeleton is shown
in Appendix B.

Aside from the **proto** command, which you can develop for your own use to
speed up the coding process, UNIX provides a series of commands to aid the
programming process. They are shown in Table 11.1. These commands handle
concerns like structuring the code for readability, printing the code, and docu-
menting what the code does.

The C language beautifier, **cb**, lets the programmer enter the code in any
format and then transforms the code to one of several standard conventions. It
straightens up the code and makes the logic more visible. The readability of the
code is enhanced and so is the maintainability. **Cb** provides a consistent format
for the code.

List and **nl** provide two means of printing C language listings. **List** works on
object files that contain symbolic debugging symbols. **Nl** provides a numbered
listing of C source code. Either can be combined with **pr** to produce a clean listing
of a C program:

TABLE 11.1   C Language Coding Commands

Command	Description
cb	beautifier
cflow	flow analyzer
cxref	cross reference listing
list	print listing
lint	syntax checker
nl	print numbered listing
vgrind	listing formatter for troff

```
# clist cnames.c
for file in $*
do
    nl $file | pr -h "Source listing for $file"
done
```

In Berkeley systems, there is a formatting program called **vgrind**, which emboldens keywords and sets comments in italics. Its output is in **troff (-t)** format. **Vgrind** can be invoked as follows:

```
# cprint files.c
vgrind -t $* | lpr -t
```

What if you don't have **vgrind** on your system? In Chapter Thirteen we'll look at how to write your own filters, to format code in any way you want.

As programmers create programs, they often include data names that are not used, statements that cannot be reached, or other problem code. **Lint**, the C program checker, finds all kinds of stylistic problems and bug-prone code. The output produced by **lint** can be selected, cut, pasted, and reported in ways that help clean up the code before compilation. **Lint** also helps spot C language portability problems, when invoked with the -p option. **Lint** is an important tool in the development of portable, bug-free C language programs.

Cflow and **cxref** help document how the program works—which module calls another, which data names are referenced and where, and so on. **Cflow** works on any combination of C, **yacc**, **lex**, assembler, and object files. **Cxref** works only on C language files.

By keeping all of the source code for a single program in a single directory, **cflow** can be executed simply as:

```
cflow *.[closy] | pr -h "Cflow listing for program `pwd`" | lp
```

Similarly, **cxref** can operate on all C language files:

```
cxref *.c | pr -h "Cross Reference for `pwd | basename`" | lp
```

The commands presented—**cb**, **cflow**, **lint**, and so on—are not the only ones that can be used during the coding process, but they are the major ones. Inventive toolsmiths will find others that can aid the coding process.

You can also call the Shell from a C language program using the **system** call. This is especially helpful when cobbling together the first draft of a system. Use Shell calls to handle stubs of modules that you will construct later. The Shell calls then serve as pseudocode for the routine you will ultimately construct. System calls are as simple as:

```
system(who; date);
```

After your program has been coded using the finest tools available, it must then be compiled and tested.

COMPILING

C language programs are created in three separate steps: preprocessing, compiling, and loading (see Figure 11.3). The commands that perform these processes are shown in Table 11.2. The Shell is the glue that links these commands together.

There are five major preprocessors for C language: the C language preprocessor (**cpp**), which is invoked automatically by the C compiler; **lex**, which generates lexical analysis programs; **yacc**, which generates grammar analysis and parsing programs; **m4**, which allows for macro substitution; and **regcmp**, which compiles regular expressions for use with **regex**, the function that examines text in much the same way as **grep**. Simple commands to preprocess lexical analyzer or **yacc** code into C language and then compile it look like this:

```
lex file.l && cc lex.yy.c -ll
yacc file.y && cc y.tab.c
```

The **m4** macro processor was designed as a preprocessor for C and assembly code. It allows the definition of macros which are then expanded by **m4** prior to compilation. Many of the abilities of **m4** are included in the C preprocessor. Only on rare occasions will a programmer need to use the macro preprocessor. Some of the assemblers (**as**), however, use **m4** as a preprocessor. It can be invoked whenever needed:

```
m4 file.m > file.c && cc file.c
```

The regular expression compiler, **regcmp**, performs most of the work done by the C function by the same name. It allows regular expressions to be compiled (an expensive process) before a C language program is compiled or tested, thereby saving execution time. It creates an output file, file.i, which can be included

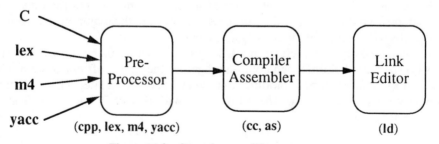

Figure 11.3   Steps in compiling a program

TABLE 11.2   Preprocessing and Compiling Commands

Command	Description
as	assembly language compiler
cc	C language compiler
dis	object file disassembler
ld	link editor
lex	lexical analyzer preprocessor
make	compile and assemble programs
m4	macro preprocessor
regcmp	compile regular expressions
strip	strip symbol tables
yacc	yet another compiler compiler

directly into C language code. Once compiled, regular expression analysis can be performed directly by **regex**:

```
regcmp regfile && cc file.c
```

where file.c contains a statement of the form:

```
#include "regfile.i"
```

Once all of the preprocessing is out of the way, the compiler **cc** and assembler **as** can be brought into play. As previously stated, these two invoke their own preprocessors **cpp** and **m4**. The output of these two processors is then compiled into object modules that are passed to the linkage editor (**ld**). Unless **ld** is told otherwise, the output of the linkage editor phase is stored in a file named a.out. Simple C language programs can be compiled and tested easily:

```
cc file.s && a.out
cc file.c && a.out
```

More complex programs containing several modules must be compiled and then linked into an executable module. The linkage editor (**ld**) is automatically invoked by **cc** when needed:

```
cc file1.c file2.c file3.c -o ctest && ctest
```

In this example, all of the C files are compiled into their respective object files: file1.o, file2.o, file3.o, and file4.o. These are then linked together by **ld**, which is executed automatically by **cc**. The output of the linkage editor phase will be the executable program **test**.

For improved efficiency, the linkage editor or **strip** can be used to strip the symbol tables out of an executable program. The benefit of removing the symbol tables is that the programs load more quickly and require less disk space. The drawbacks are that the program cannot be easily debugged without the symbol tables, and the executable program may not be portable between different releases of the UNIX operating system. Only final, production versions of programs should be stripped of their symbol tables.

Because the Shell scripts to accurately preprocess, compile, and link large programs would be overly complex, UNIX provides the **make** command to handle the complexity of preprocessing, compiling, and linking programs. A makefile prototype is available in Appendix C.

Make knows about all of the different file types in UNIX: SCCS (s.filename.c), C language (filename.c), assembly language (filename.s), lex (filename.l), yacc (filename.y), object files (filename.o), and libraries (library.a). **Make**, for example, knows that to create an object file, it must first compile a C language or assembly language file by the same name. It also knows that it may have to get the file from SCCS if it does not exist. **Make** decides what to do based on the last modification time of each file. If the object file is newer than either the SCCS or C language file, **make** assumes that the object file is the most current and does not compile anything. If the SCCS file is newer, **make** gets the file from SCCS and compiles it to create the object module. The makefile to accomplish this task for a single source file would be as follows:

```
OBJECTS = cmdname.o          # name of the object file
cmdname: $(OBJECTS)          # command depends on cmdname.o
  cc $(OBJECTS) -o cmdname    # compile & link cmdname
```

Make automatically knows to look for the SCCS (s.cmdname.c) and source files (cmdname.c). Once a makefile is created, correctly compiling a program is as simple as:

```
make
```

The output from this command using the previous makefile would be:

```
get -p s.cmdname.c > cmdname.c
cc -c cmdname.c
cc cmdname.o -o cmdname
```

Since the date on s.cmdname.c was newer than either the C or object files, **make** executed **get** to retrieve the file from SCCS. Then, **make** executed the C compiler to create an object module (cmdname.o) from the source file. Finally, **make** executed the C compiler to link the object file into the executable program (cmdname).

Sometimes, a C language file will include a data header file, filename.h, which may change and affect the resulting program. **Make** can know about these files and invoke the compiler when the header file changes:

```
OBJECTS = cmdname.o                # name of the object file
cmdname: $(OBJECTS)                # command depends on cndname.o
  cc $(OBJECTS) -o cmdname         # compile & link cmdname
cmdname.o: cmdname.c cmdname.h
```

Similarly, a single program may depend on many object files. **Make** can be instructed, via the makefile, to compile all of the modules and link them together:

```
OBJECTS = file1.o file2.o file3.o file4.o
cmdname: $(OBJECTS)                # command depends on all objects
    cc $(OBJECTS) -o cmdname       # compile & link the command
file1.o: file1.c file1.h           # object depends on header
```

This makefile will instruct **make** to compile all of the objects including file1.c, which also depends on file1.h. All four objects are created and then linked together. Since these larger compilations take longer to accomplish, the C language programmer should put the whole process into background and continue working on other activities:

```
nohup nice make&
```

A listing of commands executed by **make**, and the resulting errors, will be stored in the file nohup.out for later examination.

Besides the variable OBJECTS, there is another important **make** variable used to set the C compiler flags for all compiles and links—CFLAGS. This single variable can affect how all modules are compiled. To optimize the output of the compiler, for example, set CFLAGS to -O:

```
CFLAGS = -O    # optimize executable code
```

Similarly, to include the regular expression and lexical analyzer library (**PW** and **l**) with the resulting executable program, set CFLAGS as follows:

```
CFLAGS = -O -lPW -ll    # optimize and include RE & LEX libs
```

To invoke the inclusion of test code defined in preprocessor statements, use CFLAGS to set the -D flag:

```
CFLAGS = -DTEST
```

which would cause the inclusion of code like the following:

```
#ifdef TEST
    fprintf(stderr,"Entering Main\n");
#endif
```

Using this technique, instruments can be left in the code to test its functioning, but turned on and off with the **make** variable CFLAGS.

In summary, UNIX comes with a variety of preprocessors, compilers, and a linkage editor, which facilitate the construction of C language programs. The Shell and **make** are both useful for executing these commands in the proper order to create executable programs. Once compiled, however, C language programs must be tested and debugged.

TESTING AND DEBUGGING

The major UNIX commands that aid testing and debugging are shown in Table 11.3. **Adb** and **sdb** are the two major debugging facilities. **Prof**, **time**, and **timex** help to determine a program's efficiency. All of these commands are useful for testing.

Adb, a debugger, is available with various versions of UNIX. **Sdb**, the symbolic debugger, is available with virtually all systems. When a program aborts or requires specialized testing, these debuggers can analyze compiled C language programs, core images of the program when it failed, and aid the programmer in analysis of the problem. To maximize the effectiveness of **sdb**, the program must be compiled with the -g option and the symbol table must not be stripped from the executable file:

```
cc -g *.c -o ctest && ctest || sdb ctest
```

Or, the CFLAGS variable could have been changed to include the -g option and the program compiled and tested as follows:

```
make && ctest || sdb ctest
```

This command stream will compile all C language modules in the current directory, link them into a program called **ctest**, execute **ctest**, and if it fails, invoke **sdb**. Since most programs are compiled without the -g option or the symbol tables,

TABLE 11.3   Testing and Debugging Commands

Command	Description
adb	a debugger
diff	file comparison utility
dump	dump object file
od	octal dump
prof	execution profiler
sdb	symbolic debugger
time	time commands
timex	time commands and generate a system activity report

this compilation and retest are required to generate all of the information needed by **sdb**.

A simple use of **sdb** traces the path the program took before it ended abnormally. After executing **sdb** and receiving the **sdb** prompt (*), enter a lower case "t":

```
sdb ctest
*t
doprnt()
sub1()
main()
```

In this example, the program ended in **doprnt** (a printf function) and was called from **sub1**. **Sub1** was called from **main**. The C programmer can now trace potential paths of error in the subroutine **sub1**. To get a more specific trace, **ctest** would have to have been compiled with the -g option, but this example is sufficient for tracing most errors.

Sdb can also execute a program a line at a time, allowing the programmer to watch its progress as it steps toward completion. **Adb** works much like **sdb**. Both of these facilities are useful when testing and debugging programs.

The three commands **prof**, **time**, and **timex** can help identify programs that are resource hogs. **Time** and **timex** both give rudimentary indications that a program takes too many resources, either cpu or disk. **Prof** encourages a more exacting analysis of a program's efficiency. These three commands can be executed as follows:

```
time command
timex command
cc -p *.c -o command && command && prof command
```

The last command compiles the command with a -p option to invoke the creation of the mon.out file readable by **prof**. The command is then executed and **prof** profiles the execution of the command using mon.out. The output of **prof** can be directed to a file, printer, or terminal as required.

Each of these commands—**time**, **timex**, and **prof**—allows analysis of a program's execution in ways not possible with **sdb**. Once a program has been executed, however, analysis focuses on the program's output.

The remaining commands—**diff** and **od**—help analyze the results of a program test. **Diff** compares files, while **od** generates an octal dump of a file. **Diff** is useful with standard files that end with a newline character (\n). **Od**, on the other hand, prints the unprintable, showing normally unreadable octal characters as their octal value. Because many terminals require control strings that may be unprintable, **od** provides a simple means to examine the output of commands that generate terminal control strings. Other files, like SCCS files, have embedded octal characters that cannot be detected without **od**. Both **diff** and **od** help analyze test results.

Diff, a file comparison utility, can examine two output files and display only those lines that differ. It shows which lines were added, changed, or deleted from the test output. This comparison aids a technique called regression testing—comparing the old to the new to ensure that only the desired changes occurred. Eliminating identical information from both tests helps the programmer determine the success or failure of a change:

```
oldcommand [args] > oldstdout 2>oldstderr
newcommand [args] > newstdout 2>newstderr
diff oldstdout newstdout | pr
diff oldstderr newstderr | pr
```

Examination of **diff**'s output should indicate that the changes were made successfully or incorrectly.

Diff has several sister commands: **bdiff**, **sdiff**, and **sccsdiff**. **Bdiff** works on larger files than **diff** can handle. **Sdiff** gives a side-by-side difference listing, and **sccsdiff** compares two versions of an SCCS file. **Sccsdiff** is one of the best ways to determine the changes that occurred between two versions of a program's code, provided that the source code is stored in SCCS in the first place. SCCS is a major portion of the change control and configuration management facilities of UNIX.

CHANGE CONTROL AND CONFIGURATION MANAGEMENT

These stuffy words—change control and configuration management—simply describe the way that programs are built and changed in an orderly fashion. Working with UNIX and SCCS (Source Code Control System), you are fortunate to have some of the best tools available. SCCS stores C language code, documents, shells, or anything consisting of text. The available SCCS commands are shown in Table 11.4. When you are developing new shells or C language programs and you complete an early working version, store the version in SCCS so that you can recover it later if required. When changing a program, get the source code out of SCCS, change it, store it back, and then build the program from the SCCS source.

SCCS can hold all versions of a program, from its infancy through adulthood until it is scrapped. Most library systems will hold only the most current version of the source; the older versions are backed up on tape somewhere. Recovering old versions is no fun. With SCCS, however, it is simple. Even programmers on single-user systems will find SCCS of immeasurable value for controlling changes to software and documentation.

SCCS files can be kept in any directory, but for convenience it is best to store them in one location so that shells for accessing them can be built easily. Normally, they are stored under a directory called sccs which can exist under the user's home directory or the group's file system (see Figure 11.4). Some users prefer to store

TABLE 11.4   SCCS Commands

Command	Description
admin	add a file to SCCS
comb	combine two versions of an SCCS file
delta	create a new version of an SCCS file
get	get a file from SCCS
prs	print a description of an SCCS file
rmdel	remove a delta
sccsdiff	compare two versions of an SCCS file
val	validate an SCCS file
what	look for *what* strings in an SCCS file

documentation with the program; others favor a separate directory. Once the organization of SCCS directories is decided, Shell interfaces can easily be created to add or change SCCS files.

The command to add files to SCCS is **admin**. It has a variety of options that are often unclear to new users. A simple Shell interface would accept the type of file, program name, and source name, and then add the file as follows:

```
#cadd program file
sccsdir=$HOME/sccs/C
if [ $# -eq 2 ]          # two arguments?
then
    if [ ! -d $sccsdir/$program ]     # new program?
    then
        mkdir $sccsdir/$program     # create a directory
    fi
    echo "Enter one line description"
    read desc
    admin -n -i$file -y"${desc}" $sccsdir/$program/s.$file
else
    echo "$0 syntax: $0 program file"
fi
```

A user could add a program to SCCS easily with the following command, and the code would be equally easy to retrieve:

```
cadd prg1 main.c
```

Similarly, to edit an SCCS file would require the following command:

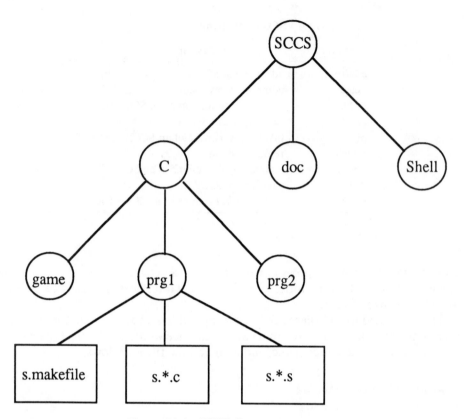

Figure 11.4   SCCS directory structure

```
#cedit program file
if [ $# -eq 2 ]
then
    sccsfile=$HOME/sccs/c/$program/s.$file
    if [ -r $sccsfile ]
    then
        get -e -s $sccsfile
        echo "$file has been retrieved for editing"
    else
        echo "File $sccsfile does not exist"
    fi
else
    echo "$0 syntax: $0 program file"
fi
```

A user could retrieve the source as follows:

```
cedit prg1 main.c
```

To save the changed file back into SCCS requires a similar command:

```
#csave program file
if [ $# -eq 2 ]
then
    sccsfile=$HOME/sccs/c/$program/s.$file
    if [ -r $sccsfile ]
    then
        echo "Enter one line description of change"
        read comments
        delta -y"$comments" $sccsfile
    else
        echo "File $sccsfile does not exist"
    fi
else
    echo "$0 syntax: $0 type program file"
fi
```

A user can save the changed source as follows:

```
csave prg1 main.c
```

SCCS also provides numerous ways to print information about SCCS files and the changes applied. **Prs** prints the status of various releases and levels of the source code. **Get** can retrieve the source code with the release and level number preceding each line of text. A simple command to print the history of changes to a file would be:

```
#chist program file
if [ $# -eq 2 ]
then
    sccsfile=$HOME/sccs/c/$program/s.$file
    if [ -r $sccsfile ]
    then
        prs -e -d":I: :D: :P: :C:" $sccsfile | pr -h "$file"
    else
        echo "File $sccsfile does not exist"
    fi
else
    echo "$0 syntax: $0 program file"
fi
```

Executing **chist** on an SCCS file would print a listing of changes (:I:), the dates the changes were created (:D:), the programmer who made the change (:P:), and the comments associated with the change (:C:). Reports of this type are useful to managers, analysts, and programmers for various activities.

Programmers, however, can get more out of a program listing containing the program code and the deltas associated with each line. A command similar to **chist** could be built to get this information:

```
get -p -m $sccsfile | pr -o8 -h "Source listing for $file"
```

The output of this command would contain the SCCS release and level number from which each line was retrieved, a tab character, and then the source code line:

```
1.1 main(argc,argv)
1.1 int argc;
1.1 char **argv;
1.1 {
1.2 char c;
2.3 char *ptr;
```

Bugs are often found in recent modifications to a program. This facility of SCCS enables the programmer to quickly locate recent code changes. Managers can also track errors back to the release and level number of the source code.

The SCCS keywords can be used to automate version and run control in C language programs. The version number of each C source file can be stored in a variable using the SCCS keyword "%A%":

```
static char *version = "%A%"; /* SCCS Version information */
```

When retrieved from SCCS, the keyword would expand to a **what** string that contains the source type, the source file name, and its release, level, branch, and sequence number:

```
static char *version = "@(#) clang filename.c 2.3.1.1 @(#)";
```

This information can be extracted from the *executable* program using **what** to check for proper version information:

```
what filename
clang filename.c 2.3.1.1
clang sub1.c 1.2
clang sub2.c 1.3.1.1
```

The version information can also be printed or written to run control files to log the execution of the command. The SCCS keywords give the programmer a strong tool for tracking and controlling change in C language programs.

Similar friendly interfaces to SCCS can be built around the remaining commands: **comb**, **rmdel**, **sccsdiff**, **val**, and **what**. The Shell can handle many functions that will not only improve change control and configuration management, but will also improve productivity and the quality of the resulting system. Many people, especially some of the UNIX gurus, question the need for all of this control, but as system complexities increase, the need for SCCS control becomes more intense.

SUMMARY

Shell will meet the personal computer needs of a programming staff for word processing, editing, graphics, and similar tasks that require quick response time. UNIX in a minicomputer environment will allow for sharing of data via electronic mail, SCCS, project management, decision support systems, and other applications where information must be shared. UNIX can provide highly productive facilities to handle most of the development and maintenance tasks. It will not, in most cases, be responsible for testing (unit, integration, or system test) on the host or target system. It is widely used to emulate microcomputer environments, however.

Because it is a highly productive, cohesive environment for building and maintaining software for a variety of target systems, UNIX will continue to provide a quality environment for software development. Its ability to handle CAD/CAM applications will further its use for automation of software design. Its ability to communicate with diverse hardware and software will encourage its introduction for distributed data processing applications.

UNIX, contrary to popular opinion, will not off-load a mainframe. It will make programmers and analysts more productive to the point that they will bury the existing mainframe or host system.

UNIX, with all of its tools and facilities, does not provide a 1,000 percent boost in productivity, but it delivers an expandable environment that will increase productivity by several hundred percent over several years. How does it do so? By improving every development and maintenance task by a few percent. When added all together, these little productivity improvements yield a huge increase in programmer productivity and the quality of delivered systems.

Where will the other hundreds of percent of improvement come from? Partially, from the application of the power of the microcomputer, which will achieve significant improvements. High-speed data communication networks will add to productivity and quality. Online testing tools and application generators on the host systems will add another jump in productivity.

Shell alone will not yield a 1,000 percent productivity improvement, but neither will application of mainframe tools or microcomputers alone accomplish the productivity leaps needed to meet the growing software demand. It is only through the introduction, training, and use of an integrated set of tools in all of these environments that productivity and quality can be maximized. This is the challenge facing managers and programmer support staffs: to design an integrated software development and maintenance environment that will meet the growing demands of programmers and users alike; to go after those 5 to 10 percent improvements that will ultimately yield the 1,000 percent improvement overall.

It is not easy to implement such an environment and it takes many years. It cannot be just a casual overnight commitment. There is no magic, but there are ways to improve productivity and quality, and UNIX has its rightful place in the center of many of these activities. It takes planning, resources, time, and support. For an investment of 1 percent for a support staff, 5 percent for training, and a capital investment to meet the resource needs of the programming staff, big productivity gains are achievable. With the help of UNIX, you can obtain productivity gains of 200 to 300 percent—an excellent return on investment.

The Shell provides many tools that aid the development and maintenance of C language programs. The Shell can be used to develop working prototypes of C language programs to test the correctness of their design, and to automate much of the coding, compiling, testing, and debugging processes. Even the control of changes to C language source code, documentation, and other text files can be orchestrated by the Shell. Every development project needs a toolsmith to create these productivity tools. The examples in this chapter provide a starting point for further development and enhancement of the C programming environment.

User friendly interfaces to all of these commands can also be constructed to present the user with menus or windows into the C language. But the Shell can still automate most of the activities required during software development and maintenance. Use its facilities to maximize productivity and quality.

EXERCISES

1. Use the Shell to prototype a program that interactively prompts users for their name, street address, city, and state. Put the output into a file for later use.

2. Use the Shell to prototype a program to select information from the /etc/passwd or /etc/group files. Format the output with **pr**.

3. Use **awk** to prototype a data selection and report program that selects the second, fourth, and fifth word from each input line and prints them in reverse order.

4. Write the statement to interactively compile and test the C language prototype in Appendix B.

5. Use **admin** to create an SCCS file using the C language prototype in Appendix B.

6. Use **get** to retrieve the file for editing.

7. Use **delta** to store the changed file back into SCCS.

Chapter Twelve

Shell Mastery

> Order and simplification are the first steps toward the
> mastery of a subject—the actual enemy is the unknown.
>
> *Thomas Mann*

Any hack can cobble together a few tools. Making them robust enough to withstand the brutality of daily use is another kettle of fish. A major concern of advanced Shell programming is not special tools, fancy techniques, or exotic human-machine dialogues, but a concern for quality. Shell, like any other programming language, can be used elegantly or shoddily. Quality is the highest concern of a Shell guru. But what is quality?

> It is easier to confess a defect than to claim a quality.
>
> *Max Beerbohm*

Quality consists of several factors: reliability, maintainability, reusability, efficiency, portability, and usability. Each has a place in advanced shells. Reliability is concerned with shells that rarely fail and always perform the correct actions. Maintainability ensures that a shell can be enhanced or repaired easily when the need arises. Reusability demands that Shell programs be as flexible and reusable as any other UNIX command. Efficiency cares about the machine resources used. The fewer the better because new machines are expensive and the longer their purchase can be delayed the better. Portability is a key factor in the popularity of UNIX; Shells should remain as portable as possible. Usability is a key feature of Shell: Native UNIX is not overly friendly, but Shell is the means to overcome that problem.

> Trouble is easily overcome before it starts.
> Deal with it before it happens.
> Set things in order before there is confusion.

> *Lao Tzu*

Shell Wizardry is to ballet what hacking is to hockey. Shell programs are born in the fire of creative activity. These draft programs, however, must be edited and improved to maximize their usefulness. The evolution of draft Shell programs that lead to quality is the essence of advanced Shell programming. The Shell, in its creator's wisdom, provides many facilities that encourage quality programming. The following sections discuss their use.

RELIABILITY

The costs of reliability problems can be found easily: scrap, defect investigation, rework, retest, downtime, and productivity losses. *Scrap* costs involve the machine and user time lost when a command fails or works incorrectly. *Defect investigation* is the time it takes to identify the cause of a defect in a Shell program. *Rework* includes the labor to fix and then to rerun the command. *Retest* includes the resources necessary to test a repaired command. *Downtime* includes the cost of the users' inability to do their work. *Productivity losses* include all of the costs of delaying work.

Shell facilities to handle reliability fall into two broad areas: default actions and fault handling. Default actions help eliminate scrap, rework, and downtime. Fault handling reduces scrap, defect investigation, rework, retest, and downtime. Both help eliminate productivity losses.

Default Actions

One of the simplest default actions occurs when a user executes a command that requires certain input parameters. If the user executes the command without any parameters, a simple Shell command will exit with an error message. An advanced Shell program, however, will prompt for the missing arguments and will exit only if the user interrupts the processing.

What if the user fails to give a file name on the command line? The Shell will prompt for the missing information. On the other hand, if the user gives many file names, the Shell will process each file. In either case, the Shell can prevent scrapping this execution of the command and the rework of reentering the command with the proper arguments.

Variable substitution offers another means of taking default actions. If a variable has no value, a default value can be substituted. If a variable has a value, a default value can still be substituted. Or, if the variable has no value, do not change it; do not issue an error message and exit from the Shell. Invoking these defaults instead of using undefined variable names will help make any shell more reliable. Consider the output of the following commands:

	Output	${name} becomes
`name=/usr/bin`		
`echo ${name}`	/usr/bin	/usr/bin
`echo ${name:-"/dev/null"}`	/usr/bin	/usr/bin
`echo ${name:="/dev/null"}`	/usr/bin	/usr/bin
`echo ${name:?"Error"}`	/usr/bin	/usr/bin
`echo ${name:+"/dev/null"}`	/dev/null	/usr/bin
`name="" # set name to NULL`		
`echo ${name}`		
`echo ${name:-"/dev/null"}`	/dev/null	NULL
`echo ${name:="/dev/null"}`	/dev/null	/dev/null
`echo ${name:?"Error"}`	Error	NULL (exit program)
`echo ${name:+"/dev/null"}`		NULL

Omitting the colon (:) in any of these examples causes the Shell to check only the variables' existence. The Shell will not check for a null variable. In the previous example, the variable name is set, but has a null value. The results change as follows:

`name="" # set name to NULL`		
`echo ${name}`		
`echo ${name-"/dev/null"}`	NULL	NULL
`echo ${name="/dev/null"}`	NULL	NULL
`echo ${name?"Error"}`	NULL	NULL
`echo ${name+"/dev/null"}`	/dev/null	NULL

Other examples of using default actions require a look at the Shell constructs IF-THEN-ELSE and CASE. To display the best Shell programming style, every IF should have an ELSE and every CASE should have a default action:

```
if [ -r $filename ]
then
    process $filename
else
    while [ ! -r $filename ]
    do
        echo "File $filename does not exist"
        echo "Please enter the correct filename"
        read $filename
    done
    process $filename
fi
```

```
case $TERM in
    vt100)
        tabs
        ;;
    630)
        tabs
        TERM=450
        ;;
    *)  # default
        echo "Setting up terminal as tty37"
        TERM=37
        ;;
esac
```

In either of these two examples, a default action prevents the unexpected from occurring. The absence of a default path is one of the hardest errors to find in programs. IFs without ELSEs and a CASE without a default are often suspect when a Shell program is unreliable.

Taking intelligent default actions is one of the cornerstones of UNIX philosophy. Advanced Shell programs echo that philosophy. Errors and faults are usually avoidable in most Shell programs—an extension of UNIX reliability.

Fault Handling

Fault handling is another feature of the Shell. The two major commands that handle error detection and correction are **test** and **trap**. **Test** helps detect errors before they occur; **trap** catches interrupts and takes intelligent default actions.

As shown in previous examples, **test** can check for the presence of files, directories, or devices (see Figure 3.1). It can compare the value of two variables or test the value of a single variable. **Test** can prevent many errors from happening and thereby prevent scrap, rework, downtime, and productivity losses.

Some Shell programs are made to run in either foreground or background. A file run into the background should not interrupt the user with spurious errors. It should mail them for later reference. **Test** can help direct error messages to the terminal or the user's mail as follows:

```
# if the terminal is associated with standard input
if [ -t 0 ]
then
    echo "Execution message"
else
    echo "Execution message" | mail $LOGNAME
fi
```

Test can also check for the presence of a variable:

```
# if $1 is non-null
if [ "$1" ]
then
    process $1
else
    echo "Enter file name"
    read filename
    process $filename
fi
```

Test is important because it can detect problems before they occur and then take an intelligent default action.

Trap works with system interrupts like the break or delete keys. The most common interrupts are hangup (1), interrupt (2), quit (3), alarm clock (14), and software termination (15). (All of the available interrupts were shown in Table 4.4.) Another useful interrupt (0) occurs at the successful termination of a Shell command. With it, **trap** can take default actions upon completion of the command.

Trap is often used to clean up after a shell when it ends. Temporary files are created in /tmp, /usr/tmp, or the user's directory. Whether the command ends or is interrupted, these files should be removed:

```
trap "rm -f /tmp/tmp$$ tmp$$; exit 0" 0 1 2 3 14 15
```

Trap can also identify the last file processed when a process is interrupted:

```
trap "echo $filename | mail $LOGNAME" 1 2 3 14 15
```

Trap can also ignore interrupts while the Shell does tricky stuff that is not easily fixed after the command has been interrupted; **trap** resets itself after the operation is complete:

```
trap "" 1 2 3 14 15            # ignore common signals
cp /tmp/tmp$$ /etc/passwd      # copy updated password file
trap 1 2 3 14 15               # reset signal traps
```

Trap can handle increasingly complex jobs as required. These few simple examples are a beginning. Reliability is integral to UNIX and fault handling with **trap** is an important method of achieving that reliability

MAINTAINABILITY

> Though a program be but three lines long,
> someday it will have to be maintained.
>
> *Geoffrey James*

Maintainability depends on quality factors called consistency, instrumentation, modularity, self-documentation, and simplicity. *Consistency* recommends doing things in the same way from shell to shell. *Instrumentation* gives indications of the success or failure of the shell as it processes its input. *Modularity* is one of the keys to the success of UNIX; Shell programs should be modular. *Self-documentation* assumes that the Shell program will document itself. *Simplicity* says it all—a simple command is easily understood, modified, and maintained.

One facet of maintainability that is difficult to quantify is programming style. The examples in this book attempt to present a "good" and consistent programming style. To improve consistency, use the skeletal Shell program in Appendix A as a starting point for all Shell programs. It contains most of the information needed for good self-documentation and online help facilities. Indenting Shell control structures to show the structure of the program is another form of consistent programming style (see Figure 12.1). Programming style is also concerned with simplicity. Because of the wealth of operators available with UNIX, any required program can be created in a number of different ways. Only a few of those ways will be simple and easy to maintain. Programming style is also reflected in the use of program development tools, like SCCS, to manage change to Shell programs and thereby simplify maintenance.

As Shell users become more sophisticated, they will begin to see new opportunities for the use of existing commands. This means that Shell commands, no matter how well written, will need to evolve to meet those opportunities. Keeping shells in SCCS will help track the evolution of a command. The reasons for changing the commands will be stored with the SCCS file, so there is no documentation to lose. A list of changes and their reasons is as close as the **prs** command. Furthermore, as one UNIX machine grows to two or three, or three dozen, the process of administering changes to the system can be simplified by extracting commands only from the SCCS libraries.

Before the commands are stored in SCCS, however, they have to be developed. Self-documentation is an important part of that development. Comments can be inserted easily into the code: they can be on a line by themselves or after an executable statement. The pound sign (#) begins all comments:

```
# If the user supplies an argument use it
if [ "$1" ]
then
    process $1
else # prompt for an argument
    echo "Enter file name"
    read filename
    process $filename
fi
```

These comments are essential to program maintainability when Shell commands become more complex. If the developer is struggling to understand how all

IF-THEN-ELSE

```
if [ conditions ]            if ( conditions ) then
then
    process1                     process1
else                         else
    process2                     process2
fi                           endif
```

CASE

```
case $var in                 switch ($var)
    match1)                      case match1:
        process1                     process1
        ;;                           breakswk
    match2)                      case match2:
        process2                     process2
        ;;                           breaksw
    *)                           default:
        default process             default process
        ;;                           breaksw
esac                         endsw
```

FOR

```
for variable in list         foreach variable ( list )
do
    process $variable            process $variable
done                         end
```

WHILE

```
while [ conditions ]         while ( conditions )
do
    process                      process
done                         end
```

Figure 12.1   Shell programming style

of the commands fit together to accomplish the task, imagine what the person who later maintains it must think.

Just about every Shell programmer runs across ways of doing things that are more elegant than others. Whenever possible, store these methods; use them in new shells or to replace complex code in existing shells. Simplicity should prevail over complexity. Otherwise, it eventually becomes impossible to maintain all of the existing shells without an army of Shell gurus.

Keeping things simple is why modularity was invented. Cars are made of small modular components, which are easier to design and build than complex hand-built components. The parts are also easier to replace when they fail. The same is true for Shell programs. Modularity will improve maintainability.

Modularity can be obtained in two ways: simplifying processing and creating sub-shells. Any Shell program over two pages in length is too complex. Sometimes the program can be simplified. The shell may have one central process with various input and output filters. A simple, modular design would be:

```
choose input filters
choose processing parameters
choose output filters
execute input filters | major process | output filters
```

An example of this modular program was presented in Chapter Nine.

Creating sub-shells allows the main shell to control the actions of several others to obtain the required result. Rather than write one huge shell, each sub-shell can do its unique part and then pass control back to the parent shell. Sub-shells are also an important feature of reusability.

Modular shells can execute as follows:

```
edit inputfiles
update datafiles
select reportdata
print reports
```

Each sub-shell creates outputs that are used by future processes. The sub-shells can be executed individually when required, or directly inline with the parent shell's code so that the sub-shell can access and modify any of the parent's variables:

Bourne Shell	C Shell
`# parent shell`	`# parent Shell`
`variable=/usr/bin`	`variable=/usr/bin`
`. subshell`	`source subshell`
`# subshell`	
`cd $variable`	
`ls -l`	
`variable=/bin`	

From a pure programming standpoint, this is somewhat dangerous because the sub-shell can change the parent's variables. Otherwise, the parent would have to export the variable, for the sub-shell to have access to it:

```
# parent shell
variable=/usr/bin
export variable
subshell
```

In this example, sub-shell would have access to the variable but would not be able to change it. Also, any changes made by the sub-shell to the current environment (such as changing directories) would not affect the parent shell.

Making small, modular Shell programs helps improve maintainability. Small programs are easily understood. Modular programs also affect reusability.

REUSABILITY

One of the reasons that Shell is so popular is that each command is modular and reusable. Each command can be easily mated with other commands via the pipe. In the process of building commands to automate repetitive tasks for users, functions are repeated from shell to shell. Creating a separate shell for these functions improves maintainability (there is only one copy to maintain). All of the shells that need the reusable function can then invoke it as a sub-shell.

When using Shell to prototype C language programs, reusable shells often indicate the need for reusable C programs as well. Current technology has demonstrated that as much as 80 percent of a program's code is reusable, leaving only 20 percent to be developed uniquely. This can increase programmer productivity and quality by a factor of two to five.

A simple way of affecting reusability is to create a library of generic Shell programs that can be copied and then enhanced to fit a particular need. These skeletons should include all of the quality features described in this chapter. A good skeleton for Shell development is shown in Appendix A. As described in Chapter Eight, there are five basic types of programs: input, output, query, update, and interface. A reusable Shell skeleton can be built for each.

EFFICIENCY

"Techies" often worry about efficiency, to the exclusion of effectiveness. To maximize efficiency, focus on people effort first and machine effort second. Once you've minimized the effort required to use and maintain a Shell program, then worry about improving the machine efficiency.

Shell runs on a wide variety of hardware, but it still concerns itself with efficiency. Spending money for additional hardware is never easy, so it makes sense to take efficiency into consideration whenever building a shell. Some efficiencies are handled by the system administrator; others are available to the common user.

The system administrator (superuser) can set the "sticky bit" on a program. Once the program has been loaded into memory, a copy is retained until the system is brought down. Keeping a copy of the program means that it can be swapped in when requested rather than read from a disk, thereby speeding up processing. UNIX programs that are used extensively in Shell programs should be stored in memory using the sticky bit:

```
chmod 1777 shell_pgm
```

Each user can further improve efficiency by simple actions. The most obvious one is to run commands during nonprime time. Commands can be queued via the **at** command (if it is available on your system). The **at** command can off-load the processor during prime time and improve response time. The following example would execute a Shell accounting report called **acctrpt** at 6 P.M. on Sunday:

```
at 6pm Sunday acctrpt
```

Shell efficiencies involve the number of variables, commands, and files. The number of bins searched for commands, and their ordering, are often prime candidates for efficiency improvement. These two criteria are established by the PATH variable:

```
PATH=:/bin:/usr/bin:/global/bin
```

The search order for this PATH is the current directory, /bin, /usr/bin, and /global/bin. If the user rarely uses the current directory and almost always /global/bin, then efficiency can be increased by switching the search order:

```
PATH=/global/bin:/bin:/usr/bin::
```

Users will sometimes put all possible bins into their PATH:

```
PATH=:/bin:/usr/bin:/global/bin:$HOME/bin . . .
```

To find the requested command, the Shell must search through many directories and hundreds of files. A simple solution is to invoke the Shell itself as a sub-shell with the expanded PATH list:

```
# home
PATH=$HOME/bin:${PATH} PS1="HOME> " sh $@
```

This command will change the PATH variable to include $HOME/bin and change the prompt to "HOME> " so that the user is aware of the change. When finished using commands in $HOME/bin, the user types a control(d) to exit from the sub-shell.

Another way to improve efficiency is to change into a directory rather than use a long path name repeatedly. This eliminates the need for the Shell to search through directory after directory for each file:

```
cd $HOME/RDBMS/employee        for file in $HOME/RDBMS/employee/*
for file in *                  do
do                                 process $file
    process $file              done
done
```

The user can also affect efficiency by reducing the number of temporary files used in a shell. Pipes and better selection of commands can reduce the number of temporary files:

```
cut -f1,5 /etc/passwd > /tmp/tmp$$
pr -h "Password listing" /tmp/tmp$$
rm /tmp/tmp$$


cut -f1,5 /etc/passwd | pr -h "Password Listing"
```

In this example, the number of commands is reduced by one, and temporary files are eliminated totally. Pipes do create temporary files of their own, but **pr** can begin executing as soon as the **cut** has passed a line to the pipe. Herein lies the advantage of the pipe.

This example also shows how programming style can reduce the number of commands required. Similarly, the commands **fgrep** and **egrep** can be more efficient than **grep** for special data selection requirements. There are a multitude of available commands in UNIX. Often, one can be substituted for several others, thereby reducing complexity and improving efficiency.

The number and length of variable names can negatively influence efficiency, but the advantages of having good variable names and using them to represent only one variable instead of many outweigh the efficiency considerations.

Use built-in commands instead of called programs. Slowness occurs in Shell programs when the system must create a new process (**fork**), search the PATH to find a given command, and then execute it. Built-in commands are executed directly, so use **read** (csh: $<) instead of **line**, and so on.

And, as we've demonstrated in other examples, put *reducing* filters—**grep**, **cut**, and **awk**—first in a pipe, to reduce the amount of data that must be transferred by the Shell:

```
grep $1 employee.db | sort | pr
```

For users running System V, there is a facility that allows users the same capabilities of the "sticky bit." The Bourne and Korn Shells allow the use of Shell functions, which can be included in the user's .profile—or anywhere, for that matter. Once a command containing the function is executed, the Shell retains a memory copy of the function for later execution. When the user executes the command again, the function is invoked from memory instead of from a disk. Response time is much faster. Shell functions are formed as follows:

```
functname()                    alias functname shell_command
{
    Shell commands
}
```

For commands that are frequently executed, Shell functions will be the fastest way to obtain a response. (For more examples, see Chapter Seven.)

Efficiency is still a concern in the UNIX system. As UNIX users learn more about the system, their ability to use its resources expands exponentially, making it hard to obtain enough hardware to satisfy their cravings. The commands **time** and **timex** can examine resource usage of commands and be used to improve efficiency. Efficiency is one way of ensuring that there will be plenty of resources for all.

PORTABILITY

Portability is another major concern of the UNIX system. Shell programmers should be concerned because: there are three different Shells—C Shell, Bourne Shell, and Korn Shell; there are many different versions of UNIX; and the C Shell and Bourne/Korn Shell are incompatible in many of their control constructs. These incompatibilities raise portability issues. The same utility (e.g., **pr**) may perform differently in different systems.

Every UNIX system provides new tools that are not part of standard UNIX. These are then used in Shell programs, and the programs lose their portability. Binary copies of UNIX sold by third parties often have nonstandard utilities that are not portable to other systems.

To maximize the chances that shells can be ported from one machine to another, stick to the standard UNIX commands contained in /bin and /usr/bin. A Shell command using any other commands will need some work when moved from a micro to a minicomputer or mainframe environment. But standards are not the only key to portability. Portability consists of three key elements:

- design for portability
- management for portability
- standards

To achieve portability of your Shells, you must begin with the design. To achieve *any* quality, for that matter, you begin with design. By simply focusing on a quality like portability, you will be more likely to achieve it. Then, as you move forward with development, manage the evolution of the shell to ensure portability. Shell checkers, like **lint** for C, are under development and should appear soon. Finally, use standard commands (e.g., those defined by POSIX).

USABILITY

Probably the major problem with UNIX is its usability. Users complain, for example, of cryptic commands. Shell is the bridge to improve usability. The best shells will need default actions, help facilities, and possibly online instruction.

Usable Shell commands should not give cryptic error messages and exit when the argument list is deficient. They should prompt for the proper information, as described in the reliability section of this chapter. Usable Shell commands should anticipate the users' needs and meet them wherever possible. Use of the **trap** command to handle interrupts is another means of making a shell more usable; a shell that cleans up after itself and restores order before exiting is more usable than one that does not.

Online Help

Online help facilities are another usability concern. The files contained in /usr/lib/help are not very beneficial, but they can be beefed up by the system administrator. User-developed Shell commands have other possibilities. Embedding help information in the Shell command is a good way to improve self-documentation and provide help facilities for locally developed commands.

Since shells should be stored in SCCS, the **what** command provides a facility for extracting help information from shells. The **what** command extracts lines from files containing the SCCS keyword string "%Z%" which expands to @(#). This keyword can be embedded in Shell commands:

```
# %Z% syntax: command [parameters] [files]
```

which expand as follows when the file is retrieved from SCCS:

```
@(#) syntax: command [parameters] [files]
```

What can examine the Shell file and produce the following:

```
syntax: command [parameters] [files]
```

Grep can also be used. Some users will require just a simple example of the command's syntax; others will need more extensive assistance. Two levels of help information can be provided by combining **grep** with **what**:

```
#localhelp
grep "@#@" $1                    # print syntax line
echo "More Information?"
read answer
if [ ${answer} = "y" ]
then
    what $1                      # print extended description
fi
```

Examples of the **grep** and **what** strings are shown in Appendix A. The local help command can be enhanced to look for the command in any of the bins specified by $PATH:

```
bins=`echo $PATH | tr ":" " "`      # remove : delimiters
bins="$bins `pwd`"                  # add current directory
for dir in $bins                    # check each bin
do
    if [ -r ${dir}/$1 ]             # if command exists
    then
        localhelp ${dir}/$1         # print help information
        break                       # leave FOR loop
    fi
done
```

This help command can be enhanced as required. Online help for Shell commands, as shown in these examples, is a necessary part of productive use of UNIX. Usability is a major factor in the acceptance of UNIX and new commands. Online tutorials, like the ones available with microcomputer packages, will be essential to reducing the training costs for new users. Local commands will need to take advantage of these packages to ensure that proper training is received by all users. Training is a major part of usability. Developing a shell is often easy. Creating help and training materials often takes longer, but is perhaps more important than the resulting shell.

Documentation

All words are pegs to hang ideas on.

Henry Ward Beecher

A system is composed of more than just software or Shells. A system includes the hardware, software, documentation, and training to help make users effective. Effective, high quality Shell programming requires the development of **man** pages and other supporting documentation. A basic outline of a **man** page is shown in Figure 12.2. Use it to document local commands. Manage the document's evolution using SCCS, just as you would the code.

Shell is a simple language compared to written language. Shell has but a few hundred verbs (e.g., **grep**), while written language has tens of thousands of verbs and words. But do not look down on the written word; it is the complex programming language of the mind.

SUMMARY

Expert Shell programming is concerned with the quality of the programs produced. It demands reliability, maintainability, reusability, efficiency, portability, and usability. A shell could be complex and intricate, a brilliant piece of

```
.TH COMMAND–NAME [8]
.SH command_name
.SH SYNOPSIS
command_name syntax
.SH DESCRIPTION
text description
.SH OPTIONS
-flags description
.SH FILES
associated files (if any)
.SH SEE ALSO
related command_names
.SH DIAGNOSTICS
error messages
.SH BUGS
Why would you have any of these?
.SH EXAMPLES
demonstrate how to use the thing effectively!
```

Figure 12.2   Man page boilerplate

work, but without self-documentation and maintainability, it cannot be what I call expert.

> It is a simple task to make things complex,
> but a complex task to make things simple.

Appendix A contains a skeleton of a shell that can be used to improve reliability, maintainability, and usability. The principles that involve advanced Shell programming are not ones of complexity, but ones of simplicity and elegance.

EXERCISES

1. What is the single, major concern of an advanced Shell programmer?

2. What are the major factors that make up quality?

3. What is, in your words, programming style?

4. What Shell commands and features help provide reliability, maintainability, reusability, efficiency, portability, and usability?

5. Write a Shell program to test the various default values assigned to a variable that is:

   a. not set
   b. set but has no value (NULL)
   c. set and has a value

6. Write the **trap** command to ignore the interrupt and quit signals. Use it in a Shell command and test its performance with the break or delete key on your terminal.

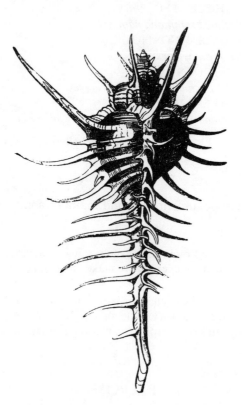

Chapter Thirteen

The Shell Filter Builder

Shell does 98 percent of what you will need for most prototyping and tool building. Sometimes, however, you will need to write a custom filter. Although it's a bit afield from Shell, **lex**—the lexical analyzer—can do wonderfully complex filtering, allowing you to design and build your own custom filters.

Lex is a powerful tool for looking at text—documents, C language, or data—to either transform or analyze it. **Lex** lets you build filters quickly and easily.

You can use **lex** to specify regular expressions (REs) for words or strings or constants and then generate a C language program from the **lex** source specifications. You can then execute the compiled program to process the matched regular expressions. **Lex** acts as program generator: It takes your specifications and generates the C language statements to lexically analyze input text.

Programs written in **lex** can act as filters—transforming the input according to your rules (Figure 13.1)—or they can pass information about matched text strings back to a calling C language module.

You can use **lex** to create filters if the change depends on only the expressions found. If you need to know the grammar or *syntax* of the input (e.g., a compiler or English analyzer) to process it, then a module that understands syntax (e.g., **yacc**) should call **lex**. **Lex** then returns a value that the syntax analyzer can understand, called a token, which the analyzer uses to examine the syntax.

Figure 13.1   Lex filters

LEX SOURCE STRUCTURE

Let's look at the structure of the **lex** source shown in Figure 13.2. First, in the *definitions* section you can specify global data used within the *rules* and *user routines*. **Lex** also has a number of internal tables. As the number of regular expressions grows, these tables need to grow. The **lex** parameters allow you to specify sizes for these tables. Don't worry about them initially; **lex** will let you know when you exceed one of the parameters.

Then, in the *rules* section (within the %% delimiters), you can specify up to 256 rules. Each rule consists of an RE to be matched and the actions to take when a match occurs. For example, a simple **lex** filter might have the specifications shown in Figure 13.3. Given these rules, the resulting program takes three actions:

1. When the analyzer program finds the word "lex" it prints "LEX" on standard output.

2. When it finds a string of one or more alphabetic characters, the **lex** statement, **ECHO**, prints the matched text on standard output.

3. The program passes any unmatched characters onto standard output. This is the default action for all unmatched input.

This example also highlights one of the major *ambiguous rules*: **lex** always prefers the longest match. Without the second rule, the first one would match the first three characters of words like *lex*ical; the output would be 'LEXical'. These ambiguous rules are essential to the simple specification of lexical programs.

```
%{
  /* global C language data and definitions */
%}
lex parameters (%e, %p, etc.)

%%
RE { actions }
%%

C language subroutines called by actions
main( )
{
...
}
yywrap( )
{
...
}
```

Figure 13.2   Detailed lex structure

```
%%
lex    printf("%s", "LEX"); /* print uppercase LEX */
[A-Za-z]+ ECHO;     /* match longer words like LEXical */
%%
```

Figure 13.3   The longest match rule

The *user routines* section is a good place to put *actions* that would otherwise clutter the *rules* sections. Write subroutines to handle complex actions and call them from the *rules* section. Sometimes, you will want to perform some processing *following* the lexical analysis. At end of input, the program generated by **lex** automatically calls **yywrap**. You can code your own **yywrap** and include this subroutine in the *user routines* section, to handle any postprocessing, or compile and link it separately. It should return a value of one (1) for end of input or zero (0) if there is more input.

LEX FILTER PROGRAMS

Let's look at more examples and compare them to Shell commands. The first example is a simple translator from lower to upper case. The command to accomplish this is:

```
tr "[a-z]" "[A-Z]"
```

When a lexical analyzer program finds text that matches an RE, it puts the matched text in an external character array called **yytext**. Using **yytext**, an identical translator could have been written as shown in Figure 13.4.

The **lex** statement, **ECHO**, uses **yytext** to reproduce matched input on standard output. **ECHO** is defined as **printf("%s",yytext);**.

Another example (Figure 13.5) specifies a simple filter to embolden passive verbs (is, was, were) in **nroff** text. The output could be piped into **nroff** to aid the

```
%{
#include <ctype.h>
char *c; /* character pointer to matched text */
%}
%%
[a-z]+ {
        /* convert matched lower case to upper case */
        for(c=yytext; *c=toupper(*c) ;c++);
        printf("%s", yytext);
    }
%%
```

Figure 13.4   A filter to translate lower to upper case

```
%%
[Aa]m   |
[Aa]re  |
[Bb]e   |
[Bb]een  |
[Bb]eing  |
[Ii]s   |
[Ww]as  |
[Ww]ere  {
        printf("\\fB%s\\fR", yytext); /* BOLD to Roman */
      }
[A-Za-z]+ {
        /* match longer words that contain the above
             like care, his, aware */
        ECHO; /* print them as is */
      }
%%
```

Figure 13.5   A filter to embolden passive verbs in nroff text

writer in finding passive verbs. In this example, rather than repeating the action
for each word found, the vertical bar (|) symbol works as a logical OR to connect
many regular expressions with the same action.

By now, you're probably wondering how this **lex** source code becomes an
executable program (Figure 13.6). Suppose the **lex** code, for this example, was in a
file called passive.l. (The makefile, Figure 13.7, recognizes files with a .l suffix as
lexical analyzer code.) To generate, compile, link, and execute passive.l, you
would enter the following commands:

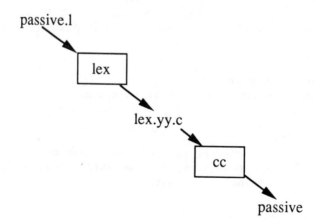

Figure 13.6   Lex filter creation

```
CFLAGS = -O
OBJECTS = main.o lex.yy.o yywrap.o
LIBS = -ll
shellmet: $(OBJECTS)
    cc $(CFLAGS) $(OBJECTS) $(LIBS) -o shellmet
main.o: shellext.h
lex.yy.o: shellmet.h lex.yy.c
lex.yy.c: shellmet.l
yywrap.o: shellext.h
```

Figure 13.7 `Shellmet` **makefile**

```
lex passive.l                 # generate lex.yy.c
cc lex.yy.c -ll -o passive    # compile and link lex (-ll)
passive < textfile | nroff
```

The command **lex passive.l** creates a function called **yylex()** in the file lex.yy.c. The **yylex** function will process the input according to the specifications in passive.l. Next, you have to compile the generated C language (lex.yy.c) and link in the **lex** library (**-ll**), which contains default **main** and **yywrap** routines.

Of course, redirecting standard input can be tiring. To specify file names on the command line, you can write your own main module that calls **yylex** (see Figure 13.8). This module will reopen standard input and call **yylex** for each file on the command line. The main module can do most of the preprocessing that any lexical analyzer requires. Any postprocessing can be handled by **yywrap**.

```
#include <stdio.h>
main(argc,argv)
int argc;
char **argv;
{       /* for all arguments */
    for(argc-,argv++ ; argc > 0 ; argc-,argv++)
    {                               /* for all arguments */
        if( freopen(*argv, "r", stdin) ) {
            yylex();                /* call yylex */
        } else {                    /* NULL */
            fprintf(stderr, "Unable to open %s\n", *argv);
        }    /* END IF */
    } /* END FOR */
}
```

Figure 13.8   Listing of `main` **module that calls** `yylex`

A SHELL QUALITY ANALYZER

Let's use these three parts—preprocessor, lexical analyzer, and postprocessor—to write a complexity analyzer for Shell script programs. Complexity is a function of the number of decisions and the size of a program. The verbs in the Shell programming language are: **case**, **for**, **foreach**, **if**, **repeat**, **switch**, **until**, and **while**. Let's write a lexical analyzer that counts the occurrences of each of these keywords and prints them if the decision count exceeds 7 ± 2 (one of the rigorously proven limits of human understanding).

We'll use the **main** program shown in Figure 13.8. Figure 13.9 shows the **lex** source for the analyzer, **shellmet.l**. Figure 13.10 shows the *include* file for the keyword counters, and Figure 13.11 shows the **yywrap** module that will accumulate the decision count, compare it to a maximum value, print the results, and reinitialize the counters. Figure 13.12 shows the *include* file that **yywrap** and **main** use to reference the external data declared by **shellmet.l**.

Note in Figure 13.9 that we had to make allowances for shell comments, any part of a line beginning with a nanogram (#) and ending before a newline (\n). We don't want to count the strings **case**, **for**, **foreach**, **if**, **repeat**, **switch**, **until**, and **while** if they occur *inside* a comment. Similarly, I had to define a regular expression, [A-Za-z0-9._]+, to rule out the possibility that these words would occur inside of another word. For example, consider a file name (like **case**01 or **for**eign). It's simple

```
%{
#include "shellmet.h"
%}
%%
case    case_cnt++;
for     for_cnt++;
foreach     foreach_cnt++;
if      if_cnt++;
repeat      repeat_cnt++;
switch      switch_cnt++;
until       until_cnt++;
while       while_cnt++;
#[^\n]*     comment_cnt++;
[\n]    line_cnt++;
[ \t]   ;
[A-Za-z0-9_.]+  { ; /* match and delete anything else that
                     might contain the above (e.g. filenames) */
            }
[^#A-Za-z0-9_.]     { ; /* match and delete anything else
                     (e.g. numbers, punctuation) */
            }
%%
```

Figure 13.9   The lex code for the analyzer

```
/* count decisions and lines */

int case_cnt    = 0;
int comment_cnt = 0;
int for_cnt     = 0;
int foreach_cnt    = 0;
int if_cnt    = 0;
int repeat_cnt    = 0;
int switch_cnt    = 0;
int until_cnt    = 0;
int while_cnt    = 0;
int line_cnt    = 0;

#include <stdio.h>
#include <shellext.h>
```

Figure 13.10   The *include* file for `shellmet.l`

to create regular expressions for the words you want to find, but not so easy to create the REs that represent larger strings that might include your keywords.

Also, since I didn't want any of the input to fall through to standard output, I had to include rules for blanks, tabs [\t]. and any other input [^#A-Za-z0-9. \t\n] that prevents them from passing on to standard output. The circumflex (^) causes the RE to match any character other than the ones within the square brackets.

I could have used a period (.), which matches any character, instead of the more complex RE with the circumflex, but I prefer to specify REs exactly, to simplify future maintenance. For example, '.*' matches any number of occurrences of any character. Because of the ambiguity rule (lex always looks for the longest match), this RE could easily override other REs that have been specified.

Lex also takes the *first* and *longest* match. The first and longest rule takes *precedence*. Because of these two ambiguous rules, the longest REs should be placed at the end of the rules section. Consider the order of the following **lex** rules:

```
(a-z)+ identifier action;
for keyword action;
```

In this example, the first rule would always match the word **for** because the first rule has precedence; the *keyword action* would never be executed. If you have problems with a lexical analyzer, examine your **lex** code for ambiguity and precedence violations.

A SHELL BEAUTIFIER

Looking at code hour after hour, the mind can begin to miss key constructs and keywords. To make these stand out on the printed page, we could create a **lex**

```
yywrap( )
{
#define MAX_DECISIONS 10
#define MAX_LINES  100
int decision_cnt = 0;

decision_cnt = case_cnt + for_cnt + foreach_cnt + if_cnt + repeat_cnt
             + switch_cnt + until_cnt + while_cnt;
if(decision_cnt <= MAX_DECISIONS && line_cnt <= MAX_LINES) {
   printf("Quality Okay!\n");
   printf("Comment count = %3d\n", comment_cnt);
} else {
   printf("Case  count = %4d\n", case_cnt);
   printf("For   count = %4d\n", for_cnt);
   printf("Foreach count = %4d\n", for_cnt);
   printf("If  count = %4d\n", if_cnt);
   printf("Repeat count = %4d\n", Repeat_cnt);
   printf("Switch count = %4d\n", switch_cnt);
   printf("Until count = %4d\n", until_cnt);
   printf("While count = %4d\n", while_cnt);
   printf("Total   = %4d\n", decision_cnt);
   printf("\nTotal Lines = %4d\n", line_cnt);

   if(decision_cnt > MAX_DECISIONS) {
     printf("\nDecisions exceed quality standards\n");
   }
   if(line_cnt > MAX_LINES) {
     printf("\nTotal Lines exceed quality standards\n");
   } /* END IF */
} /* END IF */

case_cnt  = 0; /* reinitialize the variables */
comment_cnt = 0;
for_cnt  = 0;
foreach_cnt = 0;
if_cnt  = 0;
repeat_cnt = 0;
switch_cnt = 0;
until_cnt  = 0;
while_cnt  = 0;
line_cnt  = 0;

return(1); /* end of input */
}
```

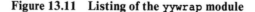

Figure 13.11   Listing of the yywrap module

```
extern int case_cnt;
extern int comment_cnt;
extern int for_cnt;
extern int foreach_cnt;
extern int if_cnt;
extern int repeat_cnt;
extern int switch_cnt;
extern int until_cnt;
extern int while_cnt;
extern int line_cnt;
```

Figure 13.12   The `shellext.h` *include* file

filter that emboldens the keywords in C language, Shell, or any other printout. A simple program, **pretty_pr**, to embolden these words would be:

```
{
#define BOLD printf("\fB%s\fR", yytext);
}
%%
if   |
else   |
switch   |
case   |
default   |
until   |
while   |
[{}]  BOLD;
[a-z]+  ECHO;
%%
```

We could then embolden and print file.c as follows:

```
pretty_pr < file.c | nroff | lp
```

OTHER LEX ROUTINES

Let's look at some of the more infrequently used features of **lex**—**input()**, **output()**, **unput()**, **yyleng**, **yymore()**, and **yyless()**. The **input()** and **unput()** routines provide a "look-ahead" capability.

input( )	gets a character from *stdin*
output( )	writes a character on *stdout*
unput( )	puts a character back on *stdin*
yymore( )	looks for additional matching characters
yyless( )	trims characters from **yytext** and puts them back on *stdin*

The two routines, **yymore()** and **yyless()**, tell **lex** to look for longer matches or cut characters from the matched text. The lexical analyzer keeps the string length of **yytext** in an external integer variable called **yyleng**. We could use these functions to analyze C language comments. In C language, comments begin with the string /* and end with */. Figure 13.13 shows a **lex** source program to strip and print comments from C language.

The **lex** rule begins with /* and looks ahead for every character up to, but not including, the next /. Using C language, I then check for a leading /* and a trailing * in **yytext** and add the trailing / using **input()**. Next, if **yytext** begins with a /*, but doesn't end with a *, then the trailing / is embedded in the comment. I use **yymore** to expand the comment. Finally, if **yytext** begins with other than /*, I delete the matched text.

I should warn you that you can get into trouble if the matched text gets too long. The **yytext[ ]** array can be up to only 200 characters in length. It isn't big enough to handle comments that span multiple sentences. To handle such problems, you'll need a *syntax analyzer*.

USING LEX WITH A SYNTAX ANALYZER

Let's use the previous example, the Shell complexity analyzer, to explain how to do this. Figure 13.14 shows the new **main** program and Figure 13.15 shows the new **lex** program that returns *tokens* to the main program. Figure 13.16 shows the definition of the tokens. The **yywrap** routine stays the same.

Notice how the **yylex** routine returns tokens to the main program, which now tallies them. Also notice that '#' is defined as COMMENT_START and that a NEWLINE is the end of a Shell comment.

```
%%
[/][*][^/]+    {
                  if(yytext[yyleng - 1] == '*') { /* end comment */

                      yytext[yyleng++] = input(); /* get '/' */
                      yytext[yyleng] = NULL;
                      print("%s\n", yytext);

                  } else

                      yymore(); /* keep looking */

                  } /* END IF */
               }
[^/]+      /* delete everything else */ ;
[/]        ;
%%
```

Figure 13.13   A lex program to strip and print comments from C language

```c
#include
#include "shellext.h"
#include "shelltoken.h"

main(argc,argv)            /* main for shellmet */
int argc;
char **argv;
{
int token = 0;

    for(argc--,argv++ ; argc > 0 ; argc--,argv++)
    {
        if( freopen(*argv, "r", stdin) ) { /* successful */

            while(( token = yylex() ))      /* NULL at EOF */
            {

                switch(token)
                {
                    case CASE:
                        case_cnt++; /* increment token counter */
                        break;
                    case COMMENT_START:
                        comment_cnt++; /* increment token counter */
                          /* delete tokens except terminating NEWLINE */
                          while(( token = yylex()) != NEWLINE);
                            /* fall through */
                    case NEWLINE:
                        line_cnt++; /* increment token counter */
                        break;
                    case FOR:
                        for_cnt++; /* increment token counter */
                        break;
                    case FOREACH:
                        foreach_cnt++; /* increment token counter */
                        break;
                    case IF:
                        if_cnt++; /* increment token counter */
                        break;
                    case REPEAT:
                        repeat_cnt++; /* increment token counter */
                        break;
                    case SWITCH:
                        switch_cnt++; /* increment token counter */
                        break;
                    case UNTIL:
                        until_cnt++; /* increment token counter */
                        break;
                    case WHILE:
                        while_cnt++; /* increment token counter */
                        break;
                    default:
                        break; /* ignore other tokens */
                } /* END SWITCH */
            } /* END WHILE */
        } else {
            fprintf(stderr, "Unable to open %s\n", *argv);
        } /* END IF */
    } /* END FOR */
}
```

Figure 13.14   The main module (syntax analyzer version)

```
%{
#include "shelltoken.h"
#include "shellmet.h"
%}
%%
case    return(CASE);
for     return(FOR);
foreach     return(FOREACH);
if     return(IF);
repeat     return(REPEAT);
switch     return(SWITCH);
until    return(UNTIL);
while    return(WHILE);
[#]    return(COMMENT_START);
[\n]    return(NEWLINE);
[ \t]    ;
[A-Za-z0-9_.]+ {    /* match and delete anything else that
                          might contain the above */
            }
[^#A-Za-z0-9_.]    { ; /* match and delete anything else
                      (e.g. numbers, punctuation) */
            }
%%
```

Figure 13.15   Lex code (syntax analyzer version)

In the main module, a return of COMMENT_START causes the logic to loop until it finds a NEWLINE to end the comment. Then, it falls through and increments the NEWLINE counter. As you can see, syntax analysis of language simplifies the regular expressions used in the **lex** code and places the burden of analysis on the calling module.

If you need to get into complicated grammars or syntax, **yacc**—the parser generator—generates programs from more easily understood syntax specifications. The two, in tandem, are powerful tools to analyze text and its grammar or syntax.

SUMMARY

I've covered the lexical analyzer and many of its robust features in just enough detail to make you dangerous. I recommend reading the documentation on **lex** to discover its other capabilities. To write your own lexical analyzer, see Kernighan and Plauger (1976). For a more thorough understanding of parsers and lexical analyzers, I recommend Aho (1985).

I hope this chapter has given you some understanding of **lex** and how to use it to build filters and syntax analyzers. I hope you are intrigued by the joy of **lex**.

```
/* shell tokens */

#define CASE            1
#define FOR             2
#define FOREACH         3
#define IF              4
#define REPEAT          5
#define SWITCH          6
#define UNTIL           7
#define WHILE           8
#define COMMENT-START   9
#define NEWLINE         10
```

Figure 13.16   The `shelltoken.h` *include* file

EXERCISES

1. Write a lexical analyzer to embolden all of the control keywords in C language: **if**, **else**, **switch**, **case**, **default** , **while**, **until**, and { }.

2. Expand the Shell metrics analyzer to count all files and variables.

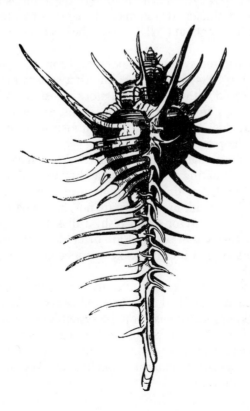

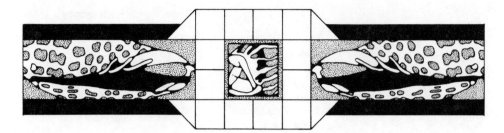

Chapter Fourteen

The UNIX System
Administrator

A well-administered UNIX system is a joy to both the administrator and the system's users. A poorly administered system can be equally painful and is the cause of much of the bad publicity about UNIX today. The key to proper system administration is the Shell.

Successfully administered systems are popular. From one mushrooms dozens of others. From 1979 to 1984, for example, the first system I installed grew to a crop of seven that coupled with a half-dozen more across U S WEST. In industry today, fields of UNIX systems—workstations, minis, and mainframes—support hordes of users worldwide. Automating the administration of your first system will greatly simplify the growth that will follow.

Shell programs can automate most of the activities of day-to-day administration and operation. Automating activities like adding users or backing up the file systems helps to ensure that nothing is forgotten or done incorrectly. Even the best of typists (which UNIX administrators are not) have a hard time entering the complete command to **volcopy** or **dump** (csh) a disk to a backup disk or tape without errors. Since file system backups are often done at night when even the best console operators are not totally awake, errors can occur unless the system does most of the work.

Other administration activities will require no human intervention at all. These can be automated with Shell and executed as required by **cron**, the clock daemon that executes commands based on the system's internal clock.

This chapter will cover how the Shell can automate many of the administrator's activities and the files used for system administration. Because of its ability to handle complex processes reliably, the Shell is the key to productive, high quality system administration.

240

ADMINISTRATION DUTIES

The UNIX system administrator has several key duties, most of which can be automated with Shell:

1. Add, change, and delete

   a. Users
   b. Software
   c. Hardware

2. Prevent problems through routine maintenance

   a. Back up daily activity
   b. Restore files

3. Diagnose and fix problems

   a. Monitor system usage—disk, cpu, network
   b. Maintain services—**mail**, **uucp**, network

4. Ensure system security

5. Provide user assistance

This chapter covers the routine activities of administration, not the nitty-gritty stuff of changing kernels. Why the day-to-day activities? Because the system never stays the same. Shell is a powerhouse for doing your daily grunt work. Let the Shell work for you. First, however, let's look at where the administrator's tools reside.

ADMINISTRATIVE DIRECTORIES AND FILES

A UNIX system administrator is directly involved with the directories shown in Table 14.1. Each of these directories contains files and commands that affect system administration.

The major files and commands of concern to the system administrator are shown in Tables 14.2 and 14.3. The file system /etc contains most of the commands required for system operation.

The UNIX system administrator is also responsible for the Shell and C commands that are locally developed. The source code, as well as the commands themselves, should be maintained on one system and *delivered* to all other systems. Shell can help automate building and delivering locally developed software to other systems. Once received, the other Shell administration systems can automatically install the software in the appropriate bin directories.

TABLE 14.1   Administrative Directories

Directory	Description
/etc	administrative and operational commands reside here as well as passwd and group files
/usr/adm	accounting directories
/usr/docs	system documentation
/usr/games	games
/usr/lib	operational logs, `cron` tables, commands
/usr/lib/acct	accounting commands
/usr/lib/uucp	`uucp` commands
/usr/lp	line printer spooling system
/usr/news	local news directory
/usr/pub	public directories
/usr/rje	Remote Job Entry system
/usr/tmp	temporary directories

TABLE 14.2   Administrative Files and Shell Commands

File or Command	Description
/etc	
/etc/brc	executed at startup by `init`
/etc/checklist	default file systems checked by `fsck`
/etc/group	listing of group IDs and passwords
/etc/inittab	event list for `init`
/etc/motd	message of the day
/etc/mnttbl	list of mounted file systems
/etc/passwd	login and password file
/etc/profile	custom shell executed by `init`
/etc/rc	startup shell executed by `init`
/etc/termcap	terminal capabilities data base
/etc/wtmp	log of login processes
/usr/adm	
/usr/adm/pacct	accounting log
/usr/lib	
/usr/lib/cronlog	log of `cron` processing
/usr/lib/crontab	event list for `cron`

TABLE 14.3   Administrative Commands in /etc

Command	Description
config	configure a UNIX system
crash	crash the system
cron	execute commands in /usr/lib/crontab
dskfmt	format a disk pack
fsck	check a file system
fsdb	debug file system errors
init	initialize the system
killall	kill all process
labelit	label a disk or tape volume
mkfs	make a file system
mknod	make a special file node (e.g., named pipes)
mount	mount a file system
shutdown	gracefully shut the system down
startup	gracefully start it up
umount	unmount a file system
volcopy	volume to volume file system copy
wall	send a message to all users

The other files that a system administrator deals with are not really files at all, but devices—terminals, disks, tapes, and line printers—that handle special functions. These are known as special files and come in two varieties: character special and block special. The various UNIX files are shown in Table 14.4. Block, character, socket, and named pipe files are created with the **mknod** command.

Shell commands write to character special files directly; block special files require special commands. Character special files act just like regular files, except that they are hardware devices. The following examples echo the system date onto the console, copy the contents of a directory to a tape, and print a file on the line printer:

```
date > /dev/console      # print date on console
find . -cpio /dev/rmt0   # backup a directory to tape
pr file > /dev/lp        # print a file on a line printer
```

Special files can also be restricted with **chmod** to prevent users from writing to them. For example, terminals (/dev/tty) should be mode 700 to prevent other users from writing directly onto their terminal while they are working. Only **/etc/wall** overrides this protection.

Most of the block and character special files are the province of the system administrator. They facilitate disk and tape backups, console messages, terminal communications, and so on. Administrators will gain the most familiarity with their use and benefits when used in the Shell. Again, any activity an administrator

TABLE 14.4   File Types

File Type	Description
Regular	standard UNIX file
Directory	standard UNIX directory
Character devices	
/dev/acu	auto call unit (cu, uucp)
/dev/console	system console
/dev/rdsk*	disk
/dev/rmt*	tape
/dev/lp	line printer
/dev/tty	terminals
/dev/vpm	virtual protocol machines (RJE)
Block devices	
/dev/dsk*	disk drive
/dev/mt*	tape drive
Named pipe	FIFO pipe created with mknod
Hard link	
Symbolic link (BSD)	
Socket (BSD)	similar to a named pipe

performs on an hourly, daily, weekly, or monthly basis should be automated with Shell.

Aside from locally developed commands and special files, the administrative files, commands, and directories can be broken into several categories: daily administration, automated administration, system startup, and system shutdown. Each of the following sections will cover the application of Shell to these activities.

DAILY ADMINISTRATION

Day-to-day work is where Shell truly shines as an aid for productive system administration. Hardly a day goes by when the administrator is not asked to add or delete a user or group from the system, restore a file, or inform the users of changes in commands, operations, or whatever. Each of these activities represents a varied level of the effort required of the system administrator. Possibly the most frequent activity required is the addition of a user.

Add, Change, and Delete Users

Adding a user is not as simple as it sounds. Entries must be made in the passwd and group files. Directories and files must be created. Environment variables must be established to point the user's login toward correct line printers, RJE lines, and so on. Because remembering all of these things is difficult, we can follow Einstein's advice: never keep anything in your mind that you can look up. Rather than miss your vacation, it makes sense to automate this activity with Shell. To add a user, the passwd file must be updated first:

```
usrno=`tail -1 /etc/passwd | cut -f3 -d:`  # get last user no
usrno=`expr $usrno + 1`                    # increment user no
echo "Which group will user belong to?"
read group                                         # get group number
grpno=`grep $group /etc/group | cut -f3 -d:`
echo "User's login name?"
read logname
echo "User's name and phone?"
read usrname
echo "File system?"
read fs
csh: echo "${logname}:..,:${usrno}:${grpno}:${usrname}: \
    /${fs}/ ${logname}:/bin/sh" \
        >> /etc/passwd        # add user entry to password file
```

Next, **adduser** will have to create the user's directories and files:

```
homedir=/${fs}/${logname}
mkdir ${homedir}                # make login directory
mkdir ${homedir}/bin            # make other required directories
mkdir ${homedir}/doc
mkdir ${homedir}/rje
mkdir ${homedir}/src
cp /unixfs/proto/profile ${homedir}/.profile   # add profile
chmod 755 ${homedir} ${homedir}/*              # all dirs readable
chmod 777 ${homedir}/src ${homedir}/rje        # writeable
chmod 700 ${homedir}/.profile                  # unchangeable
#
#      make all files and directories owned by user & group
#
chown ${logname} ${homedir} ${homedir}/* ${homedir}/.profile
chgrp ${group} ${homedir} ${homedir}/* ${homedir}/.profile
```

These few Shell commands comprise the basic needs of the **adduser** command. As the user population requires more hooks into the additional subsystems of UNIX—**lp, lpr, rje**, and so on—the **adduser** command should be enhanced to establish all of the environment variables required to make the user's entrance into the system as comfortable as possible. Taking care of all of these details when adding a user to a system not only helps the user, but keeps the administrator from having to answer numerous phone calls from frustrated users.

The command to add a group to the /etc/group file would be similar in format to **adduser**. **Addgroup** can be created easily with a few modifications to the commands shown.

The next frequent requirement is to delete a user. All references to the user must be removed from the system, including /etc/passwd, /etc/group, and /fs/logname. Using the same variable names as used in **adduser**, **deluser** executes as follows:

```
# deluser - remove /etc/passwd entry
sed -e "/^${logname}/d" < /etc/passwd > /etc/opasswd
cp /etc/opasswd /etc/passwd          # replace passwd file
ed /etc/group <<!        # remove group entry
g/${logname},/s///
g/,${logname}/s///
w
q
!
cd /${fs}/${logname}# change dir to user directory
if [ $? -eq 0 ]              # successful cd?
then
    rm -rf *                        # remove all files and directories
    cd ..
    rmdir ${logname}    # remove user directory
else
    echo "OOPS -- /${fs}/${logname} not found"
fi
```

Again, as more hooks are added to a system's users, **deluser** will need to delete more references to the login name. Aside from administering logins, the system administrator must restore files and directories when a user inadvertently removes a semiprecious file. Note that this is less likely to happen in a C Shell system when the user has the **noclobber** variable set.

Add, Change, and Delete Software

Figure 14.1 shows a UNIX environment of the future—workstations in a local area network (LAN) tied into larger, distributed systems which include both UNIX and other operating systems via various network protocols. The challenge for power administrators will be to develop, build, install, and maintain all of the software from a central point and distribute it to remote sites. To meet this challenge, you will need to create a system that:

1. builds the software from SCCS

2. sends the software via the network or **uucp**

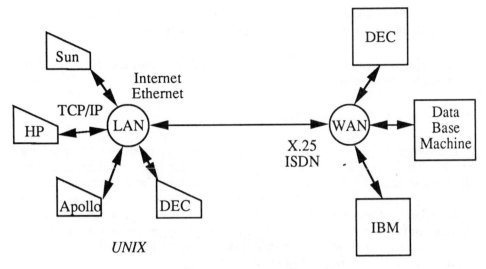

Figure 14.1   Network configuration

3. loads the software on the remote systems during off hours

4. sends confirmation of installation to the administrator

Because of differences from environment to environment, you will want to develop such a delivery system for your individual configuration. Automating this process in Shell took only a couple of days and saved countless thousands of hours over the 10-year life of the seven-system configuration implemented for U S WEST.

Much of the daily administration work occurs in off-hours, while users and administrators rest. The tool that pilots this work is **cron**.

Cron

Cron reads /usr/spool/cron/crontabs and executes the commands found, according to the time specifications. **Cron** gives the system administrator a handy way of being everywhere and doing everything, without having to be on the system.

Crontab entries have six fields. The first five fields tell **cron** when to execute the command: minute (0-59), hour (0-23), day (1-31), month (1-12), and day of the week (0-6; Sunday = 0 and Saturday = 6). To match a number of different times or days, a field may contain comma-separated numbers. To match a particular time or day, an asterisk (*) can be used in any of these fields. The sixth field contains the command to be executed.

A simple crontab will have entries to print the date and time on the console every 30 minutes and to **sync** the superblock every 10 minutes:

```
0,30 * * * * date > /dev/console; echo "\n" > /dev/console
0,10,20,30,40,50 * * * * /bin/sync > /dev/null
```

To execute the **calendar** program every weekday morning at 5 A.M., add the following line to crontab:

```
0 5 * * 1-5 /usr/bin/calendar -
```

The system administrator should use **cron** to handle as many routine tasks as possible. These include activities like monitoring disk usage, cleaning up temporary files, validating SCCS files, keeping system logs to a reasonable size, printing accounting reports (**acctcom**, **sar**), administering subsystems like **lp**, **lpr**, and **rje**, or any related administrative task. The system can handle all kinds of detective work in nonprime hours, when the administrator is home having dinner or sleeping. Use **cron** like an army of administrators and have it send detected errors to the real administrator for resolution.

Cron is started when the system is brought up and stops when the system is shut down for backups. Both of these two activities—start up and shut down—can be automated with Shell, to further reduce operational costs and errors.

Start Up

> Trouble is easily overcome before it starts.
>
> *Lao Tzu*

Starting the system is handled by **init**. The /etc/inittab file controls the actions of **init** in each of its states—mounting disks and bringing all of the terminal devices (/dev/tty) on line.

/etc/rc checks all of the file systems for errors using **fsck**, mounts the file systems, and starts process accounting, **cron**, the RJE, **lp**, **uucp**, and anything else that should be available when users enter the system.

Since /etc/rc is a shell, it can be modified to ensure that the system comes up cleanly, ready for users. /etc/rc can execute special shells to handle the requirements of the system administrator, like mailing the date and time of system startup. All of these files are under the control of the system administrator and should evolve to simplify system operation.

Shutdown

> Give as much care to the end as to the
> beginning, then there will be no failure.
>
> *Lao Tzu*

How the system is shut down is probably more important than how it is started. Rash actions like halting the machine from the console before all commands are killed, all file systems are unmounted, accounting and subsystems are stopped, and so on, can generate all kinds of problems. These can be avoided by using the **shutdown** command. Since **shutdown** is a Shell command, it can be modified to improve system reliability.

Once the system has been gracefully shut down and placed in single user mode, and file systems have been checked, the **shutdown** command should ask the operator about disk or tape backups and execute these commands as required.

ROUTINE MAINTENANCE

A system administrator can reduce the possibility of lost files by requiring nightly back ups and by automating the backup process with Shell commands to mount the proper backup disk or tape and **volcopy** the file systems. Disk and tape backup commands are fairly similar. The following command will back up the **root** and **usr** file systems:

```
# diskbackup
day=`date +%a`                          # get day of week Sun-Sat
echo "Backup volume name is bck${day}
echo "Mount backup pack labeled FILE SYSTEM = root"
echo "Hit return when ready"
read answer
mount /dev/rdsk14 /bck > /dev/null       # mount root backup
volcopy root /dev/rdsk0 unix0 /dev/rdsk140 bck${day}
volcopy usr /dev/rdsk2 unix0 /dev/rdsk142 bck${day}
umount /dev/rdsk14 > /dev/null            #unmount backup drive
```

The command could also use **labelit** to check the volume name of the backup pack before continuing. Disk and tape backup commands should be developed for each system to ensure the accuracy of the backup procedures. There is nothing more vicious than a user who has lost data and work. Do not let this happen to the users on your system.

Restoring files requires that the operations staff mount the correct backup disk or tape. What better way to ensure that the most current backup copy is used than to let the Shell request the backup disk from a history log? Assuming that the disk backup command creates a log of the file systems backed up and the volume names of the backup disks, a command called **file_restore** could determine which disk to use:

```
# file_restore
echo "Enter full path name: /fs/userid/dir.../filename"
read path
fs=`echo $path | cut -f2 -d"/"`
backup=`grep $fs /etc/backuplog | tail -1`   # get latest log
backupvol=`echo ${backup} | cut -f2 -d:`      # get volume
special=`echo ${backup} | cut -f3 -d:`        # get special name
echo "Mount $backupvol on backup drive"
echo "Hit <return> key when ready to continue"
read answer
mount ${special} /bck                         # mount backup as bck
file=`echo $path | cut -f3- -d/`              # cut filesys from path
cp /bck/${file} $path                         # copy backup file
umount ${special}                             # unmount backup drive
echo "${path} restored from /bck/${file}"
echo "Remove $backupbvol from backup drive"
```

If the backup log contained the following information:

```
unix1:bkuptues:/dev/rdsk140
unix2:bkuptues:/dev/rdsk142
unix1:bkupwed:/dev/rdsk140
unix2:bkupwed:/dev/rdsk142
```

then the command to back up the file /unix1/lja/src/main.c would ask the system administrator to mount the disk labeled bkupwed on the backup drive (in this case dsk14). The **file_restore** command would then mount the backup file system as /bck and copy the previous version of the file into the requested directory and file.

DIAGNOSING AND FIXING PROBLEMS

No computer system is impervious to errors. You will, however, find it much easier to prevent problems than to fix them when they occur. Prevention is also less costly. Prevention involves monitoring the system's functions and taking corrective action *before* problems occur. Fix it before it breaks!

Monitoring System Usage

> Because the sage always confronts difficulties, he never experiences them.
>
> *Lao Tzu*

The first thing to manage on most systems is disk usage. The disk free (**df**) command can help pinpoint rapidly growing disk usage. If the amount of free space under a file system drops below a certain level, you will want to request free spaces from the user community or consider expanding their file system:

```
df /userfs
```

You may also find it useful to fully automate this process so that the system tracks changes in disk usage, comparing one day against the next, and notifies you of any untoward activity. You may also want to monitor remote systems using **uux**:

```
uux 'df / | mail home!yourself' remote_system
```

Then you can use the disk usage (**du**) command to identify the 20 percent of the users who use 80 percent of the disk space. (Pareto's rule often holds true for all system resource usage.)

CPU and access times can be monitored via the accounting data. In my experience, UNIX systems experience a slow initial growth rate, then modest growth, and toward the end, massive growth. By tracking and plotting the trend, you will have sufficient advance warning to install hardware upgrades and tune the system to meet the demands.

You will need to develop additional commands to monitor the other services on the system: **mail**, **uucp**, **lp**, **lpr**, and networking.

ENSURING SYSTEM SECURITY

The Shell administrator has four key jobs with respect to system security:

1. prevent unauthorized access

2. maintain system integrity

3. preserve data privacy

4. prevent interruption of service

To prevent unauthorized access, you need to make sure that all of the users and groups have passwords and that there are no duplicate user IDs:

```
awk -f: 'if ( $2 == "" ) { print }"' /etc/passwd /etc/group
cut -f1 -d: /etc/passwd | sort | uniq -d
cut -f1 -d: /etc/group | sort | uniq -d
```

To maintain system integrity, you will need to manage the permissions on executable files and directories. Following are the three permissions that allow the user to assume someone else's identity, even the superuser's, for the duration of the command:

4000 set user ID	changes to the owner of the executable program
2000 set group ID	does the same for the group
1000 sticky bit	keeps a program in memory

The most dangerous of these, of course, is the first, especially when the owner is **root**. To find these programs, **cron** should periodically search the system as follows:

```
find / -user root -perm 4000 -exec ls -lg {} \;
find / -perm 2000 -exec ls -lg {} \;
find / -perm 777 -type f -print
```

To preserve data privacy, the administrator will need control of the **mount** and **umount** commands, and file and directory permissions. Mounting and unmounting file systems stays in the control of the superuser who has access to /etc/mount and /etc/umount. Controlling data security is augmented by the **umask** command, which determines the default file permissions. To prevent anyone except the users and their group from accessing files created by the users, we could put the following statement in */etc/profile* or *.cshrc*:

```
umask 027
```

As a backup procedure, we could periodically check for directories that can be read and written by anyone in the "world":

```
find / -perm 777 -type d -print
```

We could also encourage users to set their own default security and use **crypt** for really important files. All of these activities are designed to help prevent loss of data or loss of the system. To further prevent interruption of service, we could place external users in a restricted Shell (**rsh**).

Restricted Shells

Occasionally, the administrator will need to allow a group of users access to the machine without giving them all of the power of UNIX. In these instances, the system administrator can create a restricted environment that lets new users perform some necessary work, but prohibits them from going crazy in the system.

Creating restricted Shells is easy. First, the administrator creates a restricted login that points to /bin/rsh instead of /bin/sh. When the new user logs in, he or she will be prohibited from executing the **cd** command, changing the value of PATH, redirecting output, or executing commands beginning with "/". These restrictions are enforced only after **login** has executed the commands in the new user's .profile.

By creating the proper .profile and not allowing the new user to change it, the system administrator can put the user in any directory, supply any commands required with PATH, and rest assured that the user can do little damage.

The commands required are often linked from /bin and /usr/bin to a set of restricted bins: /rbin and /usr/rbin. A simple *profile* to restrict a user's activities would be:

```
PATH=:/rbin:/usr/rbin
cd /unixfs/rdir
export PATH
```

The new user could then execute the commands in the current directory, /rbin and /usr/rbin, but would be restricted from moving about the system.

This will only be occasionally useful, but it is an option for good system administration. Use it sparingly; the goal of administration is to help the users do whatever they need to do.

PROVIDING USER ASSISTANCE

The final requirement of daily administration is to communicate all system changes to the user population. A knowledgeable user population minimizes the number of phone calls an administrator will receive. The commands that handle user communication are **mail**, **news**, and **wall**. The file /etc/motd, message of the day, can also be used to provide daily information when the user logs into UNIX. The following example shows various entries for /etc/motd:

```
/etc/motd
The system will be down for preventive maintenance Sunday,
July 17 from 9AM to 6PM. Please refer questions to x1234.
```

News is used for changes to the system or system commands. Users can read the daily news (**rn**) when they have time. **News** files are kept in the directory /usr/news. **Mail** communicates directly with specific users or groups of users. **Wall** writes to all users who are logged in, when immediate communication is required (e.g., when the system is coming down for emergency maintenance).

Shell programming can aid the system administrator in all phases of daily administration. Shell commands should be developed to automate any activity that happens frequently, like adding or deleting users, or restoring files. Other administration tasks must occur on a set schedule. Rather than demand that these be done by the administrator, they can be executed automatically by **cron**.

Help

Nothing is more frustrating to a UNIX user than to need help and not know where to call to get it. Consider building a simple command, called **helpme**, that prints the administrator's work and home phone numbers. If there is more than one administrator and each specializes in certain UNIX subsystems, then include that information too:

```
# helpme
cat /global/help/oncall       # print list of administrators
```

Periodically, check all of the system logs for signs of trouble. As certain kinds of errors rise to the surface, develop Shell commands to **grep** for errors in the logs and mail them to the system administrator nightly using **cron**. The sooner errors are detected and corrected, the sooner the administrator can kick back and spend his or her time developing new and better tools to support the user population.

SUMMARY

The UNIX system administrator has as much to gain from Shell usage as any UNIX user. Much of the work of administering a system can be handled with Shell commands, **cron**, and the startup and shutdown procedures. Productive UNIX administration relies on extensive use of the Shell and all of its facilities. From the UNIX guru to the simplest user, Shell is the way to help users accomplish their goals. May you spend your time collecting rare and beautiful shells to satisfy your every need.

EXERCISES

1. Write the command to allow users to create news files in /usr/news.

2. Write the command to send mail to groups of users by extracting their user IDs from the /etc/group file.

3. Write the command to back up file systems to tape on your system. (Look up your device types for magnetic tape.)

4. Write the commands to restore files and file systems from tape.

5. Modify the backup command to include all of the disks and file systems on your UNIX system.

6. Write the crontab entry to print the accounting reports in /usr/adm/acct/fiscal on a line printer.

7. Write the crontab entry to validate all of the SCCS files on the system and send mail of the corrupted files to the system administrator.

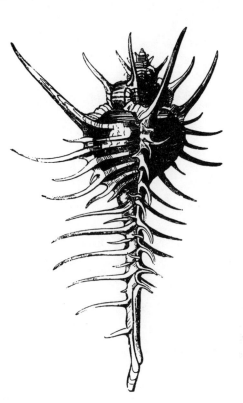

Appendix A

Reusable Shell Code

```
#
#  %M% %Y% %I%
#
#  Most recent update: %G% at %U%
#
#%Z% Function -
#%Z%
#
#@#@ Syntax -
#
#%Z% General Instructions -
#%Z%
#%Z% Parameters -
#%Z%  Required -
#%Z%
#%Z%  Optional -
#%Z%
# store the flags
while [ `echo $1 | cut -f1` = "-" ]
do
      parms="${parms} $1"
      shift
done
```

```
case $# in
    #    if they don't give any files, prompt for them
    0)
         echo "enter filename"
         read filename
         ;;
    #    if they give exactly the right number, do something
    1)
         filename=$1
         ;;
    #    if they give a whole bunch, process all of them
    *)
         filename="$*"
         ;;
esac
#describe actual processing
for file in ${filename}
do
    process $file
done
```

Appendix B

C Language Prototype

```c
char mainrel[] = "%A%";

#include <stdio.h>
#include <string.h>
#include "cobext.h"

main(argc, argv)
int argc;
char **argv;
{
  /**********************************************************
  *                                                        *
  * main program:                                          *
  *                                                        *
  * program description:                                   *
  *                                                        *
  * subroutines called or required:                        *
  *                                                        *
  * reference: (job definition, ipo, etc)                  *
  *                                                        *
  *                           %A%                          *
  **********************************************************
  */
char *cmdname;
```

```
cmdname=argv[0];      /* save pointer to the commandname */
argc--; argv++;
/*
      check for control flags
*/
while (argc>1 && *argv[1]=='-') {

   switch(argv[0][1]) {

   case 'f': /* flags */
                /* insert -f processing */
     break;

   default:
     fprintf(stderr, "%s: invalid parameter %s\n",
             cmdname, *argv);
      return(1);
      break;
   } /* END SWITCH */

   argc-;       /* decrement the argument counter */
   argv++;      /* increment the argument pointer */
 } /* END WHILE */

 while(argc>0){
  /*
      if the file exists reopen it as standard input
  */

  if (freopen(*argv, "r", stdin) == NULL) {
      fprintf(stderr,"%s: can't open %s\n", pgm, *argv);
      return(1);
  }
 } /* END WHILE */
}
```

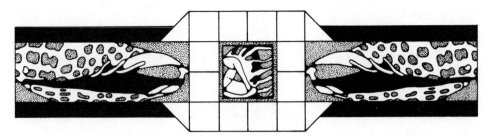

Appendix C

Makefile Prototype

```
OBJECTS = main.o sub.o lex.yy.o y.tab.o
LIB = -ll -lm
CFLAGS = -O
BIN=/usr/local/bin

command: $(OBJECTS)
      cc $(CFLAGS) $(OBJECTS) $(LIB) -o command

main.o: command.h main.c

sub.o: command.h sub.c

lex.yy.o: command.h lex.yy.c

lex.yy.c: cobmet.l
        lex cobmet.l

y.tab.o: command.h y.tab.c

y.tab.c: command.y
        yacc command.y

clean:
        rm *.o

install:
        cp command $(BIN)
```

Bibliography

AT&T. *The Bell System Technical Journal,* **57**(6), part 2 (1978).

Aho, A. V., B. W. Kernighan, and P. J. Weinberger. *The AWK Programming Language.* Reading: Addison-Wesley, 1988.

Aho, A. V., R. Sethi, and J. D. Ullman. *Compilers, Principles, Techniques, and Tools.* Reading: Addison-Wesley, 1985.

Boar, Bernard. *Application Prototyping.* New York: John Wiley & Sons, 1984.

Boehm, B. W., et al. "A Software Development Environment for Improving Productivity," *IEEE Computer* (June 1984), pp. 30–34.

"Trends," *ComputerWorld* (Nov. 13, 1989), p. 136.

James, Geoffrey. *The Tao of Programming.* Santa Monica: Info-Books, 1987.

Kernighan, B. W., and P. J. Plauger. *Software Tools.* Reading: Addison-Wesley, 1976.

Peters, Tom. *A Passion for Excellence.* New York: Random House, 1985.

Rifkin, G., and J. A. Savage. "Is the U.S. Ready for Japan's Software Push?," *ComputerWorld* (May 8, 1989), pp. 1, 114–116.

Stevens, W. P. "How Data Flow Can Improve Application Development Productivity," *IBM Systems Journal,* **21**(2) (1982).

Thadhani, A. J. "Factors Affecting Programmer Productivity during Application Development," *IBM Systems Journal,* **23**(1) (1984), pp. 19–35.

Unger, John. "One Man's Experience," *Byte* (May 1989), pp. 237–242.

Index